G000241484

THE BARBARIANS

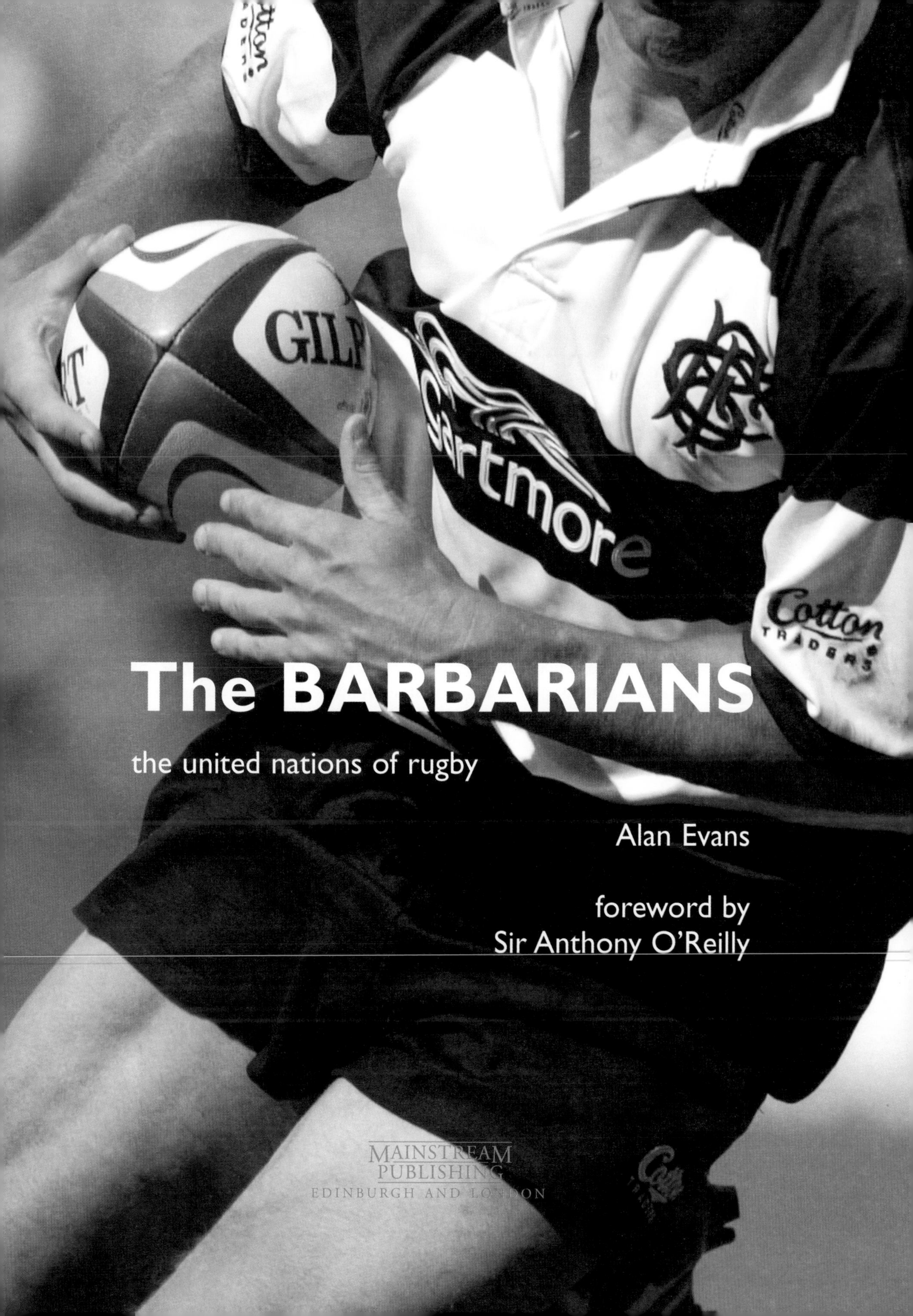

The BARBARIANS

the united nations of rugby

Alan Evans

foreword by
Sir Anthony O'Reilly

MAINSTREAM
PUBLISHING
EDINBURGH AND LONDON

Copyright © Alan Evans, 2005
All rights reserved
The moral right of the author has been asserted

First published in Great Britain in 2005 by
MAINSTREAM PUBLISHING COMPANY (EDINBURGH) LTD
7 Albany Street
Edinburgh EH1 3UG

ISBN 1 84018 970 3

No part of this book may be reproduced or transmitted in any form or by any
other means without permission in writing from the publisher, except by a
reviewer who wishes to quote brief passages in connection with a review written
for insertion in a magazine, newspaper or broadcast

A catalogue record for this book is available
from the British Library

Typeset in Apollo, Baskerville and Gill

Printed in Great Britain by
The Bath Press Ltd

To Barbarians of the past, present and future

and all that they represent

ACKNOWLEDGEMENTS

The author wishes to thank the following people for their help and support in the preparation of this book: Gordon H. Brown, Steve Cannon, John Dawes, Michael Gibson, Gareth Griffiths, Billy Hullin, Brian Jones, Haydn Mainwaring, Sir Anthony O'Reilly, Brian Price, Adam Robson, Fergus Slattery, Micky Steele-Bodger, Kevin Stewart, Bob Wilkinson, Bleddyn Williams, Geoffrey Windsor-Lewis.

CONTENTS

FOREWORD

To be a Barbarian is to be one of a proud universe of people who believe in their hearts that rugby football should be a game – and a fun game at that. The criteria for admission are simple and twofold: you have to be a footballer and a gentleman.

Many great gentlemen failed to make the Barbarians and many great footballers – well, need I complete the sentence?

Today, the criteria would be different. The huge, attractive, vital, theatrical, gladiatorial, televisual and professional game has captured the imagination of an excited public, and has made the game in its competitiveness and velocity something that demands total commitment in time, in thought and in one's whole being.

What a contrast to the first ambitions of the founder of the Barbarians in 1890, William Carpmael, and that long line of Corinthian figures that you will discover in this book. The Barbarian ethos is incorporated in the words of the Barbarians' song:

> For it's a way we have in the Baa-Baas
> And a jolly good way, too.
> For it's a way we have in the Baa-Baas
> And a rule that we play to;
> For the rugby game, we do not train
> We play it with a will,
> For it's a way we have in the Baa-Baas
> And a jolly good way, too!

In essence, this is the very antithesis of modern rugby, and it is a measure of the flexibility of the Barbarians that they have maintained a certain magical hold upon the public's mind that has made them still able to field teams of distinction and quality throughout the world.

This book is a splendid one, and because I first played for the Barbarians 50 years ago, it also allows me to ramble down the corridors of the Club's history with a knowledge of many of the main players and officials.

I was first chosen for the Barbarians on the Easter tour of 1955. Many of us had been selected for the British Lions to tour South Africa that summer, but in a way, an even greater distinction was to be selected for the Baa-Baas.

On that first of many Easter tours, I learned many things about the Baa-Baas, my fellow players and the 'alickadoos' who populate these pages and those tours.

The Big Four games at Easter each year started with a game against Penarth, led in those days by an indestructible scrum-half shaped like a fire hydrant, called 'Slogger' Templeman. That was the easy game. On Saturday, we played Cardiff, who were then one of the greatest clubs in the world. This was followed by a weekend of golf and salacious song, and then the prescribed visit to the Esplanade Ballroom on the pier at Penarth on Sunday night to chase, if possible, the amorous Welsh ladies. At eleven o'clock, the beady eye of Micky Steele-Bodger, the deputed official, was cast across the road from the hotel to the ballroom to decide who would be playing against Swansea on the Monday. That was an eye we all sought to avoid, particularly if we had played against Cardiff on the Saturday.

Swansea on the Monday was followed by a gruelling game against Newport on the Tuesday, another truly great team in those days. Ray Prosser from Pontypool, a club across the river from Newport, when playing against Newport, always announced, 'You know, I 'ate these overseas games!'

The Easter tour in 1957 led to our first tour to Canada, beautifully described in this book. It was a tour which Andrew Armstrong Mulligan, our elegant scrum-half, observed as being 'one of the few tours in which the team were in charge of the officials'.

Missionary in nature, it proved extraordinarily difficult when playing against British Columbia, the strongest team in Canada. I marked George Puil, a Canadian sprint champion, that day and, being somewhat careful of myself, was quite happy with the game. Afterwards, a representative of the Los Angeles Rams approached me and said, 'I'd like you to consider signing professional terms for the LA Rams as a wide receiver.' Suitably honoured, I demurred and said, 'Well, I'm a law student, sir, in Dublin, hoping to complete my studies. Why did you think I might be able to play American football?' And he said, 'I watched you play today, and you can look after yourself. You're the most elusive coward I've ever seen.' I still wonder at the compliment.

Canada was followed by South Africa in 1958, and for those of us who had toured with the Lions in '55, it was like *The Last Remake of Beau Geste*. Cliff Morgan was at his glittering best and enthralled the crowds in this his swansong. But the memory of the tour for me involved the graceful, swift and ghostly Arthur Smith scoring truly spectacular tries in both of our Transvaal matches against the pick of the Springboks. He was the captain of the 1962 Lions and died tragically of cancer at 42. He was a great athlete and a very distinguished scientist and the very essence of a true Barbarian.

The Barbarians have existed as an ideal and as a club. At the centenary dinner, I recalled the story of Lord Birkenhead, F.E. Smith – 'the Thunderer' – one of the great QCs of his time. He lived in Mayfair and crossed to the House of Lords each day, pausing to relieve himself at the Athenaeum Club, of which he was not a member. This greatly irritated the members, who deputed the doorman to enquire of his status. One day, emerging from the gentlemen's toilet, he was accosted by the hall porter, who said, 'Excuse me, my Lord, but are you a member of this club?'

'Good God,' said Birkenhead, 'you mean to say it's a club as well?'

The Barbarian Football Club is somewhat like Birkenhead's concept of a club, in that it has never had a permanent home, and yet it has an eternal home in the minds and the ambitions of every rugby player of quality and sensitivity who has played rugby for the past century. It owes its eminence to a great succession of extraordinary presidents, but none more than Micky Steele-Bodger. Bodger epitomises that quality in the Club, which, if you are a footballer and a gentleman, you will find is a hospitable place to play. Its style of rugby is that of the Lions at their best. It has an unquenchable belief in the beauty of the game of rugby football and in spreading the gospel of the game to an ever-widening audience.

In all of this, Steele-Bodger and his loyal committeemen have been the foot-soldiers in their determination to combat the crasser aspects of professionalism and to remind everyone that the very heart of rugby football is not entertainment, though it can be entertaining, but that it is a game of football played by gentlemen.

Tony O'Reilly
Barbarians, Ireland and
British Isles
March 2005

11

INTRODUCTION

Throughout the Barbarian Football Club's long and distinguished history it has been blessed with the opportunity to invite the great players of the day to wear the famous black-and-white jersey. And ever since 1890 when the Club was founded, countless articles have appeared in newspapers and magazines lauding the spirit of adventure and ability displayed by those invited to play.

It is hoped that in these pages there is captured that essential spirit of the Club which some might think more appropriate to the Corinthian age of sport than its modern-day incarnation. But the Barbarian Football Club has always believed in encouraging players to enjoy themselves, to play without fear of making mistakes, to have confidence in their teammates and to play attacking rugby which is as exciting to watch as it is to play. With such an approach it has proved possible for our scratch sides to take on some of the best club and national teams in the world and make an even match of it.

As a club we have defeated all three of the great southern hemisphere countries – Australia, New Zealand and South Africa – something that several national teams have yet to achieve, and on our short summer tours, introduced in 2000, with matches against the Home Unions, we have played fifteen and lost only two.

For their generous support in helping us to bring the official history of the Club up to date, we owe thanks to our Club sponsors, Gartmore Investment Management, with whom we are expecting a long and mutually beneficial relationship.

We also thank Cotton Traders, our official kit suppliers, who have given financial support to this book and who provide the players with the much-sought-after Barbarian playing kit.

My thanks to Sir Anthony O'Reilly, the renowned Irish businessman and generous benefactor, for giving his time to write the foreword. As a famous sportsman and the Club's most capped player (thirty matches) and top try-scorer (thirty-eight tries, including seven

in one match), there could not be a better-known Barbarian to convey the *joie de vivre* of the Club given the experiences on which he can draw, from matches both in the UK and on overseas tours.

My thanks also to Morton Speyer and BCMB for the design on the book cover and finally to Alan Evans, the author, who has dedicated many, many hours to first the research and then the writing of the manuscript. He has been with us on every possible occasion throughout this past year and we are most grateful to him for both his endeavour and the result.

I am sure that this book will be enjoyed by its readers and I hope that they will have the opportunity of watching Barbarian rugby at first hand in the near future and for many years to come.

Micky Steele-Bodger
President, Barbarian Football Club
March 2005

I

BARBARIANS AND GENTLEMEN

'We must make sure that our future is a happy and successful one, thus rewarding all those who in the past have contributed so much while at the same time acknowledging their contribution.'
— Micky Steele-Bodger, 1990

If Micky Steele-Bodger had not been born, the Barbarians would have had to invent him. For 60 years and more, from budding sportsman to archetypal alickadoo, he has epitomised everything that is best and unique about the Club and its traditions. He has served it faithfully as a player and committeeman and, since 1988, has presided over it with an almost indefinable cocktail of gentle persuasion and iron-firm opinions, self-deprecating personality and charismatic presence, that has cajoled and convinced the rugby world at large that, whatever the challenges thrown up by the ever-changing priorities of the professional game, his beloved Barbarians were not about to disappear over the horizon. He would be the first to assert

that nothing would have been possible without the loyal support and commitment to the cause of successive members of the committee over the years; but every one of them would be equally certain that Micky has been the Club's — and their — driving force, a man with what must surely be the most comprehensive address book in the sport and a direct line to all the movers and shakers that matter.

Not that the man himself is one to stand on ceremony or to give all his time to the great and the good at the expense of anyone else. In his world, everyone is important and deserving of respect, even if this sometimes comes in the form of a mischievous remark, which he has developed into a fine art. That fools no one who

knows him. To a man (and woman) the most common assessment of him is that he is 'loyal', whether to friends and colleagues or to the many organisations he has been associated with over the years. The cornerstone of them all, though, is undoubtedly the Barbarian Football Club and never more so than during the challenges it has faced since the higher echelons of the Union game went professional in 1995. As the great Irish flanker Fergus Slattery says, 'Micky is an English bulldog, overflowing with determination, and he is totally committed to everything he is involved in and especially the Barbarians.'

That determination may well be traced back to the vicissitudes of his own playing days in the years immediately after the Second World War. To say that a promising career was cut short in its prime would qualify as a massive understatement. By the age of 24 he had already progressed in almost textbook fashion through university, club and representative rugby and been ever-present for England in two international championship campaigns. Born and bred in Staffordshire, he was sent, appropriately, to Rugby School and then the universities at Cambridge, Edinburgh and Dublin, where he completed his veterinary qualifications. All four institutions gave him the perfect opportunity to develop his sporting prowess as well. He won his first Blue at Cambridge in December 1945, combining his university matches with other first-class experience at the Harlequins. His diminutive height of 5 ft 8 in. had dictated that his schoolboy rugby had been played at scrum-half, then prop, but at university he had blossomed into an international-class wing-forward. In that same 1945–46 season he had played three times for England in the 'Victory'

internationals, a home-and-away series for the five European nations for which caps were not awarded but which in every other respect had all the trappings of Test matches. Equally prestigious was the New Zealand Kiwis tour that season, and Micky played against them for both a Midlands XV and a Cambridge University team, which he captained.

With his reputation growing match by match, he resisted any attempts to move him back into the front row, even when he attended his first pre-season trial for the Harlequins at Teddington. As he recalls, 'I was keen to play club rugby when not required by Cambridge, but when I went to the Harlequins, Adrian Stoop [the President] asked me to play at hooker for the A-team. Having converted to the back row because I was too light for the front row, I had no wish to return there. And anyway, wing-forward suited me because I had a good sense of anticipation, though I was often accused of being offside!'

He used his size and speed to good advantage, not only to shoot off the ends of lineouts and sides of scrums to disrupt the opposing backs in the open spaces – the legendary Welsh centre and lifelong friend Bleddyn Williams still claims that on the field Micky was 'a bloody nuisance, always offside' – but also to indulge in nefarious skulduggery in the close exchanges. With more than a hint of a chuckle Micky admits to conceding a penalty against Ireland in the 1946 Victory international by jumping over an opponent in a lineout. 'Our captain, Jack Heaton, wasn't amused and told me I'd better make amends for giving away the three points by scoring a try. So I did.' England won the game 14–6.

The following year at Lansdowne Road, this time in a full-scale official international, he was at it again and the Irish took full revenge. 'I was told to stand at the front of the lineouts to guard the blind side. This annoyed their prop, John Daly, who had huge hands and used them to good effect. A punch blinded me in one eye. It was a bitterly cold day but the Irish were better prepared than us – they wore vests and even the teetotallers among them had the benefit of a tot of good Irish whiskey. After the game I went back to the Shelbourne Hotel and soaked in a hot bath with a raw steak over my damaged eye. This was a terrible waste at a time when there was still post-war meat rationing!' Elsewhere, the entire England team must have been nursing their bruises: Ireland had won the game 22–nil.

Micky clearly relished the physical side of the game, as evidenced by his tactics as skipper of an underdog Cambridge team against their gifted Oxford adversaries in the 1946 match. Realising that his team were in danger of being run off their feet by the unbeaten Dark Blues, his game plan was based on what he called 'aggressive defence'. It almost worked. In front of a then record 40,000 crowd he scored a captain's try to establish a 5–3 lead before his side was overhauled in the closing stages. It was a rare defeat in a distinguished career. When official international matches were resumed in January 1947, he won the first of his nine consecutive caps as England beat Wales 9–6 at Cardiff Arms Park.

But perhaps the most significant benchmark in his playing days, and arguably in all his subsequent life, had occurred 11 months earlier. On Thursday, 28 February 1946 M.R. Steele-Bodger had made his debut for the Barbarians against the East Midlands at Northampton. It was only appropriate that his first wearing of the famous black-and-white

Micky Steele-Bodger's first England cap was against Wales in Cardiff in 1947. Here (third from the right) he follows a foot-rush that was typical of forward play in that era.
(© Steele-Bodger Collection)

jersey was in the Mobbs Memorial Match, the most traditional and ceremonial of all the Club's regular fixtures, and one that he has been instrumental in ensuring still survives to this day. The Barbarians won the 1946 game by 20 points to 6, with Micky in a back row that also featured his Cambridge captain of a couple of months earlier, Eric Bole. His next Barbarian landmark followed almost immediately: selection for the Easter tour of South Wales. It was the beginning of an unbroken run as player and committeeman that stretched to 50 consecutive Easters until the demise of the tour in 1996.

For Micky, everything about the annual pilgrimage, from the Thursday arrival at the Esplanade Hotel in Penarth, through the four games themselves that sandwiched the Sunday golf tournament at the Glamorganshire club,

and the singalongs late into every night, was like manna from heaven. Underpinning everything were the characters – some of whom, in 1946, were in the latter stages of their own long-term service while Micky was starting out on his – and the antics they got up to. From the outset he knew that this was a great adventure with a subtle balance of social and sporting activities that he wanted to remain a part of. He describes each Easter tour as an exercise in 'organised chaos', something that obviously appealed to his own sense of fun and penchant for the absurd. He describes one individual whose very presence epitomised the environment he now found himself in: 'Charlie Hopwood had been on the committee since 1930 and had played for the Baa-Baas before that. He had somehow managed to play over sixty games for Cambridge over three years without winning a Blue. A solicitor by profession, he was the "Good-time Charlie" whose self-appointed role every Easter was to give out the Club's ties and collect the money in. That wasn't as simple as it sounds for Charlie. Typically, he was found fast asleep in the corner of the bar with only three of the thirty ties left. The treasurer, Hughie Glyn Hughes, had no hesitation in asking him for the £57 to cover the sale of the missing ties. The ties were returned next morning and the debt was cancelled. This was a situation not unusual for Charlie. Once, on a Cambridge tour to South Africa, he received a bill for six bottles of champagne from a hotel in Pietermaritzburg when the team had been nowhere near that town on the entire trip.'

Of course, Micky also loved the competitive nature of the rugby against the top Welsh clubs. The opening game against Penarth on Good Friday may have been the least demanding of the four fixtures (though the Seasiders intermittently recorded famous victories), but Micky was happy to play in the fixture and then again on the Monday at Swansea on his first tour in 1946. The following year he completed the full house by being selected for the Cardiff and Newport games. And all the time he was becoming more and more steeped in the Baa-Baas' way of doing things. 'The only rule on tour was that the players selected for the following day's match were expected to be in bed by 11 p.m.,' he says. Sometimes the bedrooms themselves could throw up unexpected surprises. 'The Barbarians were always terribly attached to Penarth and the Esplanade Hotel in particular. It was nothing grand. Every year I was allocated room 10, which was rather small but comfortable. But one year I checked in, went to the room and detected a funny smell. I thought nothing of it until the following morning when one of the team popped in to see me, made a face, and asked whether I was suffering from athlete's foot. It was time to inspect the room further. Eventually, on top of the wardrobe, we discovered the skeleton of a chicken. I had eaten it in the room 12 months earlier and it was still there!'

Micky was by then qualified as a veterinary surgeon so he recognised the comic element in the situation. Easter in Wales was to be enjoyed and the proverbial wild horses, indeed real-life infected cows, couldn't keep him away. As one Bank Holiday weekend approached, a problem arose that probably could only happen to him: 'It was the Wednesday before Easter and I was called out to a farm in Middleton, near Tamworth, to examine a cow which at evening milking was found to be distressed. Within minutes of my arrival the cow died, haemorrhaging as she fell and covering my hands with blood. Anthrax was at once suspected and later confirmed by microscopic examination. Being a notifiable disease, it required reporting to the Ministry of Agriculture and a request to their laboratory for the urgent despatch of anti-serum by passenger train from London. This arrived late that night and, returning to the farm, I worked through the night injecting all the livestock. By morning several more that had appeared ill had died, but the rest of the cattle had survived. But I also needed to be put on a course of treatment myself, so, 24 hours later, there I was in the Esp needing penicillin in my buttocks at regular intervals and all enthusiastically administered by a Penarth doctor who enjoyed nothing more than an evening in the bar with the Baa-Baas.'

It shouldn't happen to a vet; certainly not a Barbarian one.

In January 1947 Micky was invited to join the Barbarian committee as the Cambridge representative. His Oxford equivalent was Ossie Newton-Thompson. It was an impressive group led by the president, Emile de Lissa, and including four of his eventual successors, Jack Haigh Smith (then honorary secretary), Hughie Glyn Hughes (treasurer), Herbert Waddell and Micky. And Micky's playing days were far from over. He was still in the England team, played again on the Easter tour and at the end of the year captained the Club when making the second of his four appearances against Leicester. Early in 1948 came another great honour with his selection for the Barbarians in their first-ever match against an international touring side, the Wallabies, at Cardiff Arms Park. He still considers the occasion and the match to be one of the Club's greatest days in

its long history, not only because of the quality of the game itself, which the Barbarians won 9–6, with Micky scoring the first try, but also because 'playing the Wallabies turned us into a world side'. By that he meant that the Club now had a worldwide identity. In more recent times, with the regular selection of players from all over the globe, it has come to mean something else.

Another notable event occurred later in 1948, marking the beginning of Micky's role as an organiser and selector in the game. He was asked by a fellow Barbarian committeeman, Dr Windsor H. Lewis, to invite a team to play Cambridge University as the final preparation for the Varsity match. The notion appealed to Micky immediately. An earlier fixture against J.E. Greenwood's XV had lapsed after 1938 and since then Cambridge had gone to Twickenham rather underprepared for the annual clash with

Micky Steele-Bodger (centre) closes down Pebeyre of France at Twickenham, 1947.
(© Steele-Bodger Collection)

the Dark Blues. Oxford, on the other hand, still had their traditional pre-Twickenham encounter with Major R.V. Stanley's XV. In November 1948 Cambridge redressed the imbalance. They would play M.R. Steele-Bodger's XV. Micky, who by then was in the latter stages of his veterinary studies at Edinburgh University, didn't let his old Alma Mater down. He had made two provisos in accepting the challenge: he must always have a free hand in team selection and there must always be a post-match dinner. Well over half a century later the fixture and its traditions still survive. Back in 1948 he realised that for the rehearsal for the big day to be meaningful, he needed to put together a strong side, and he did just that with the Wales and British Isles superstars Bleddyn Williams and Haydn Tanner at half-back and a host of other internationals. They were good enough to win the inaugural University v. Steele-Bodger's XV match 13–9.

Micky was still only 23 when he masterminded the first Steele-Bodger's XV but his own playing days were approaching a premature end. He had never been far from the thick of the action on the pitch and he had regularly been in the wars in club and international matches. Against France in Paris in 1948 he broke a thumb; he had broken his nose in a club match at Gloucester; while in Scotland he was stretchered off at Galashiels after tearing ankle ligaments playing for the Co-optimists against the South of Scotland. The latter injury, almost inevitably, was not without its funny side. 'As they carried me off, I was set to be the first emergency admission in the new treatment room they had built but they couldn't get the stretcher through a narrow doorway – when it was designed they forgot to allow for the extra width of the hands

of the carriers being outside the stretcher – so they asked me to get off it and hop through and then get back on again.'

As well as the injuries he suffered himself, in an era when replacements were not allowed, Micky was often pulled out of the pack to cover backs who had been forced to leave the field. He saw out more than one international on the wing but in the 1948 Calcutta Cup match at Murrayfield he was moved to scrum-half. In a tempestuous encounter England's centre and captain Keith Scott broke his jaw and scrum-half Richard Madge tore ligaments. Before long Micky was concussed but played on despite advice to the contrary: 'Someone in the crowd shouted out, "Take the poor boy off and put him to bed." They didn't say whether I should be alone or with somebody.'

Unfortunately, within a couple of years or so there was less cause for a chuckle and a twinkle in the eye. In September 1950 Micky was again due to go to Scotland to play for the Co-optimists in the Selkirk Sevens. He was now living and working in the Midlands so he went for a training run with his new club at Moseley. Disaster was about to strike. 'I had only turned up to go for the run but there was also a club trial match scheduled and as one of the selected wing-forwards was delayed, they asked me to fill the gap temporarily. I only expected to be on the field for about ten minutes before I would hand over to the other chap. Moments before this was due I was dribbling the ball past the opposing full-back but he dived to fall on it; he missed but caught my knee and snapped the ligaments. I was taken to hospital and then in an ambulance home to Tamworth in great pain. The injured knee was 19 inches thicker than the good one. It eventually required two operations and for two years I was on a walking stick. I never played again.'

Micky was barely 25 years old, with a playing record that encompassed 9 England caps, 2 Blues at Cambridge, 13 games for the Barbarians and club rugby with the Harlequins and Moseley. He was still, of course, on the Barbarian committee and that was a major consolation as he came to terms with his new situation. He also had a fine professional career to look forward to and this he soon achieved as new responsibilities were taken on board. His father had established a veterinary practice in south Staffordshire in 1923 and as he finalised his own qualifications in the profession, Micky might have contemplated the setting-up of a

By the 1960s Steele-Bodger was involved with the England team as national selector and tour manager. (© Barbarian Archive)

new practice elsewhere. Any such thoughts disappeared with the sudden death of his father, Harry, and he and his brother Alasdair took over the family practice. It was divided into two areas, with Micky based in Tamworth and the surrounding villages and farms. He still lives in the town today and, among all the local organisations and regional sports councils he has served on over the years, one of his proudest claims is that he has been president of Tamworth Rugby Football Club since 1952.

It was only a matter of time before Micky was rising through the ranks of the Rugby Football Union as well and in 1953 he began a 15-year stint as an international selector. He was soon ranked among the most widely travelled and best-known administrators in the game. When England went on their first overseas tour, to New Zealand and Australia in May 1963, Micky was the assistant manager; when the side next went abroad, to Canada four years later, he was manager. His deft touch in matters of man-management, his unfailing good humour and his comfortable manner in the corridors of power won him many admirers. When one of the most talented squads ever assembled, the RFU President's XV, came to England for the centenary celebrations in the spring of 1971, he was the natural and popular choice to be its manager. For him, guiding the likes of New Zealand's Colin Meads, the Springbok Frik du Preez or France's Jo Maso across the shires of England on a dazzling four-match tour that culminated in a capped international against England at Twickenham came as naturally as debating the great issues of the day as a delegate on the International Rugby Board. The presidency of the Rugby Football Union followed in 1973–74, the chairmanship of the IRB was another office

he held, and as chairman of the Four Home Unions Tours Committee he was also responsible for the selection of several British Isles teams to the southern hemisphere.

And all the time he was a committeeman for the Barbarian Football Club. He seemed destined to one day become the Club's president. He is the first to admit that he served a long apprenticeship but one in which he had the best possible role models and tutors. Longevity is a quality very apparent with the Baa-Baas. When Micky first played for them in 1946, the president was Emile de Lissa, and he was only the second man to hold the office since the Club's birth 56 years before. To be strictly accurate, the position of president had only been introduced in 1913 and its first holder, appropriately, was Percy Carpmael, the man who had founded the club in 1890. In the intervening 23 years Percy had been secretary and treasurer while also pursuing his work in the family business of chartered patent agents. The parallels between his background and interests and those of his successors are almost uncanny. Born and educated in Streatham, London, he went to Jesus College, Cambridge, and won his Blue in the 1885 Varsity match. His later rugby was played for Blackheath, then one of the most influential clubs in the British game. William Percy Carpmael played in 20 of the first 23 fixtures undertaken by the Barbarian Football Club between 1890 and 1893 and was to continue leading it off the field until his death in 1936.

In that year the presidency passed seamlessly to Emile Ernest Vere de Lissa, another club member at Blackheath, a big friend of Carpmael's and an enthusiastic chronicler who had been secretary and then treasurer of the Barbarians since his first Easter

W.P. Carpmael, founder and first president of the Barbarian Football Club.
(© Barbarian Archive)

tour in 1905. Emile, as he was known by all who came into contact with him, was unique among the Club's presidents in that he was not a distinguished player. But that hardly mattered because he was widely respected and had a proven track record as secretary at Richmond Athletic Ground, then a centre of sporting prowess to rank alongside Blackheath. He was, in effect, a pioneer among alickadoos – and as such perfect presidential material. Not that the term 'alickadoo' is in itself an easily defined reference for future office. Over the years it has been taken to mean anything from camp-followers to members of an older generation who by their very presence maintain and promote the values of the past; but it always describes folk who do everything short of actually playing to promote and nurture the game in general and the Barbarians in particular. On the Club's 1969 tour to South Africa the current secretary, Geoff Windsor-Lewis, with surely more than a whiff of mischief, which Baa-Baas past and present would approve of, defined for the benefit of the local press what he, as an alickadoo, was: 'All I can do . . . is talk.' Apparently, several scribes fell for that one and also faithfully recorded Geoff's other revelation that the Oxford English Dictionary was planning to include the word in its 1990 edition in recognition of the Barbarians' 100th birthday.

The presidency of de Lissa continued until 1955, when he died at the age of 85. It marked the end of an era not only because he had been a link with the game from the early years of the century but also because he had presided over the Club during the difficult war years and had been a much-respected figurehead in the decade since then. Amidst the general sadness of his passing there was further cause for regret in that he did not live to see one of his dearest projects reach fruition. In 1933 he had edited the first definitive history of the Club, *Barbarian Records 1890–1932*, and, in 1955, an updated volume was being prepared under the professional guidance of two notable historians and writers, Andrew 'Jock' Wemyss of the *Daily Express* and O.L. Owen of *The Times*.

The death of de Lissa in the summer of 1955 meant that the next president would be the most senior member of the committee. This was H.A. 'Jack' Haigh Smith, who had been honorary secretary for the previous 30 years. He was a former Trojans and Blackheath player, and had been selected three times for the Barbarians on the 1913 Easter tour. Once again he was someone who would bring a deep

Emile de Lissa was the second president and the editor of the first official history of the Club, published in 1933.
(© Barbarian Archive)

knowledge of the game to his position. He had been assistant manager on the British Isles tour to South Africa in 1938, had been touch judge for England in every international played at Twickenham between 1930 and 1949, and had worked with de Lissa in organising services internationals at the Richmond Athletic Ground during the war. But his term of office as Club president was to be cut cruelly short. There is in the Club's archives an endearing record of a five-way exchange of correspondence between Wemyss, Owen, Haigh Smith, Hughie Glyn Hughes and Herbert Waddell as, throughout the month of September 1955, they strove to complete the

The presidency of H.A. Haigh Smith was cruelly cut short by illness in 1955.
(© Barbarian Archive)

expertise, the others typical Barbarian commitment and enthusiasm. One issue that seemed to exercise all their minds unduly was the use of the word 'dribble' in an account by Wemyss of a match against Swansea in the 1920s. On 11 October Owen wrote to Wemyss: 'Now for a serio-comic matter mentioned by Haigh while we were having tea at Richmond on Saturday. It would seem that Herbert Waddell had laid some objection to your use of the word "dribble" . . . in your article. How serious his objection is I really don't know – it would seem to have some bearing upon Ernie Crawford's [another committee member] association of the word dribble with p—dle.' Not even Owen could bring himself to write the offending word in full. Whatever the hilarious undertones to this linguistic debate of half a century ago, there was darker news in the same letter from Owen when he reported that 'Haigh was carted off to hospital on Sunday night and is still there having X-rays and the like. Chronic indigestion apparently has had a flare up and – well, one must hope that nothing really serious has developed.'

Unfortunately it had. Yet from his sick bed on 14 October Haigh wrote to Wemyss to reassure him that, 'I have written to Herbert [Waddell] and more or less told him not to be silly. No one can take exception to the word "dribble" and anyhow, you are the editor and he had better talk to you.' There then followed three pages of analysis of what needed to be done to improve the book. That was almost the new president's last contribution to the project. On 26 October, Glyn Hughes wrote to other members of the committee: 'Haigh had to go back into hospital over the weekend for an operation on a very bad appendix; the old boy is far from well and very weak and tired. I go in

new book in time for the Christmas market. Little did they know that long before the festive season they would have lost another president and that, by then, Hughie would be president and Herbert in the newly created post of vice-president.

On 16 September Haigh wrote to Jock Wemyss: 'We are now working full blast at the new Barbarian book with a view to getting it published this season, I hope by Christmas . . . though [this] is a very big job.' Over the next couple of weeks further letters from Haigh, who was obviously the driving force behind the project, were mailed to the others in the working group covering everything from the rearranging of contents to photographic captions. Owen and Wemyss provided the every day and will keep you informed but in the meantime do not worry him with any letters or documents.' Two days later Jack Haigh Smith died. The Club prepared to appoint its third president within almost as many months.

Brigadier Hugh Llewellyn Glyn Hughes had been born in South Africa and brought up in Swansea before becoming a distinguished soldier and physician, a fine rugby player and a widely admired administrator. On the rugby field he was a hooker for Epsom College, United Hospitals, Blackheath, Exeter, London, Middlesex, Devon and 20 times for the Barbarians; later, he became a top-class referee. Off it he was president of Blackheath, assistant manager of the 1936 British tour to Argentina and, from 1928, treasurer of the Barbarians. He held a similar post on the Four Home Unions Tours Committee. And on the battlefields of two world wars he had an even more extraordinary record. In the First World War he was a subaltern in the Royal Army Medical Corps (RAMC), was awarded the Distinguished Service Order (DSO) and bar, and finished as a captain. At the outbreak of the next global conflict in 1939 he was a 47-year-old lieutenant of the Army reserve but again returned to the theatre of war and won a second bar to his DSO, some 30 years after his first, and was made a Commander of the Order of the British Empire (CBE), won several other awards from France, the USA and Israel, and was promoted first to colonel and then to brigadier. He was also the first medical officer to attempt to deal with the atrocities of Belsen. In peacetime he became honorary physician to the Queen. But to every Barbarian he was simply Hughie. As he himself wrote, 'Barbarians must be good players – and good fellows.' Yet again the Club was being led by an extraordinary president.

'The Brigadier' or 'Hughie' . . . whatever he was known as, H.L. Glyn Hughes was regarded as another great president.
(© Barbarian Archive)

By the time Hughie began his presidency, which was to last until 1973, Micky Steele-Bodger was well established as a committeeman. In an appreciation of the Club in *The Times* O.L. Owen described a typical scene in the Esplanade Hotel at Easter-time: 'To be in the little bar . . . with Hughie and other alickadoos is to savour the important social side of rugby at its best. H. Waddell, vice-president and prepared to talk all night; A. Wemyss, wondering if he is wearing his correct glass eye; and M.R. Steele-Bodger, veterinary surgeon and with himself the constitution of an ox.'

Micky was also playing a proactive role in the effective running of the Club. On 16 January 1957 he wrote to Jock Wemyss about

his concerns for the effectiveness of the committee: ' A committee of 11 trying to pick a side is impossible . . . Last Sunday I had a meeting with Hughie [Glyn Hughes] in town and we thought quite definitely that an executive must be appointed, the only difficulty being not who should go on the executive but as to how those left off it should be notified of that fact. It will, I am afraid, merely appear that we attempted to run in a democratic fashion, found it was too much bother and went back to the autocratic ways. Really, I suppose we all agree that semi-autocracy is the ideal thing.'

Of course, then as now, team selection for all the Barbarian teams and tours was done by a combination of telephone and Royal Mail. Not that it was without its sweeping generalisations, disagreements and hilarious assumptions, and in all these respects correspondence from the mid-1950s provides some classic examples. As the various selections for the Easter tour were being considered in 1956, Herbert Waddell noted in letters to Jock Wemyss that a certain English wing might be invited 'if [he] is a decent chap' but 'we can check with Micky Steele-Bodger'; another English centre should definitely be chosen because 'he is a good, loyal Barbarian'; and Waddell himself had 'up my sleeve a good new man for the Barbarians . . . who has got a beautiful sidestep and is fast'. But woe betide any player, however eminent, if they had failed to impress individuals on the committee. As permutations were mulled over for the Club's first overseas trip to Canada the following summer, one British and Irish Lion was discounted because 'he is blind' and another forward with international experience because 'he is stupid'. This tone probably illustrates a

businesslike and brusque style rather than one of disdain, though to the modern eye it might be seen as politically incorrect. Witness another early Waddellism when trying to arrange a Barbarian delegation to the Selkirk Sevens in September 1957: 'I told [a fellow committee member] not to take his wife as no women went to these games or to the pubs afterwards. He phoned up last night somewhat apologetically and said he would have to take her. Who wears the trousers? I can't stand women on rugby tours. There is a place for everything and everybody.'

It is only fair to report that during his own presidency after 1974 Herbert Waddell and his wife, Bee, were the firmest champions of the notion of wives of the committee forming a fellowship and new traditions and events were built up around a succession of 'better halves'. Even so, Micky Steele-Bodger can still not resist the occasional barbed comment which is almost used as bait to dangle in front of (and probably test) the most respected of modern career women. In an interview with the *Daily Telegraph*'s Sue Mott in 1997, arranged, inevitably, at his London base, the East India Club in St James' Square, he said, 'If you had been wearing trousers there could have been trouble – and 15 years ago you'd have had to come in the back way.' Mott passed the test with flying colours, reporting that Micky's 'grin was as deep as his chauvinism'.

All this, however, is a distraction from the real business of the Barbarians, which is playing the game, in every sense, on the field. Looking back, there is no disputing that Hughie Glyn Hughes' leadership between 1955 and November 1973 coincided with a glorious era in Barbarian history. The first overseas tours, to Canada in 1957 and South Africa in

Barbarians and their ladies. By the 1980s the fairer sex played a full part at committee gatherings with the president, Herbert Waddell, surrounded by a galaxy of better halves. The alickadoos at the back are (left to right) Geoff Windsor-Lewis, Micky Steele-Bodger, Adam Robson, David Chisholm, Gordon Ferguson and Vic Roberts.
(© Barbarian Archive)

1958 and 1969, were undertaken and he managed them all with great style and dignity. Nearer home, the great matches against the international touring teams were again staged at Cardiff Arms Park every three years, with the Wallabies beaten in 1958, the Springboks in 1961, and, most famously, the All Blacks in 1973. It was also a period when the regular fixtures in the Midlands and in South Wales continued to be the highlight of the domestic calendar. Hughie died on 24 November 1973. Earlier that day he had watched Scotland play Argentina at Murrayfield and attended the post-match dinner for the teams. He died in his sleep at the North British Hotel. He was 81 years old and the tributes flowed in, not only from the sporting world but also from many other walks of life. The *British Medical Journal*

noted that, 'Medicine has lost one of its great driving forces of recent years and many of us have lost a loyal friend.' At his thanksgiving service in London two months later the address was given by another man of stature in the game, Judge Carl Aarvold. He said, 'As a sportsman [Hughie] had no doubt that a man should play a game not to achieve renown, or wealth, or the claim of the unstable fan, but for the sheer exhilaration and enjoyment of skill and competitive effort, for the thrill of being one of a team whom you must never let down, and the more guts it needed – the better.' Somehow it summed up the man and the Barbarians.

Once again the similarities between the late and new President were remarkable. At the age of 71 Herbert Waddell had had literally a lifetime's preparation for the role he now took on and, like Glyn Hughes and the others before him, he was widely regarded as a rugby statesman but one with a considerable profile in the world at large. He had joined the Barbarian committee in 1926 when he was still one of the most talented fly-halfs of his generation. He was a proud Scot who had been educated at Glasgow Academy and at Fettes College, two renowned staging posts for budding internationals north of the Border. He advanced through the Scottish Schools team to senior club rugby with the Glasgow Academicals club that dominated Scottish rugby throughout the 1920s. It was a golden era for the national team as well, with its greatest day being 21 March 1925. It was the cause for multiple celebrations as Murrayfield hosted an international for the first time and Herbert marked the occasion with a late drop goal that secured the Calcutta Cup, Triple Crown, Grand Slam and International Championship. He had won the first of his 15 Scottish caps in France a year earlier as a 21 year old and had done so well with three tries and another drop goal during that season's championship that he had been a popular selection for the British Isles tour to South Africa. Further success followed with fifteen matches, including three Tests, on that trip and it was a country with which he was to have many affiliations throughout his life. An injured shoulder and a threatened ulcer had hampered his playing career before his final international appearance in 1930 – highlighted by another match-winning Murrayfield drop goal against Wales – and then his progression to the higher echelons of the administrative side of the game.

Meanwhile, and again like Hughie Glyn Hughes, Herbert gave distinguished military service in the Second World War, where he

Herbert Waddell became the fifth president in 1974, having already held similar office with the Scottish Rugby Union, and was also an honorary vice-president of the South African Rugby Board. (© Barbarian Archive)

commanded the 11th Highland Light Infantry and, later, the 141 Royal Armoured Corps (RAC) – The Buffs – ending with the rank of colonel and a mention in dispatches. He was equally successful in civilian life. He had been a member of the Stock Exchange since 1927 and the firm of Spiers and Jeffrey since 1929. He became senior partner there, a role he continued in until 1979. Barbarian tours were often an opportunity to share his knowledge of the financial markets with any players who showed an interest or ambition in that volatile sphere.

Immediately after the war, Herbert was elected to the committee of the Scottish Rugby Union and became a national selector for six seasons, and was a delegate on the International Rugby Football Board from 1952 until 1963 when he became president of the SRU. He was already president of Glasgow Academicals, an honorary vice-president of the South African Rugby Board and vice-president of the Barbarians. The latter two honours were perfectly juxtaposed in 1958 when the Club toured South Africa and Herbert was assistant manager to Hughie on a trip that further enhanced the Barbarians' reputation in the rugby world. Eleven years later, when the Barbarians returned to South Africa, Herbert went as a camp-follower rather than in an official Club capacity – Hughie Glyn Hughes was manager and Geoff Windsor-Lewis his assistant – but was also invited as a guest of the SARB. Thus the tour party had the best of both worlds, with the president, vice-president and secretary all travelling with the players.

Herbert's own presidency of the Club was as successful as his predecessors'. Over the next 14 years special matches were arranged with several clubs in Scotland, England and France who were celebrating their own centenaries. The keynote matches against the Springboks, Wallabies and All Blacks continued as before but now with Twickenham as well as Cardiff attracting sell-out crowds. It was arguably at Twickenham in 1977 that the most prestigious match of all was staged, a game between the Barbarian Football Club and the British Isles; more specifically, the Lions' team that had recently returned from a 26-match tour of New Zealand. The game was held in honour of the Silver Jubilee of Queen Elizabeth II, attracted a capacity crowd of 70,000 and resulted in an unparalleled sum of £100,000 being donated to the Silver Jubilee Fund. It was another candidate for the accolade of greatest day in the Club's history.

But there were also difficult issues to confront during Herbert's era as president, not least the gradual diminution of the Easter tour of Wales. The final fixture with Penarth was in 1986, a decision that hit the local club hard and which required all the presidential skills of diplomacy and explanation often under extreme pressure. Herbert was more than equal to the task. When Herbert died on 5 January 1988, Geoff Windsor-Lewis informed the other members of the committee, concluding his official letter, 'Herbert was a great man and will be sadly missed by all of us.' At his funeral service a week later the Rev. J. Hay Hamilton, who as a boy had marked him in schools rugby and as a young man had served under him in the Highland Light Infantry, summed up Herbert's legacy to perfection: 'And so we say farewell . . . to this man of many parts, of many gifts of mind and spirit; a man with a great zest for living, happy in his home and family and who enjoyed life to the full; one whom his country delighted to honour with the CBE medal.'

Later in 1988 the Barbarians played Glasgow Academicals in what was designated the Herbert Waddell Memorial Match. Great names of a new era, like Finlay Calder, Donal Lenihan, Jonathan Davies and Will Carling, had no hesitation in accepting invitations to play. The match itself was a 13-try extravaganza won by the Barbarians and followed by a gala dinner. Herbert would have approved.

The death of Herbert Waddell was the signal for the election of the Club's sixth president in 98 years. On 15 January 1988 Geoff Windsor-Lewis wrote again to the committee:

It is in the best interests of the Club to elect a new president and vice-president following Herbert's sad death. In order

to save time and expense, and in accordance with the Club rules that business may be carried out by correspondence, I would like to set out the following proposals:

Micky Steele-Bodger to become president – I am delighted to propose him and Gordon Ferguson has seconded this proposal.

David Chisholm has proposed Vic Roberts as vice-president and Jeff Herdman has seconded this nomination.

Any other nominations should reach me by 30 January 1988.

No one expected there to be any such further nominations and neither were there. Michael Roland Steele-Bodger was duly installed as president in time for the Mobbs Memorial Match of March 1988. Beyond that there were many significant events looming on the horizon: the Easter tour to Wales, albeit truncated, with only Cardiff and Swansea now on the itinerary, a month later; and, at the end of the year, a fixture against the touring Wallabies at Cardiff Arms Park. Micky was 62 years old, the youngest president to take up office since Percy Carpmael in 1913, and, typically, he approached everything with boundless energy and enthusiasm. Looming on the horizon was the Club's centenary season in 1990 and it was the perfect project for the new president to become immersed in. In the course of the next two years, fixtures were confirmed against England, Wales and Argentina, a poignant return would be made to Bradford, where the local club had been the Barbarians' second-ever opponents in 1890, and, of course, there would be a series of other events with the centrepiece being the centenary dinner to be

held at the Hilton Hotel in Park Lane, London, on 28 September 1990. Micky was in his element. It was to be a landmark moment in the Club's history but also the perfect launch pad for another exceptional presidency.

Since 1988 Micky's leadership has benefited from the presence of several equally committed lieutenants on the committee. Vic Roberts, his old back-row teammate for England and the Barbarians in the 1940s, was his loyal vice-president until his death in March 2004. Gordon Ferguson was a marvellous Mr Fix-it as well as honorary treasurer before being succeeded by Mike Weston. Adam Robson, another ex-president of the Scottish Rugby Union, was a huge support after 1985 until an untimely illness forced him to stand down in 2003. Great players like Andy Ripley, Kevin Flynn, Gareth Davies, Dusty Hare, Simon Halliday, John Jeffrey, John Spencer, Jeff Probyn, Derek Quinnell and Donal Lenihan have often combined their work for the Club with other responsibilities on national rugby unions and in the business world. There was no better example of a readiness to adopt new approaches than the invitation to the former All Black Zinzan Brooke to join the committee in 2002. This was part recognition of the increasing number of players from the southern hemisphere representing the Club and also further evidence that with the Barbarians there have never been national boundaries or constraints to work within. Other long-serving committee members down to the present day are the former Wales international Haydn Mainwaring and Syd Millar, who also became chairman of the International Rugby Board. Mainwaring is forever associated in Barbarian folklore with the resounding tackle that poleaxed the giant Springbok lock and skipper

Avril Malan en route to the famous win in 1961 at Cardiff. He says of the president, 'Micky has an incredible knowledge which effectively saves the rest of the committee time. He knows everyone and they know him. This opens doors when we are negotiating fixtures and trying to secure player availability. And on a personal level, he is also a very caring and loyal person.'

The most significant ever-present colleague of the Steele-Bodger era remains the honorary secretary, Geoff Windsor-Lewis, who came straight onto the committee in that role in the summer of 1966. He was an ideal recruit with all the correct credentials. His father, Dr Windsor H. Lewis, was a Cambridge Blue and Welsh international fly-half who had played in the same Barbarian sides as Herbert Waddell in the 1920s before serving on the committee in the early 1930s and again for many years after the war. Geoff had followed in his father's footsteps in every respect, winning three Blues including a winning captaincy in 1958, a couple of caps in the centre for Wales in 1960 and four appearances for the Barbarians, and had been the mainstay of the Oxfordshire county side for several seasons before leading them to two consecutive championship semi-finals. It was Micky who approached him to take on the post of Club secretary. 'Micky phoned one Saturday evening to arrange a meeting the following day. I had just retired from playing and had known Micky and the rest of the committee for many years. The next afternoon we sat in the garden discussing the Barbarians when he proposed that as he was then chairman of the England selectors, he needed to relinquish the secretaryship of the Club. Would I take it over? I realised immediately that it was a huge honour to be invited so he was a bit taken aback when I

asked if I could think about it over the weekend. But I knew that it was an opportunity that was unlikely to come around again and there was no doubt that I would jump at the offer. I haven't regretted it for one moment since then.'

Geoff Windsor-Lewis is now approaching his 40th year as honorary secretary and he reckons he hasn't missed a Club fixture in that time. He has worked with three presidents and has benefited from all of them as his role has become very different over the years. 'Hughie [Glyn Hughes] told me at the outset that he would give me all the help he could and I quickly learnt that there were several unwritten rules. The old military discipline was evident when he believed that with any meeting if you weren't five minutes early, you were five minutes late. His advice to the teams was always that we should keep the game simple and play hard, a lesson I still try to instil when I speak to our teams these days. And another great thing about Hughie was that he wouldn't tolerate swearing and particularly when addressing a team formally. Herbert [Waddell] was slightly more detached than Hughie and he was happy to let me get on with running the day-to-day administration and I certainly grew into the role as a result. I have to say, though, that Micky is a one-off. He has a phenomenal enthusiasm and incredible energy levels underpinned by a burning desire to succeed. At home he has benefited from his marvellous marriage with [his wife] Muff, and they are a true partnership.'

Like everyone else, Geoff is amazed at the stamina and determination of a man approaching his 80th year whose working week invariably entails at least two return rail journeys from his home in Tamworth to the East

India Club in London, where he is also president. With a mixture of admiration and jest, he added, 'Micky is the only Barbarian I know who commutes over 100 miles to his gentlemen's club,' because Geoff knows that from his office there in the shadow of St James' Square Micky works long hours communicating with people from all over the rugby world, and all in the interests of the Club.

For Micky Steele-Bodger himself, however, no individual is bigger than the Club. At the outset of the centenary season in September 1990, he wrote: 'We must make sure that our future is a happy and successful one, thus rewarding all those who in the past have contributed so much while at the same time acknowledging their contribution.' He also noted, 'The achievements of the past surely . . . entitle the Club to enter its second century with confidence even though circumstances and attitudes in rugby football have changed . . .' Nearly twenty years into his presidency the Barbarian Football Club is still thriving. As Geoff Windsor-Lewis concludes, 'I don't think there will ever be another like him.'

II

CENTENARY CELEBRATIONS

'This illustrious touring team ... are unique and the epitome of the original design of rugby as a most magnificent attacking game demanding the highest levels of sportsmanship, courage and skill and playing for fun.'

— Clem Thomas, 1991

The centenary season of the Barbarian Football Club was always going to be something special. It officially began on 28 September 1990 and was set to encompass a gala dinner, matches against England, Wales and Argentina as well as the traditional Welsh opponents of Newport, Cardiff and Swansea plus Leicester and the East Midlands in England. At the start of the following season the celebrations were still continuing. Such was the popularity of the Club that special requests to be part of its landmark year could not all be included within the confines of the 1990–91 season. Thus, in September 1991, the Barbarians travelled north to play Scotland at Murrayfield and, the following week, went west across to Ireland to play two other clubs with centenaries of their own: Constitution in Cork and Old Wesley in

Dublin. It was, in every sense, a birthday and a half.

No stone was left unturned as Gordon Ferguson and the rest of the committee trawled the world to find contact numbers to invite all surviving former players to join the party at some stage. It was important that old traditions and friendships were recognised as they always had been by the Club. So the itinerary for the first week of celebrations included not only matches at the modern citadels of Twickenham and the National Stadium at Cardiff Arms Park, but also a match and dinner at the Bradford and Bingley Rugby Football Club in Yorkshire. The Barbarians were returning to their roots, to the city where the very concept of the Club was formulated by Percy Carpmael and his friends on 9 April 1890.

The occasion then was a light-hearted supper held at Leuchter's Restaurant in Bradford during a four-match tour of the Midlands and the North by Carpmael's team of Southern Nomads. Obviously imbued by the spirit of camaraderie and sporting exhilaration of a trek that took in games against Burton, Moseley, Wakefield Trinity and the Yorkshire county cup-holders, Huddersfield, the tourists resolved to broaden their horizons and establish a new touring club. Carpmael's men at that supper, the menu for which may or may not have included oysters, as was assumed in original Barbarian folklore, were primarily from the London clubs of Blackheath, Richmond, Harlequins, Rosslyn Park, St Thomas's Hospital and Middlesex Wanderers. From further afield the clubs of Castle Cary, Manchester, Dublin University, Wellington and Wiveliscombe were also represented. The Southern Nomads had enjoyed their travels around the rugby heartlands of the regions and had lost only to Huddersfield, by a try to nil on the afternoon of 8 April. But now, as the clock ticked past midnight, the seeds of the Barbarians' birth were sown. The official record book of the Club, written in impressive copper-plate style, succinctly sums up the result of their deliberations:

Barbarian Football Club
It was resolved to form the above club at 2 a.m. on April 9th 1890 at the Alexandra Hotel, Bradford, by the members of a scratch team captained by W.P. Carpmael. This team played the following matches on:-
April 4 Burton – Won 1 goal to 1 try
April 5 Moseley – Drawn
April 7 Wakefield Trinity –

Won 2 goals 2 tries to 1 try
April 8 Huddersfield – Lost 0 to 1 try

The Alexandra Hotel was the team's base for their three days in Yorkshire but they had adjourned to Leuchter's Restaurant during the evening and that is where almost certainly their resolution was passed. As for the name of the Club, O.L. Owen had explained in Emile de Lissa's *Barbarian Records 1890–1932* that '[the Barbarians were] dignified by the famous victory of Arminius over Varus and his legions . . . about two thousand years ago'. Less impressively, de Lissa's handwritten note inserted into the original archive says that the name was 'in derision, it is presumed, of people who apply the epithet [barbarian] indiscriminately to all players of the rugby game'. In his research for the book, de Lissa had also corresponded with a leading figure in the Corinthian club, N. Lane Jackson. In a letter of 21 July 1932, Jackson had written, 'I believe that "Tottie" Carpmael really started the Barbarians after a long chat with me at the sports club [in St James' Square] when I told him all about the origin of the Corinthians. As I played rugger for seven years before I took up soccer, I was much interested in his ideas.' The conclusion drawn by de Lissa was that the rules and constitution of the Club had been framed on those of the Corinthian Football Club. Clearly, Carpmael had done his research in the months leading up to the formation of the Barbarians.

It would still be nearly eight months before the Barbarian Football Club played its first fixtures, again, appropriately, in the north of England at Hartlepool and Bradford. Before then several other matters of detail had to be completed. Pride of place went to the rules of the Club and they had been prepared by Carpmael together with three other founder members, Frank Evershed from Blackheath, W.N. Mayne of Moseley and M.T. Scott of the Northern club, during the late summer. They proposed five rules for the new Club: that it be called the Barbarian Football Club and that the colours be a white jersey with black monogram on the left breast, dark shorts and stockings; that the members be limited to sixty-five and that there be no entry fee or subscription; that a committee of between four and eight members and an honorary secretary and treasurer should be elected at the annual general meeting and then be responsible for the entire management of the Club; that a general meeting be held in the month of October in each year for the election of the committee and officers, to pass the accounts and to remove from the list of members those who are unlikely to further assist the club; and that any alteration to the rules could only be carried by a two-thirds majority of members at a general meeting.

The next entry in the official records is minuted succinctly:

> At the first Annual Meeting held on Oct 1st 1890 at 24 Southampton Buildings at 5 oc'k. The rules were passed as presented with one alteration proposed by W.P. Carpmael (in the absence of A.B. Perkins) & seconded by R.F. Chaldecott, i.e. in rule 4 'October' read September – carried.

Carpmael would be the honorary secretary and treasurer, Mayne the assistant secretary and, as well as Evershed and Scott, the first elected committee included P.F. Hancock of Wiveliscombe and J.H. Rogers of Moseley.

The official record book that outlines the resolution to set up the Club on 9 April 1890 and its subsequent first annual meeting on 1 October of the same year.
(© Barbarian Archive)

Preparations now went ahead for the first games at the end of the year and in due course subtle amendments were proposed to the rules. The irony is that the first annual meeting of 1890 turned out to be the last of its kind. The committee quickly established a modus operandi based on communication by post and this was written into the rules the following year. At the same time the colours became the now familiar black-and-white jersey with black shorts. It was also decided that all the members should resign annually but that they should also elect 50 new members by the end of September each year; the committee had the

NOW READY ! ORD'S RUGBY GUIDE. NOW READY !

HARTLEPOOL ROVERS
Colours:—Red, White and Black.

Full Back :
J. W. HORN

Three-quarter Backs :
Right : Centres : Left :
T. A. F. CROW HILL D. McPHERSON
F. H. R. ALDERSON A. E. EMMERSON

Half-Backs :
Left : Right :
G. SMITH A. O. SCOTT

Forwards : T. GULLY
F. C. LOHDEN J. COATES
F. E. PEASE C. M. HUNTLEY
J. SNOWDON W. YIEND, Capt.
A. HILL Hunter T. BURT

Touch Judge—Mr. W. H. ALLEN
Referee—Mr. T. M. Swinburne, Pres.
Durham Co. Rugby Union.

First Half	G	PG	T	M		TOTAL	
						G	PG
Second Half						1	

ORD'S
OFFICIAL PROGRAMME.
(B. T. ORD, Introducer of the Football Programme in the North.)

HARTLEPOOL ROVERS
versus
BARBARIANS.

Friarage Field, H'pool,
SATURDAY, DEC. 27th, 1890.
Kick off 2·30 p.m.

ADMISSION 3D. GRAND STAND
(ENCLOSED) 6D. (UNENCLOSED) 3D.
STAND 1D.

B. T. ORD, PRINTER, HIGH ST., HARTLEPOOL.

BARBARIANS.
Colours—

Full Back :
— BOUCHER.

Three-quarter Backs :
Left : Right :
Centre :
A. E. STODDART (Capt.) R. L. ASHTON,
McGREGOR or GEORGE. J. H. ROGERS,

Half Backs :
R. R. ESCOTT, E. W. SENIOR,

Forwards :
R. D. BUDWORTH, A. ALLPORT,
S. M. J. WOODS, P. F. HANCOCK,
W. W. MAYNE, W. H. MANFIELD,
P. P. CARPMAEL, CAREY

Touch Judge—TREGELLAS

First Half	G	PG	T	M		TOTAL	
						G	PG	T	M
Second Half						3	-	-	1

NOW READY ! ORD'S RUGBY GUIDE. NOW READY !

The official programme for the inaugural game against Hartlepool Rovers. The touch judge, T.S. Tregellas, played in the Club's next match, two days later, against Bradford.

discretion to add a further 15 nominations during the course of a season. Further amendments were made over the years, the most important of which was undoubtedly the decision in 1913 that the office of president be created. There was little doubt that the first president should be the man who had done more than anyone to establish and foster the Club and Percy Carpmael was duly elected. Other refinements included the introduction of an official tie in 1895, a blazer in 1929 and, a year later, the distinctive Club badge. The latter was the work of I.M.B. Stuart, a forward who had played twice for Ireland in 1924 and who had played for the Barbarians on six Easter tours. His ingenious design incorporated into two overlapping shields the emblems of the four national unions in the British Isles — the rose, thistle, shamrock and Prince of Wales feathers — and the silver fern of New Zealand, the springbok of South Africa and the waratah of New South Wales. Above the shields two lambs were depicted chasing a rugby ball. It soon became one of the most recognised and admired badges in rugby union.

The Club's first matches were arranged for the Christmas period of 1890 and on the evening of Boxing Day the team assembled at the most appropriate place imaginable, the Alexandra Hotel in Bradford where, eight months earlier, Carpmael and his cohort of Southern Nomads had gathered on the weekend of their grand plan. Now the Barbarians were about to see the light of day in an inaugural fixture against Hartlepool Rovers. The captain for the match was to be A.E. Stoddart, one of the most celebrated sportsmen of his generation. Andrew Stoddart had already captained the British team that toured Australia and New Zealand in 1888 and England against Wales two years later, as well as achieving cricket immortality when he led England on a triumphant Ashes tour Down Under in 1894–95. The Club could have no better figurehead to lead it onto the pitch for the first time. With him were seven members of the Southern Nomads' trailblazers of the previous spring – Alfred Allport, Randolph Aston, Richard Budworth, Philip Hancock, W.N. Mayne, E.W. Senior and, of course, Carpmael himself. All of them, except Mayne of Moseley and Senior of St Thomas's Hospital, were members of the Blackheath club. Having stayed overnight in Bradford, the team travelled the following morning by rail to Hartlepool, were not too disconcerted by a 45-minute delay and at 2.40 p.m. kicked off in front of what was described as 'an admiring crowd'. The Barbarians' presence at the Rovers ground, the Friarage, was a recognition that their opponents were among the strongest teams in England at the time and the occasion was certainly a success. In the Hartlepool Rovers history published in 1901, Fred Theaker wrote:

The team that beat Devonshire four months later was again captained by A.E. Stoddart. In the first season the monogram on the players' jerseys consisted of a skull and crossbones; this was soon changed. (© Barbarian Archive)

> The feature of the season . . . was a visit from the Barbarians, comprising players drawn from the English, Scottish and Welsh clubs, including A.E. Stoddart, R.L. Aston, Gregor McGregor and S.M.J. Woods, and after a well-contested game the visitors won by three goals and one try to one goal and one try. It was a splendid exposition and one of the best matches I have seen and, as an object lesson, it ought to have been witnessed by all other players, and probably some of them learned how happily the laws could be put into operation, and as long as the Barbarians and Rovers can meet and show the same skill, the games will be delightful to watch. Individual brilliancy may have its merits, but the game is intended for a team. The Barbarians did not make the mistake of playing the game of individuals but as a team gave an exhibition worthy of the traditions of the game.

Two days later the Barbarians took the field again, this time against Bradford. Nine of the team had played against the Rovers and although the match ended in a draw, it was not without incident. In an amusing diary of the tour published by 'One of Them', it is reported that 'once Stoddart had a clear run but someone in the crowd blew a whistle and he stopped'. He did, however, finish off another move with one of the Club's two tries and reputations were preserved all around. A third fixture, scheduled

THE BARBARIANS

THE DIARY OF THE BARBARIAN F. C. TOUR.

BY ONE OF THEM.

Xmas 1890

December 26.

5.30 p.m.—Kings Cross Station was enlivened by the presence of P. F. Hancock, S. M. J. Woods, A. E. Stoddart, A. Allport, W. P. Carpmael, E. W. Senior, W. H. Manfield, H. Boucher, A. S. Gedge, T. S. Tregellas, R. B. Sweet-Escott, R. L. Aston, W. H. Carey, R. D. Budworth, P. Maud, and one spectator called "Lupus." An enterprising guard asked why he was so named, we then heard that this keen footballer once ran with the beagles in Somerset; after a time a hare was jumped and this man of panics remarked, "There goes Lupus."

5.45 p.m.—We left King's Cross.

5.50 p.m.—Cards.

10.15.—Arrived at Bradford; found Mayne and A. Rogers. Went to Alexandra Hotel, had supper, and dressed for the dance.

December 27.

2 a.m.—Supper.

4 a.m.—Most of the team in bed, but sad to relate one gay man danced until 7.30—this was the only day on which he was down to breakfast.

10 a.m.—Start on a journey to Hartlepool.

10.30 a.m.—Had a most enjoyable wait of half-an-hour at Holbeck—a place noted for its porters. If you want to hear how our secretary was scored off, ask Stoddart.

12.30 p.m.—Melton Mowbray pies and beer. Woods strongly recommends these pies to all players, they should be eaten just before playing. It is reported that since these pies have been made the price of felines has gone up.

2.10 p.m.—Arrived at Hartlepool, three-quarters of an hour late—met by McGregor and Alderson. The joint owners of the canary embraced before an admiring crowd.

2.40 p.m.—Kick-off—had a very fast and interesting game. At half-time we were leading by three goals, condition and the dance then seemed to tell, but we won pretty comfortably by 3-0-1 to 1-1-4.

The feature of the match was the passing of McGregor, and the sprint of Allport. I hear that he at once wired to N. Spurling to run him 50 yards. It will be a great race. We had a walking apothecaries' shop, touch judging for us—fortunately for him Carpmael hurt his head, but he, the apothecary judge, then produced lint, bandages, wristlets, &c., &c., and the head was then wonderfully done up by that rising surgeon, Mr. Allport, of Guy's Hospital.

Alderson and Yiend were in good form for the Rovers.

6.50 p.m.—We started by the Harrogate and Leeds express; the feature of the N.E.R. express is that it stops by snow-clad-fields instead of all stations. It is very amusing at first, but after a bit it gets monotonous.

11.15 a.m.—Arrived at Leeds. Several savages were by this time rather good understudies for the desert of Sahara. They climbed out of the saloon which was in a siding, and got to the station—but Leeds is a provincial town, and Gedge is never going to leave London again.

12.10.—We reached Bradford once more.

December 28.

All slept the sleep of the just, got up, had dinner, and went back to bed. One or two rash men who were playing for that insignificant team called the South went for a ten mile walk.

An enterprising interviewer called to-day to see Stoddart. The much paragraphed and photoed one went out to see him; somehow the reporter had vanished, but Budda got an arm-chair!

I may also mention that a hair-singeing establishment was opened with great success in the evening. I ought to have recorded yesterday that a little boy of Hartlepool gave Hancock's height as "six foot and a bally brick." Of course he said the Hartlepool equivalent for bally!

December 29.

6.30 a.m.—The army's breakfast was ready.

7.30 a.m.—The army's breakfast was again got ready.

8.30 a.m.—Ditto.

9.30 a.m.—Ditto.

11.0 a.m.—The army came down—terrible commotion—rush of waiters—awful language of the reserved forces.

11.10 a.m.—The army tackled a kipper and subsided for the day.

1.45. p.m.—The ball was kicked off in the Bradford match. We had Woods, Budworth, Allport, Aston, and Carpmael away but Alderson and Yiend assisted. As we were very hard up for forwards and had any amount of backs we played four three-quarters. We soon got a try which Aldi converted, after this the game got rather energetic. At half-time we led by two goals to one penalty goal. In the second half we had very bad luck, several times what appeared certain tries were just saved, and once Stoddart had a clear run in b... someone in the crowd blew a whistle and he stopped. Bradford got in twice, once because our forwards stopped and appealed. The other try was exceedingly doubtful. Doyle, the back, kicked the ball over our line, Bairstow (three-quarter) and Harrison (forward) rushed up, one kept Boucher off and the other touched down.

We claimed confidently for offside, and it seems impossible that it could have been otherwise, as Doyle was knocked over by Alderson and therefore put no one onside.

Anyhow the match was a draw. We should all like to see Hickson captain again. Directly he goes some of the team take to various Northern practices of a doubtful character.

Alderson, McGregor, Stoddart, and Senior played very well, the passing being excellent; all the forwards played hard, Yiend was very good.

4.40 p.m.—We heard that the South had been beaten.

6.0 p.m.—Great rejoicings—Alderson having been elected captain of England.

We then had dinner at the "Talbot," and went to the theatre.

December 30.

10.30 a.m.—The Army had his breakfast.

11.7 a.m.—Just off when the Boots rushed up the platform with No. 18's tooth-brush (he held the brush in his hand). Shouts of Mayne. The little scene reminded us of one of Leech's sketches.

11.8 a.m.—Started for Manchester.

1.10 p.m.—In the middle of lunch and of a great discussion whether there were any songs after the N. v. S. dinner—Budworth and Aston for—Woods and Allport against—a telegram comes putting off the match. Agreed to catch the two o'clock train for London.

6.15 p.m.—Arrived at King's Cross after a pleasant tour. The Army and the Baby have a farewell rag, and we part until the 31st of March at Cardiff.

An impressively thorough report of the match against Hartlepool Rovers and the social activities surrounding the first matches in December 1890. (© Barbarian Archive) for Swinton the following afternoon, was cancelled two hours before the start because of a heavy overnight frost. Instead, the party caught an early train to London. Carpmael was already planning their next get-together for Easter matches in Wales and Devon.

A century later the commendable plan of the modern Barbarians was to go to Bradford again. After playing – and losing to – the Yorkshire side in 1891, there had been no further fixtures until the Club's 75th anniversary in 1965. Then, in a short tour, the Barbarians had beaten both Bradford and Hartlepool Rovers in the space of three days. The Rovers had been visited more regularly, with the Club winning six and drawing two of the eight matches between 1893 and 1902. Another game had taken place in 1979 to mark the Rovers' own centenary. The Barbarians, with ten Lions in their side, had won that match 62–10. Now, in the Club's centenary year, it was Bradford's turn to be played in the week between the England and Wales matches.

As the planning for the centenary season gathered pace, the Barbarians received a welcome boost that in its way was further confirmation that the second 100 years of the Club would be very different to the first: they received sponsorship. The possibility of financial support from the commercial world had been in the air for several years and, though the Club had never sought sponsorship, offers had been mooted and politely declined. The only exceptions had been two matches against the touring Wallabies side in Cardiff in 1984 and 1988, which were called, respectively, the Wang Match and the Royal Bank of Scotland Match, and the All Blacks match at Twickenham in November 1989, which was sponsored by the Willis

Two popular Barbarians of more recent times, Rob Andrew (left) and Gavin Hastings, helped launch the Club's first sponsorship agreement with Scottish Amicable in the centenary season of 1990–91.
(© Barbarian Archive)

Group. Though professional rugby was still some time in the future by the start of the 1990s, the climate was clearly changing even for the Barbarians. On 28 February 1990 it was announced that Scottish Amicable and the Club had signed a sponsorship agreement worth £150,000 over three years. Over the same period the company would also provide a support spend of £750,000. Micky Steele-Bodger said, 'The Barbarians have had many offers of sponsorship but have been delighted to accept that of Scottish Amicable because their aims and objectives from the sponsorship are broadly similar to those of the Club. This sponsorship will allow the Club to move forward in the 1990s on a steady financial footing, especially important in our centenary year.' A week before the centenary dinner in

September a second announcement was made, introducing an 'Amicable Gesture' whereby £50 would be donated for every point scored by the Barbarians during the centenary season. The money would go to the youth trust of the national union of the country where the match was played – and in due course, as various Baa-Baas ran in try after try, nearly £15,000 was raised and donated within England and Wales alone. As the opening weekend of the centenary celebrations approached, the president gave an interview to *The Times* in which he said, 'As a club, we do not intend to stand still and simply reflect on a glorious first century. We are proud of what we have achieved so far but we know that we have a mission and a responsibility to the game of rugby football. In achieving our goals, while preserving the unique character of our Club, we know we have another hundred years ahead of us that will be just as exciting a challenge.' Clearly the Club was entering a new era.

On 28 September 1990 the rugby world gathered to salute the Barbarians' 100th birthday. The day began in style for the committee, with lunch at the Lensbury Club, where the Barbarians team to play England the following day were staying and training. By mid-afternoon they were on a river trip on the Thames. Then, at 7 p.m., almost 600 guests including former players and leading administrators from all over the world joined them for the centenary dinner at the Hilton on Park Lane in London's West End. Among the administrators were the presidents of eight national unions and officials from the Barbarian clubs in Australia, Fiji, France, New Zealand, Portugal and South Africa. The former players represented every decade of the Club's history since the 1920s. Pride of place went to

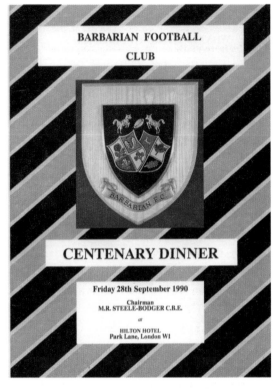

A special souvenir brochure was produced for the centenary dinner on 28 September 1990. (© Barbarian Archive)

James Richardson of Birkenhead Park and England, who had played for the Club against the East Midlands in 1924 and was now 3 months short of his 87th birthday. He was the oldest Barbarian in attendance, but not far behind him was 85-year-old William Kirwan-Taylor OBE, another England international, almost inevitably from Cambridge University and Blackheath, whose Club debut had been in 1926 against Leicester. The long-established links with Hartlepool Rovers were represented by the presence of Cliff Harrison, a wing who had played as a 19 year old in the Mobbs Match of 1931. Barbarians of a more recent vintage included eight members of the 1948 team that beat the Wallabies in the Club's first fixture against an international touring side. Micky Steele-Bodger had scored a try in that match as had the scrum-half and captain Haydn Tanner and they were joined by the Cardiff and Wales centres Billy Cleaver and Bleddyn Williams, England's Martin Turner, Tommy Kemp and Harry Walker, and the Irish hooker who had gone on to lead the 1950 Lions, Dr Karl Mullen. Six other Lions captains were there, too. If not quite an A to Z of world rugby, it was certainly a case of A to Y in a gathering of everyone from Sir Carl Aarvold to John Young, the 1959 Lion. It was the perfect preamble to the rugby on show over the next few months.

The action kicked off with another first for the Club, a game against England at Twickenham. The headquarters of the English game had been the venue for matches against the All Blacks in 1967, 1974 and 1989 and, of course, the Club had played the Lions there in 1977. Further back still the Barbarians had played London in a match in aid of the King George V Jubilee Trust Fund in May 1935 (won comfortably by 34 points to 3), and in 1985 a match against London Welsh in that club's centenary season was staged there. A match against a full England side was a new departure and a significant one. The Barbarians' selectors were taking no chances, inviting a team of all the talents from far and wide. The captaincy was awarded to the Australian captain and scrum-half, Nick Farr-Jones, who had played for the Club against the All Blacks the previous year. Partnering him at half-back was his fellow Wallaby and world-record points-scorer in international rugby, Michael Lynagh. It was by any standards a cosmopolitan back division with Ireland's Kenny Murphy in the number 15 shirt and a three-quarter line comprised of the

Frenchmen Jean-Baptiste Lafond and Denis Charvet, the All Blacks' powerhouse centre Joe Stanley and another Aussie legend, David Campese. The capacity Twickenham crowd seemed in for a treat of running rugby with the only question mark being over the quality of possession provided for the stars behind the scrum. One or two commentators wondered whether a pack made up of Richard Loe of New Zealand, the Welshman Ian Watkins and Scotland's Paul Burnell in the front row, Ian Jones (New Zealand) and Steve Cutler (Australia) at lock, and a back-row trio of France's relatively unknown Karl Janik, Phil Davies of Wales and the uncapped Kiwi Eric Rush would be able to compete with a strong England side. They needn't have worried, though the team made a tentative start, with England's lock Paul Ackford announcing his intention to dominate the lineouts from the outset. The Barbarians' much-maligned front row put down its own marker by stealing England's first scrum put-in. There was something to say for playing two tight-head props after all. When the Club then took a four-point lead in the eighteenth minute, after Murphy had appeared outside his centres to give Campese the scoring pass, the immediate future was indeed looking bright. But the good times didn't last long. Before half-time, Dean Richards had powered over for an England try and full-back Simon Hodgkinson converted and added a penalty goal. Lynagh responded with a penalty goal of his own to reduce the arrears to 7–9 at the break.

The Barbarians had a difficult third quarter as possession dried up for a while and Hodgkinson contributed another nine points with a converted try and a penalty goal. Then the Club finished the game in style. Suddenly

Four years before he won the first of his 66 international caps, Neil Back played for the Club as a replacement against England at Twickenham in 1990. The England defender (number 14) is Rory Underwood.

(© Colorsport)

Campese was propelling 30-metre underarm spin passes infield from the touch-line, replacement flanker Neil Back was gobbling up all the loose balls and restarting attacks, tap penalties were being taken from everywhere and the pace of the game was being ratcheted up a notch or two. It was from one such penalty deep in his own half that Farr-Jones inspired the best move of the game. Up the middle the Barbarians went with Loe, Rush and the ever-present Back acting as link and all playing their parts before the backs got in on the act. Campese and Stanley were on hand before Back and Farr-Jones popped up again for the final inside pass and Davies to take and flop over in the far-left corner. It was a team try fit to celebrate a centenary.

The ending wasn't quite scripted well enough. Though Lynagh converted Davies' try from the edge of touch and then added another penalty goal, England still led. Yet at the very end, with the score at 16–18, the game had one final twist. Another penalty was awarded to the Barbarians. A goal would have won the game but, as Micky Steele-Bodger recalls, 'Nick Farr-Jones wears contact lenses and the normal scoreboard was out of use because of the ground redevelopments. I think he must have misread the numbers on the other scoreboard because he decided against going for goal. We could have nicked it by a point!' Winning the game would have been a bonus but the performance had been well up to the standards set by the Club over the years. So everyone was reasonably happy and a decade later the Barbarians would return to Twickenham to enjoy several notable victories over an England XV.

In true Barbarian fashion the evening that followed was long and lively. Another dinner, naturally, this time at the Guildhall in the City, climaxed with the Royal Marines beating the Retreat at 10.30 p.m. In September 1990 the Barbarians' advance into their centenary celebrations was only just beginning. Next stop was Yorkshire and the match with Bradford & Bingley. A separate squad of players had been assembled for the midweek game, the exceptions being the Argentinian scrum-half Fabio Gomez and the Moseley prop Mark Linnett. The rest of the overseas players who had featured at Twickenham would reappear on the following Saturday against Wales. In Bradford the Club would be captained by the Ireland lock Willie Anderson and there would be a good representation of other international-class players such as Scotland's Peter Dods and Craig Chalmers and England's Mike Harrison among the backs, and another Englishman, Nigel Redman, alongside Anderson in the second row of the pack. Bradford and Bingley were two of the oldest clubs in Yorkshire, but even in their new amalgamation they were unlikely to upset the birthday celebrations with a famous win. Their president, D.J. Duttine, summed up their true intent when he wrote in his welcoming address that his club was 'taking on the best-known touring team in the world [and] I am sure the players will be proud and honoured to be taking part in this memorable fixture'. The Yorkshiremen were equally proud that one of their own, Mike Harrison, who was from the nearby Wakefield club and who had captained England in 1987, was among the Barbarian contingent. Fittingly, he scored the opening try of the match before the Club went on to build a 28–3 interval lead and a final winning margin of 52–7, including ten tries. Then it was time for the post-match dinner and a menu that, with a great sense of occasion, included Leuchter's Oysters, Carpmael Salmon Mayonnaise and, after a Centenary Roast Topside of Beef, a Barbarian Brandy Snap Nest. The following day the committee made its way south again to Cardiff to link up with the players preparing for the match against Wales.

It was again a natural choice for the Club to play at Cardiff Arms Park during this special year. By 1990 the Barbarians had met Cardiff 106 times at the famous ground, the Wallabies, Springboks and All Blacks had been the opposition there a dozen times, and, after the building of the National Stadium on the site, the Club had played the New Zealand Barbarians on the adjoining Cardiff RFC ground, still known as the Arms Park, in 1987.

The game against Wales on 6 October 1990 was initially billed as the first-ever encounter between the sides. This was far from the case,

The Club's return to Yorkshire to play Bradford & Bingley in 1990 was celebrated with another centenary dinner. (© Barbarian Archive)

though, as on 17 April 1915 a fixture had taken place in most unusual circumstances. It was one of six matches arranged by the Club to help the war effort. They had begun with a match against Shoreham Camp in December 1914 in aid of the North Sea Fleet, continued with two matches in Leicester in the late winter and spring of 1915 to help both military recruitment and the local infirmary, and a week before the Wales encounter the Barbarians had beaten RAMC (Crookham) at Richmond, the funds from which were donated to the British Red Cross. Later in the year they would return to Richmond to play

the South African Services for the evocatively named Comforts for Colonial Troops Fund. The Club's good work was typified by the 1915 game at Cardiff Arms Park, though some contemporary match reports failed to acknowledge the Barbarians' role in the proceedings. Some referred to it as Wales v. England, others as a Services (or Military) International, and others still as merely a 'recruiting match'. It was certainly the latter, with every effort made to enlist more soldiers. Beforehand the band of the 3rd Battalion of the Welsh Regiment marched through the streets and were joined inside the ground by the pipes and drums of the Cameron Highlanders, while recruiting sergeants moved among the 15,000 crowd, many of whom were already in uniform. Whatever the confusion about the team's identity, the *Daily Telegraph* correctly chronicled the game as Wales v. the Barbarians, the Club albeit made up of 12 Englishmen,

including the captain Edgar Mobbs, plus two Irish internationals, John Minch and Joseph Quinn, both of whom had played for the RAMC against the Club seven days earlier. At the time, and in subsequent histories, the Cambridge University and Blackheath half-back Arthur Horan was assumed to be a thirteenth Englishman in the team, but after the war he was also capped by Ireland.

Though Wales had lost their air of near-invincibility of the previous decade, they were still a tightly knit unit built around nine of the team that had won the final pre-war international against Ireland in Belfast in 1914. Their power lay in a pack of forwards known as the 'Terrible Eight', led by the Rev. Alban Davies, memorably described in the Welsh Rugby Union's official history as 'if not quite an angel, [he] was as holy as this Welsh side could be'. Ironically, the Barbarians chose to play seven forwards and eight backs, but only

Edgar Mobbs captained the Barbarians team that beat Wales in 1915. (© Barbarian Archive)

by force of circumstance. Having gathered at Paddington Station with only 14 players, the first recruitment of the day took place on the train to the west as they discovered John Birkett, already an eminent Harlequin, Barbarian and 21-times-capped England centre, among their fellow passengers. The die was cast: the search for an extra forward was abandoned and the Club took the field with eight backs. The occasion was a success on all fronts. The *Daily Telegraph* reported that:

> It was a serious crowd. People were invited to the match so that those in khaki might learn from Major T. Lucas, chief recruiting officer for Glamorgan, how imperative it is that those who are free to do so should join the colours. Major Lucas and other officers made the most of the opportunity that the presence of so large a crowd afforded them of making an intimate and sporting appeal for all fit and free men to rally to the flag. There was no mincing of words, and if at the end of a match brimful of sport — many days have gone by since Cardiff people were privileged to see such a great game — there were any hangers-back, no recruiting campaign, no matter how fashioned, is likely to induce them to shoulder arms.

The action on the field certainly stirred the blood with the *Telegraph* further reporting that it 'set on parade all the delights of a man's game, a game the root idea of which is to teach chivalry and self-discipline, and which offers as its greatest joy the honour and glory that come from winning'. The Barbarians must indeed have enjoyed the occasion, belying pre-match predictions that they would be overwhelmed. It was their seven-man pack that first held and then overpowered the famed 'Terrible Eight', with one of their number, F.J. Bull of Northamptonshire, scoring the first converted try. The *Morning Post* concluded that 'how those seven Barbarian forwards managed to hold the Welsh eight and to get the ball as well was one of those mysteries of the game that will occur perhaps once in a hundred times. This was the hundredth time.'

By the time the match reached the interval, the Barbarians had scored three more tries by Minch, Horan and Quinn, with the Oxford University and England forward Geoffrey 'Khaki' Roberts and the Devon county fly-half E.G. Butcher adding the goal points. Wales could only reply with a solitary try by Bryn Lewis and trailed badly 3–18. The Club's superiority continued throughout the second 35 minutes (matches were then of 70 minutes' duration) with Quinn scoring again and Birkett appropriately capping a great individual contribution with a try of his own. The home side's consolation scores came from an Ivor Davies try and a Clem Lewis drop goal. The Barbarians had won convincingly and the *South Wales Daily News* admitted that 'the England side [*sic*] were certainly the better combination than the score of 26 points to 10 would indicate'. Two weeks later the secretary of the Cardiff club, Charley Arthur, wrote to Emile de Lissa: 'I have much pleasure in sending you a cheque for £42. 4s. 0d. [£42.20] and beg to thank you and Mr Treloar [the Barbarians' honorary secretary] for all the trouble you have taken in making the match a great success, both financially and in the matter of recruiting.' Seventy-five years later, Wales and the Barbarians met again in very different circumstances.

Thankfully it was a time of celebrations and reunions rather than set to a backdrop of war. The match would nevertheless be a serious affair for 80 minutes at least, with the Welsh smarting from a Five Nations campaign earlier in 1990 that had left them with a first-ever whitewash in their own 120-year history. They would want to beat the Barbarians and begin their climb back to international respectability. The Club, for its part, would want to go one step further than the narrow defeat by England. Nick Farr-Jones was again chosen as captain and he played his part in the pre-match build-up by telling the local press, 'It's always nice to get one under your belt and the seven Australians and Kiwis will have appreciated that Twickenham run. We are confident after that match and although we lost, the beauty of the Baa-Baas is that we don't get too disappointed when we lose. If we enjoy ourselves we will have played well, and that will transfer to the crowd. We won't have a win-at-all-costs approach.' A further stimulus was given to the approaching game when the Welsh Rugby Union announced that it would be awarding full international caps to all the players in the Wales team. A controversy not of the Club's making quickly gathered a pace of its own. In the *Sunday Times* Stephen Jones conceded that 'for the Barbarians, it is a marvellous honour and thoroughly well deserved' but continued that for Welsh rugby 'it is a travesty, the final twist of a dangerously flawed policy'. Jones had in mind the new policy among the home countries to award caps for games against what were then the developing nations in the game. That was fine in itself, but was out of step with the plethora of fixtures in the 1970s and '80s when an England XV or a Wales XV had played against

New Zealand centre Joe Stanley powers over for the first of the Barbarians' four tries as Wales are defeated again in the centenary season.
(© Huw Evans Agency)

the likes of Fiji, Romania and Argentina without awarding them full status. None of this directly concerned the Barbarians, though it could be argued that Ireland in 1974 and South Africa throughout the 1980s had awarded full caps for games against various combinations known as a President's XV or a World XV, as indeed England had done in 1971. So the game played at the National Stadium, Cardiff Arms Park, in October 1990 had some unexpected subtexts. It also had no shortage of excitement as the Barbarians deservedly created an impressive 31–24 victory.

Though Farr-Jones later said that his side had gone out 'to have a bit of fun' and that the game turned out to be 'a bit loose', there was nevertheless a serious side to the play from the outset. In front of a crowd of 42,000 the

Barbarians' first points came from two penalty goals by Stuart Barnes and in reply the Wales captain, Paul Thorburn, was by the end of the match to kick five of his own. The longer the game went on, however, the more dominant the Club became. With a surfeit of possession – the lineout count was 24–5 in their favour – the side were soon able to indulge in free-flowing attacks from all areas of the field. The first try resulted from one such moment of inspiration as a tap penalty in their own 22 launched the French winger Jean-Baptiste Lafond on a mazy run that ended with an inside pass to the All Black Joe Stanley for the touchdown under the Welsh posts. Try number two came from the skipper as Farr-Jones dummied and raced over from a five-metre scrum. Wales kept in touch at 21–all at the interval thanks to a converted try by Thorburn and a drop goal by fly-half David Evans. The men in red even momentarily sighted glory early in the second half when Thorburn gave them the lead with his final penalty goal. The euphoria was short-lived, however, as the full-back then had a clearance kick charged down by Eric Rush, who pounced on the loose ball for his side's third try. At the very end the Barbarians opened up again and Jerry Guscott was at Barnes' elbow to accept the scoring pass. Barnes finished with three conversions and three penalty goals from eight attempts and the Barbarians with their unbeaten record against Wales intact.

The first part of the centenary celebrations was now almost over. After another official dinner, this time with the Wales team and hierarchy in the Royal Hotel, and a final Sunday morning drinks party for the Barbarian committee, players, wives and girlfriends, the group dispersed and went their separate ways. Before Christmas, they would return to South

Nick Farr-Jones of Australia led the team against Wales and scored a captain's try.
(© Huw Evans Agency)

Wales twice to play Newport in a fixture that had by then been moved from its traditional Easter slot in the Club's calendar, and in November another game at Cardiff Arms Park against new international opponents, Argentina. The two games were to have very different outcomes, reflecting the different set of circumstances that by 1990 applied to the selection and make-up of the Club's teams. Although the household names were still there in abundance for what might be described as the glamour matches at the great national stadiums of the British Isles, bringing together strong sides for midweek matches against other clubs, however traditional the fixtures might be, was less straightforward. The Barbarians' centenary had coincided with the first season of official leagues in Wales and Ireland; they had already been successfully launched in England three years earlier and were long since well established in Scotland. Player availability for the Barbarians would never be

straightforward again. Compromises would have to be made in selection, and fixtures carefully arranged to avoid obvious clashes with league programmes. Mercifully, in 1990 there was still plenty of leeway in the calendar. The Welsh leagues, for instance, only took up a set number of weekends and so released a fair amount of time for Anglo–Welsh 'friendly' fixtures. Newport found themselves in the second tier of the league structure but the make-up of the domestic season still accommodated money-spinning games against the likes of Cardiff, Llanelli and Swansea from the top division. The Barbarians match remained one of the highlights of their season and they fielded a team that at that point was unbeaten in league matches. They were later to win the league with only one defeat in fourteen outings. The Barbarians needed to select wisely and appeared to have done so with 11 international players in a side led, as at

Bradford a month earlier, by Willie Anderson. The star name in the backs was the Lions Test scrum-half, Robert Jones, but the original line-up didn't quite make it to the starting line. The Cardiff centre, Mark Ring, and Leicester's flying wing, Barry Evans, two of the internationals, were forced to pull out, as did number 8 Phil Davies, who had scored the Barbarians' try at Twickenham. Newport, after four losses against the Club in as many years, including two 50-points-plus hammerings, were determined to spoil the Baa-Baas' party. They did so with something to spare, building up a 19–6 lead by half-time and going on to add another 24 points without reply in the second period. At the end the Barbarians were well beaten, their only scores coming from a converted try by the Leicester and Ireland fly-half Brian Smith. It was Newport's 50th win in 84 games against the Club.

There was no point in soul-searching. A

A pause for celebration in the Cardiff Arms Park dressing-room after the 31–24 victory over Wales in 1990. (© Huw Evans Agency)

48

little over two weeks later the Barbarians would be back in Wales for another big occasion, against Argentina. By playing the Club at Cardiff Arms Park in the final match of a tour, the Pumas would join the Wallabies, Springboks and All Blacks in the history books. Though they had been less successful than their illustrious southern hemisphere counterparts, the Pumas had given a good account of themselves against Ireland before losing 18–20, courtesy of a penalty goal against them in the tenth minute of injury time. Earlier in the year they had beaten England 15–13 in a full-scale Test match in Buenos Aires, but the young team sent on tour proved no match in the return fixture at Twickenham, losing 51–nil. Nevertheless, the Barbarians knew they would be dangerous opponents, even without their world-class fly-half and captain Hugo Porta, who was ruled out with a hamstring injury. A full set of league fixtures in England meant that the Club would rely heavily on Welsh and Irish players plus a smattering of overseas stars. The All Black lock Ian Jones qualified comfortably for the latter category and with him were two other Kiwis, the centre Craig Innes and the uncapped prop Laurence Hullena. Phil Davies, by now a confirmed Barbarian favourite, was again in the pack, while the side was led by Robert Jones. The Swansea scrum-half was surprisingly out of favour with the Welsh selectors and admitted he welcomed any opportunity to play on the international stage. The side he led looked strong enough to put the birthday celebrations back on track after the damp squib at Newport. However, pre-match expectations looked way off course as the Pumas rattled up a 16–nil lead, including a penalty try for a collapsed scrum, inside the first 20 minutes. Suddenly the

Barbarians had to look to their laurels and they were rescued by the wit and imagination of Mark Ring. The Cardiff centre had been sorely missed at Newport but now he made up for lost time as first he drifted to the left and cleverly switched play for the Irish wing Keith Crossan to have a clear run to the line. Then he produced one of his trademark chip kicks for Ian Jones and the Welsh flanker Richard Webster to send Ieuan Evans over on the opposite wing. The game was still a real contest and the Nottingham full-back Simon Hodgkinson, having already converted both tries, ignored the remonstrations of the crowd by opting for a penalty kick at goal that pulled the score back to 15–16 at the interval. Another goal followed shortly afterwards and from there the Baa-Baas built on their lead with further converted tries by Craig Chalmers and Crossan. For the Club there was the perfect finale as Robert Jones dummied and darted over for the fifth try and a 34–22 victory.

One more match remained before the turn of the year. The Christmas-time game against Leicester at Welford Road had in recent years established itself as the most enduring and competitive of the Club's regular fixtures. While the Easter tour of Wales had been reduced to two matches at Cardiff and Swansea and the Mobbs Memorial Match was already showing worrying signs of becoming a try-scoring romp, the engagement at Leicester, while still played in the true Barbarian spirit of adventure, also retained a discernible edge that unfailingly attracted 16,000 capacity crowds. The Tigers had no intention of taking any Barbarian prisoners, even in their centenary year. Micky Steele-Bodger and the committee, fortunately, were able to complete a formidable side of their own to take on the likes of the celebrated

Underwood brothers, Rory and Tony, and Neil Back, though other household names like Dean Richards and Paul Dodge were missing from the home side. The Barbarians were captained by Rob Andrew, with Richard Hill inside him at scrum-half and two attacking gems outside in the midfield, Jerry Guscott and Franck Mesnel. Another Frenchman, Jean-Baptiste Lafond, having played on the wing against England and Wales, would be playing his third game of the season for the Club but this time in the number 15 shirt. The pack may have had fewer shining lights but it would be driven on from the back row by two 1989 Lions, Andy Robinson and Derek White. Robinson relished his contest with Back, a rival for the open-side berth in the England team. The Leicester man was still only 21 and the Barbarians recognised his qualities long before the national selectors, who didn't pick him until 1994. In later years Steele-Bodger was to identify Back as one of the individuals who in modern times epitomised the Barbarians' way of doing things. He said, 'Back always set himself high standards but he was also a respecter of what we as a club were trying to achieve. He appreciated the opportunities we gave him and his family were also marvellous people.' On 27 December 1990, however, the future world-class flanker and his teammates had to give second-best to an inspired Barbarians performance.

In what the *Daily Telegraph* described as 'a genuine contest of quality laced with several expertly taken tries', the Barbarians outscored their opponents by five tries to two. Lafond reprised his performance against Wales with another attack out of defence for a try of his own before Guscott took off from a standing start to score another. Utility replacement Richard Moon added two more tries and the Cambridge Blue Richard Pool-Jones added a fifth to complete a resounding win. The Underwoods shared the Tigers' two tries but they were denied a third when Tony sent John Liley racing for the line only to be recalled for a foot in touch. The touch judge holding up the flag was Barbarian committeeman and Leicester legend Dusty Hare. Somehow it summed up the spirit between the two clubs.

With the centenary season entering its second half there was still much to look forward to. As well as the matches against the East Midlands, Cardiff and Swansea, an invitation was received to send a squad to the Hong Kong Sevens in late March. This was both an honour and the source of a potential predicament. The prestigious tournament would take place a week before the Easter tour to Wales and would call for a careful management of playing resources – but it was an event that attracted a global audience and taking part in it was further evidence of the Club's high profile in the sport. Geoff Windsor-Lewis hit the right notes when he said, 'Going to Hong Kong on several occasions proved to be even more important than we first realised. It enabled us to renew valuable contacts with rugby men from the southern hemisphere and in terms of the profile of the Club it proved to be a marvellous showcase for us among the hundreds of ex-pats living and working in the Far East.' So there was never any doubt that the Barbarians would return to Hong Kong, where they had won the sevens crown at their first attempt in 1981 and been in three semi-finals in their three visits since then. As Clem Thomas wrote in the *Hong Kong Standard* before the tournament kicked off, 'No side is closer to the ethic of these [Hong Kong] Sevens than this illustrious touring team who are unique and the epitome of the original design of rugby as a most magnificent attacking game demanding the highest levels of sportsmanship, courage and skill and playing for fun.'

The Barbarians' squad for the competition reflected their desire to continue their impressive record of previous visits. England's captain Will Carling headed a lightning-fast set of backs that included Jerry Guscott, Tony Underwood and Andrew Harriman, plus the adopted Welshman Rupert Moon. The Northampton full-back and wing Ian Hunter was selected as a forward, where he joined a talented trio of back-row men in Neil Back, Chris Sheasby and Micky Skinner. They were good enough to comfortably qualify from their pool matches against Germany and South Korea before edging past Australia, captained by Michael Lynagh, 16–6 in the quarter-final. Any hope of a centenary sevens title, though, evaporated in the semi-final when they went down 22–14 to Fiji. The Islanders went on to beat New Zealand in the final. For the Barbarians, however, it had again been a worthwhile venture and a fitting shop window in a special season.

At home their domestic fixtures were continuing with mixed results. Both the Mobbs Memorial Match and the Easter Saturday game at Cardiff Arms Park attracted capacity crowds. At Northampton the Club, never slow to recognise loyal service, selected the 39-year-old Sheffield stalwart Bill Reichwald in the centre and the 6 ft 8 in. Orrell lock Bob Kimmins in the pack. Both enjoyed their afternoon in the limelight: Reichwald, after 12 seasons as captain of his Yorkshire club, alongside the Barbarians' captain and magical playmaker, Mark Ring, and Kimmins hilariously came within a hair's breadth of a

famous try on at least three occasions. Although the Barbarians won the match 46–34, the unfortunate forward never quite made it to the line. John Mason reported in the *Daily Telegraph*, 'Twice, perhaps three times, opportunities in broken play left the Kimmins Fan Club, of which membership knows no bounds, in a state of heady expectation. Alas, the fates decreed otherwise.' Reichwald, too, had his fans, with over 100 of them following him from Sheffield to see him in Barbarian colours. Any anxieties that the Hong Kong expedition would affect the Club's prospects against Cardiff a week later were soon dispelled. Tony Underwood, having scored against the Baa-Baas at Christmas, now scored four for them as the 42–25 triumph at the Arms Park represented the Club's highest points tally against Cardiff in 107 matches. The home side took the defeat well, with their secretary John Nelson, himself a Barbarian in 1958, saying, 'This is a traditional fixture the Cardiff club want to be associated with for another 100 years because it adds even more to a season now that there are so many competitions which place pressure on the players. However, the Barbarians game allows them to express themselves in an atmosphere free of the tensions of the league and cup.'

The continuing close links between the two clubs were even more evident over the Easter weekend as several of the Barbarians party, including the Scotland internationals Gavin and Scott Hastings and David Sole, took their leave as they were required elsewhere. Only half-a-dozen of the original selections were still available for the Bank Holiday Monday game against Swansea, though this was partly offset by the arrival of three Frenchmen, the ever-popular Jean-Baptiste Lafond, scrum-half

Aubin Hueber and the stylish back-rower Laurent Cabannes. With them came five members of the Cardiff side, the USA international captain Kevin Higgins and his Canadian counterpart Mark Wyatt. But they were not enough to shore up a depleted side against a Swansea unit that also had to bring in new recruits – ironically, two more of the Cardiff squad. Amidst all the birthday celebrations the Swansea fixture was a salutary reminder that the second 100 years of the Barbarian Football Club would pose new challenges. To complete a disappointing day the rain poured down and in the circumstances the Club did well to hold the All Whites close to a final score of 31–33. Nevertheless, the curtain came down on the 1990–91 season with plenty of high spots for Micky Steele-Bodger and the committee to reflect on with pride. One hundred and fifteen players, ranging from long-serving club members to international superstars, had represented the Barbarians in the nine matches and the Hong Kong Sevens and large crowds had watched them wherever they went – and after a summer's break the centenary bandwagon would roll again into Murrayfield and across to Ireland.

The three-match tour spread over nine days in September 1991 was to prove a fitting finale to twelve months of celebrations. Twenty-three players from nine countries were assembled and, to everyone's relief after what had happened at Swansea, only one reinforcement was needed by the time the squad reached the final stage of the tour to play Old Wesley in Dublin. That in itself must have been a notable physical achievement as, in true Barbarian fashion, the players and committee had crammed in a succession of receptions, dinners, dances, golf days, sailing and, ominously, what

was listed as an 'optional' visit to the Guinness Brewery and Irish Distillers in Dublin. The latter, however, came on the morning after the final match and presumably offered the ideal send-off to a set of players who had performed admirably in the three matches.

The game at Murrayfield completed a hat-trick of matches against Scotland that had begun in 1970 with a fixture in aid of Edinburgh's Commonwealth Games Fund and had continued 13 years later with a second match to mark the opening of the new East Stand at the stadium. Now it was a match to honour the Barbarians' centenary and, fittingly, it ended in a 16–all draw. Under the captaincy of Stuart Barnes the Barbarian team contained a subtle blend of overseas and home stars. The French captain Pierre Berbizier partnered Barnes at half-back but it was the pack selections that attracted most pre-match interest. The front row comprised the 39-year-old Topo Rodriguez, a gnarled Argentinian prop who had won World Cup honours with Australia, the 18-st. Tom Lawton, the most-capped Wallaby hooker, who had settled in South Africa, and, also from South Africa, another massive prop, Guy Kebble. An old friend was returning at flanker. Eric Rush had won rave notices with his performances against England and Wales at the start of the centenary season and here he was again and still uncapped by New Zealand. He was finally called to All Black colours at the age of 30 during the 1995 World Cup, but for the Barbarians he was always a popular choice. Against Scotland in 1991, though, the back-row spotlight fell on the number 8, Kari Tapper. The 28-year-old builder was the first player from Sweden to serve the Club and he was to acquit himself well on and off the field over the course of the next week.

The Murrayfield match featured contrasting

strengths and weaknesses as the Baa-Baas controlled the scrums and the Scots merrily poached the lineouts. At first it looked as if the Club would win the game with something to spare. Rush scored twice in the opening half-hour, his second try built on sharp thinking as he chipped into open space and accelerated onto the ball for the touchdown. But Scotland had their own opportunists with hooker Kenny Milne and former Lions captain Finlay Calder both scoring tries from Barbarian errors. With barely five minutes left to play, the home side led 16–10 and, camped on the opposition goal line, were in sight of a first-ever victory. It was the ideal scenario for a moment of Baa-Baas invention and derring-do. The hero of the hour was the South African full-back Andre Joubert. Taking a pass behind his own line, he burst out of defence, kicked ahead and regathered, and linked with the New Zealander Scott Pierce before fellow centre Quentin Daniels completed the breakout with a converted try at the other end of the field. It was a breathtaking end to a match played in perfect conditions.

And so to Ireland, and where better to round off a birthday party that had lasted more than 12 months? Though it would be the Club's first venture across the Irish Sea since the game against the Wanderers in Dublin in 1970, it was very much a case of being reunited with old friends. Micky Steele-Bodger recalled, 'It was very important that, having played in England, Scotland and Wales during our centenary, we also visited Ireland. The driving force behind the match in Cork against the Constitution club was Tom Kiernan and with that arranged to coincide with their own centenary, it was just perfect that we could then go on to Dublin to play another birthday club, Old Wesley.' Kiernan, the captain of the British and Irish

Lions in 1968, was a distinguished Barbarian himself and president of the Constitution club. In the side that played the Baa-Baas was full-back Kenny Murphy, who had performed so well for the Club in the opening game of the centenary at Twickenham, while the captain was Donal Lenihan, a future Barbarian committeeman. Although they were the reigning All-Ireland league champions, the local club was no match for the Baa-Baas who, having been contained to a 13–9 lead at the interval, pulled away with 26 points without reply in the second half. The Harlequins and England wing Andrew Harriman and the Llanelli fly-half Colin Stephens both scored two tries, with the others coming from Ian Hunter, the uncapped Scottish lock Andrew Macdonald and the Natal flanker Wahl Bartmann.

Two days later the Barbarians were in Dublin and their itinerary for the final 24 hours of an exhausting year summed up all that went before: players training and the committee meeting friends old and new over lunch at Castle Golf Club; a pre-match reception at Donnybrook; an early-evening kick-off to the match against Old Wesley; and finally a banquet in a marquee. It was almost incidental that the Barbarians narrowly lost the match 36–37 thanks to an Irish drop goal in the sixth minute of injury time. Once again a capacity crowd had turned out to acknowledge their own heroes and to salute the Barbarians. The Club's final try, their 67th in 12 matches since they had run out at Twickenham a year earlier, was scored by one of the finds of the year, Eric Rush. A match had been lost but a year in the life of the Barbarian Football Club had been nothing less than a triumph of tradition and style. No one would forget it in a hurry.

III

INTO THE FOUR CORNERS OF ENGLAND

'It'll be a shame if these matches ever go...You only had to see the faces of some of our youngsters when they were told they had been selected.'

– Bob Dwyer 1997

Since the Barbarian Football Club was established in 1890, its matches have been played in every conceivable corner of the rugby game in the British Isles. Over the years, too, there has evolved a distinctive pattern to the fixtures, though none of them have been, or ever will be, set in stone. There have tended to be subtle amendments to the Barbarians calendar, often reflecting the changing environment within which the game in general is played. Two developments of recent times which undoubtedly required the Club to reassess its own role were the introduction of national leagues in the late 1980s and early '90s

and, in 1995, the declaration of professionalism within the sport. Casualties were inevitable, and for the Club the reluctant but eventual abandonment of the Easter tour of Wales was the classic example. Yet one of the great qualities of successive Barbarian committees has been their ability to fine-tune the matches and their timing. Despite all that happened to rugby union at club and international level in the final decade of the twentieth century, the Club was still able to play what it regarded as the ideal quota of six matches a season. Two of those games continue to be against sides that now constitute the Barbarians' longest-established regular opponents: Leicester and the East Midlands.

The match in Leicester dates back to 1909 and the Mobbs Memorial Match against the East Midlands was first played in 1921. Together they provide the centrepiece of the Barbarians' profile in England. In their own way they are another example of how the Club mixed and matched its itinerary even in the early years of its existence. A feature of the fixture list in the first 40 years was how the players and spectators in the Midlands of England rarely saw the Barbarians. Though Percy Carpmael and the Southern Nomads had played at Burton-on-Trent and Moseley on their tour in the spring of 1890, when several of them became the pioneering Barbarians later in the year, in subsequent seasons they hardly ever returned to the area. The single exception was a match against Bedford in February 1894, when Carpmael was still captain and the local side won by seven points to three. The occasion was obviously a success, the *Bedfordshire Standard* reporting, 'It was one of the best and most exciting games ever seen in Bedford, and the Invincibles [Bedford] gained their proudest victory. The crowd – between 5,000 and 6,000 – broke into the enclosure and lustily cheered the winners, shouldering Jacob [who had kicked the winning drop goal] off the field in honour, and cheering the team right down into the town.'

The Barbarians did not return to the Midlands until 1909. The main focus of their travels within England in the early years was very much the north of the country and then the west and south-west. These were by some margin the strongholds of the game. After the historic first matches against Hartlepool Rovers and Bradford in December 1890 several other northern towns and clubs featured in the Barbarians' fixture list in the next decade. Huddersfield, Swinton, Leeds, Carlisle, South Shields, Percy Park, Liverpool, Durham and Birkenhead Park were all visited and so, in the west, were Exeter (to play Devonshire), Bath, Bristol and Gloucester. Between 1902 and 1907 Devonport Albion was added to the Easter tour of South Wales and, after that, Cheltenham was included for six seasons up to the outbreak of the First World War. The clubs of the Midlands were prominent by their absence. This was not as surprising as it might seem, a good yardstick being that the vast majority of players for the England team in the ten years either side of 1900 were drawn from Blackheath, Richmond, the universities of Oxford and Cambridge and the northern and western clubs. The first member of the Leicester club to play for England was the wing John Miles in 1903 and only three others were selected in the next five years. Ironically, there was a Leicester representative, W.H. Carey, in the inaugural Barbarian team against Hartlepool Rovers in 1890, but over the next twenty seasons only one other, P.W. Oscroft in 1896, was invited to play. A similar pattern was evident at another rugby hotbed of the future: Harold Weston was Northampton's first England cap in 1901; but it was their second, Edgar Mobbs, eight years later, who was destined to become part of Barbarian folklore.

Ever since their first season the Barbarians had undertaken a Christmas tour, though after their second venture in 1891 when they played Devonshire, Bradford, Huddersfield and Swinton between 26 and 30 December, wiser counsel usually prevailed, with the number of matches often limited to two and occasionally three. There was still a tendency to alternate

the tours between South Wales and the North-east but from 1904 the games against Cardiff and Newport became the norm. To these was added Leicester on 29 December 1909, and it was to mark the beginning of a series that ran uninterrupted except by bad weather and world wars (and then only to a limited degree) until 1996. At first, success was hard to come by for the Barbarians with a draw in the first match and then three straight defeats. Tagging the fixture onto what were invariably two hard games in Wales may have been stretching resources too far. Travel was one factor, fatigue another. The fixtures were always set for 26 December (Cardiff), 27th (Newport) and 28th (Leicester), unless the holiday fell on a weekend, when there would be some respite on a Sunday. When the Club finally beat Leicester at the fifth attempt, it was perhaps no coincidence that the match had been postponed in December because of snow and played two months later in February 1914. The first Christmas win at Welford Road had to wait until 1923, by which time the three-match tour had been abandoned and Leicester was a stand-alone fixture.

What had also made the early matches against Leicester notably difficult to win was a run of bad luck with the weather. The first game in 1909 had only gone ahead after a covering of straw had protected the pitch overnight (when, instead of the anticipated frost, there was torrential rain) and in three successive years there were again heavy conditions underfoot. But, as one of the foremost reporters of the era, Philip Trevor, noted in the *Daily Telegraph* after the first match, 'Once again it was proved yesterday that really good players can play really good football upon very heavy and slippery ground.'

The match ended as a 9–all draw, with each side scoring three tries. Leicester took the lead twice at 3–nil and 6–3 but, each time, the Barbarians came back and eventually overhauled them. A feature of the game was how both sides adapted to the wet weather, forsaking passing for the dribbling that was a revered skill at that time. The home side's first try by forward Jimmy Burdett came from such a tactic and their other two scores were the results of individual darts by George 'Pedlar' Wood, a scrum-half who was to play once for England five years later and was still turning out against the Baa-Baas in 1920. The Club hit back with touchdowns by two of their own forwards – Norman Wodehouse, a naval lieutenant, and Reginald Hands – and their captain and centre, Walter Wilson. In later years Hands was killed in the final months of the First World War and Wodehouse perished while in charge of an Atlantic convoy at the age of 54 in 1941. That remains a tragic postscript to a notable landmark in Barbarian history. Nearly 100 years later the two clubs are still playing each other and, as Philip Trevor concluded in 1909, '[The Barbarians] are frankly a scratch side but they are deservedly one of the great institutions of English rugby football, all the same.'

The first Barbarian victory over Leicester, in 1914, was a narrow one by five points to three and also notable for the fact that the winning try was claimed by a Leicester club man, Steve Palmer, playing as a late replacement in the centre. Clearly, great cooperation between the two clubs was already well established and this was further exemplified within the following twelve months or so. Although the outbreak of war had led to the cessation of official sport, the Barbarians twice played in Leicester in

January and March of 1915. As with the later fixture in Cardiff against Wales, both matches were in aid of the war effort and specifically to encourage military recruitment. In that respect they were a success, though for the Baa-Baas, victories on the field of play were again proving elusive. The opposition was listed not as Leicester but as T.H. Crumbie's XV, which, not surprisingly, was composed almost entirely of the local club's members. Tom Crumbie was the honorary secretary of Leicester and he liaised with Edgar Mobbs on the organisation of the two games. In unusually good conditions the first game, on 2 January 1915, attracted a Saturday afternoon crowd of over 5,000 and both sides fielded, by mutual agreement, only 14 men. Though the Barbarians were led by

Edgar Mobbs, already established as one of the most celebrated backs of his generation, and with him was another notable performer in the Cardiff and Wales full-back Bobby Williams, the team included nine new players and proved no match for Leicester, who won by the comfortable score of 21–6. However, it was reported that, 'It was a most interesting game from beginning to end, the play being both fast and exciting [and] the defeat of the Barbarians by a margin of 15 points came as a surprise, but they played a fine sporting game and, certainly, did not deserve to be beaten so heavily.' Mobbs and the Devon county winger E.G. Butcher had scored the two consolation tries and both played again in the second match on 27 March. For this game the Barbarians were strengthened

During the Second World War the Club played several matches at Leicester, including this game in 1944 against a Midlands XV assembled by J.E. Thorneloe. (© Barbarian Archive)

by the inclusion of another Welsh international, the fly-half Tommy Vile, and a try by G.E. Kidman of Guy's Hospital was sufficient to earn them a 3–all draw. More importantly the impressively large crowd of nearly 7,000 contributed significantly to the £2,000 appeal fund launched at the Leicester Royal Infirmary, while what was described as 'a very imposing military parade' was an obvious aid to the recruitment campaign. The Barbarians, in their own way, had played a part in the war effort and history was to repeat itself over a quarter of a century later when seven matches were staged at Leicester involving the Club against various combinations selected by Crumbie's successor as local secretary, Eric Thorneloe.

During the inter-war years, Leicester and the Barbarians each enjoyed periods of notable success in the developing series. The Tigers won seven of the nine matches played between 1919 and 1927, the most resounding scoreline being 28–10 in their favour in 1921. From 1928 onwards, however, the Barbarians redressed the balance with eight victories and a draw in the next ten encounters. This was a vintage period for the Club. Though winning matches at all costs was never a priority, all concerned could nevertheless point with satisfaction to two invincible seasons in 1932–33 and 1934–35, and their performances at Leicester were as good as any. They were selecting from the cream of British rugby, as witnessed by the game at Welford Road on 27 December 1934 when, for the first time in 14 years, they played two matches at Christmas. The previous day they had beaten Blackheath 16–13 in a match to celebrate that club's centenary. Nine of the Barbarians played again in a team of fifteen international players against Leicester. The

midfield triangle was made up of an Englishman, a Welshman and a Scotsman – Peter Cranmer and Wilfred Wooller in the centre and Wilson Shaw at fly-half – with another Scottish international, Ross Logan, leading the side from scrum-half. Even then they had to fight tooth and nail for the narrowest of victories. In his match report, Jock Wemyss was effusive in his praise:

> Once again the annual match between Leicester and the Barbarians was a great game, despite the deplorable condition of the famous Welford Road ground, and the tourists thoroughly deserved their narrow victory by two tries [six points] to one goal [five points]. Both teams gave a wonderful display. It was almost impossible to run at any speed through the mud. Any number of movements, of course, broke down, but it was astonishing that the players were able to handle and kick with any degree of accuracy at all . . . Leicester made their efforts, too, which kept a large holiday crowd in a state of great excitement, but in the end it was Shaw who gained the plaudits of the spectators. The Glasgow High School player seems to be inspired when wearing a Barbarian jersey. Without any question at all he was again a Scotland stand-off and, moreover, as against Blackheath, the match-winner as well.

Wilson Shaw scored tries against both Blackheath and Leicester that Christmas and went on to captain Scotland in the 1935 International Championship. The following December he was back at Leicester with the

Barbarians again, along with Logan, Wooller, Cranmer and several others of the 1934 team, but with a less satisfactory result – a nil–all draw. Sometimes, even Barbarians matches can be pointless. In 1936 and 1937, however, the Club totalled 12 tries and 54 points at Welford Road before the Tigers won the final inter-war match 8–6 on 27 December 1938.

The post-war series began with three straight victories for the Barbarians, with Micky Steele-Bodger captaining the side in 1947. The annual fixture was by then well established as one of the premier non-international dates on the British rugby calendar and in the 1950s another important element was added. Every third year the Barbarians would play the All Blacks, Springboks or Wallabies at Cardiff Arms Park in the final match of their respective long European tours. The opposition, as well as being illustrious, would be well-tuned teams playing together for perhaps the 30th time in various permutations over the course of four months. Even the gifted individuals in the Barbarians' line-ups would be hard-pushed to match them without some form of run-out. It became noticeable in 1953, when the Barbarians were about to play the All Blacks, that the Leicester match began to have a dual role: an important fixture in its own right, but also an invaluable opportunity to try out prospective selections for the tourists match a few weeks later. Thus, in that season, nine of the side that beat Leicester comprehensively by 39–11 took the field again in mid-February against the All Blacks. Much the same happened ahead of the Wallabies and Springboks games in 1958 and 1961, though the concentration then was on blending forward packs. At other times the Leicester match was not so much a trial for what was on the horizon as a celebration of what had

The team, captained by the Richmond and England centre Peter Cranmer, that beat Leicester by the record margin of 34–nil in 1937. (© Barbarian Archive)

gone before. The greatest example of that, undoubtedly, was the game in 1955 when the Club invited 15 members of that summer's illustrious British Isles team which had toured South Africa to regroup at Leicester. All of them accepted, though Jeff Butterfield was forced to withdraw with an eye injury. Still, 14 Lions and the Cardiff and Wales centre Gordon Wells making up the numbers was not a bad turn-out for any club side. The Barbarians provided a 17,000 capacity crowd with three sparkling tries, two of them from Tony O'Reilly, in the mud and the rain and a 12–3 victory.

In the following season the match attracted live television coverage for the first time and, in wintry weather, Cliff Morgan captained the team to another impressive victory. In *The Times* O.L. Owen observed that: 'Morgan almost has the gift of being able to bamboozle opponents by standing still when they are

The jubilee match programme of 1959 when the Club won 17–9. (© Barbarian Archive)

arriving by air just before the kick-off. The headlines, however, were grabbed by his fellow wing, Peter Thompson of Headingley and England, who equalled the Club record set by Cyril Holmes in 1947 by scoring five of the Baa-Baas' seven tries in an exceptional display of attacking rugby. O'Reilly, inevitably, and the then-uncapped Royal Navy wing-forward Jeff Clements scored the other two with another debutant at full-back, Llanelli's Terry Davies, adding a conversion. Leicester could manage only a couple of penalty goals in reply as the visitors finished 23–6 ahead.

The next encounter, in 1957, followed a very similar pattern, this time the Barbarians kicking a second conversion to their seven tries – O'Reilly scoring three of them – in a 25–6 win. Two years later the match celebrated its 50th anniversary and, with a nice sense of occasion, the Barbarians handed the captaincy to the five-try hero Peter Thompson. O'Reilly, on the other hand, was now among the opposition, playing in the centre for Leicester while on a short-term career move in the Midlands. With him were two other notable recruits, the 1950 Lions prop John Robins and a Lion from the more recent tour of Australasia, Phil Horrocks-Taylor. The Barbarians, with seven uncapped players in their ranks, were still good value for their 17–9 win.

The 50th match (as opposed to anniversary) followed in 1969 and was again highlighted by remarkable deeds. By then a new set of international stars were in the firmament and there was no shortage of them in the black-and-white shirt, with J.P.R. Williams at full-back, John Spencer and David Duckham in the centre, and the side led by the England lock Mike Davis. Together they delivered a performance remarkable even by Barbarian

looking for the suspected pranks which go with his reputation.'

The *Guardian*'s correspondent, Denys Rowbotham, concurred, noting that 'From the start Morgan showed that he could dart hither and thither over snow, check, stop, turn, accelerate, jink and sidestep like any skater in an ice ballet.' With the Welsh icon at half-back was a Barbarian debutant who was to become a Club favourite on and off the field for many years: Ireland's Andy Mulligan. O'Reilly was there again, this time giving a foretaste of his later life as a millionaire businessman by standards. In *The Times* U.A. Titley reported, 'When an exceptionally knowledgeable and unashamedly partisan rugby crowd cries for more from their opponents, and without a single penalty goal to mar the scoreboard, it is clear that something out of the ordinary is happening. That was precisely the situation at the Welford Road ground on Saturday when the Barbarians . . . won by four goals and five tries to nothing.' Nine tries without reply! And that against a gnarled Tigers team, captained by the experienced Kevin Andrews, that included streetwise performers of its own such as John Elliott, David Matthews and Graham Willars in the pack and a wily scrum-worker in John Allen. But on this day there was something special in the air. Titley explained, 'When sharp warning-flickers develop into a sustained purple patch, with success breeding success, there is seldom much that the opposition can do about it.' The Tigers were not exactly standing by and watching ('To the gallant Leicester pack went the distinction of reducing what could have become massive murder to artistic homicide,' added Titley) but certainly they seemed helpless behind the scrum as the rampant Duckham bagged five tries himself, Keith Fielding scored two and the Welshmen Bob Phillips and John Jeffery shared the other four. It was another red-letter day in the Club's history.

High-scoring points sprees were to become almost the norm in the fixture in the 1980s and beyond, but beforehand, in the '70s, the spoils were more evenly shared, with Leicester winning five of the ten matches, much to the delight of local stalwarts such as Allen and Willars, who had suffered such agonies in the jubilee match of 1969. The Tigers were benefiting from the presence of new stars of their own, such as Dusty Hare, Peter Wheeler, Paul Dodge, Les Cusworth and Garry Adey. They had all been part of a revival in the Midlands club's fortunes in the second half of the 1970s and it was to go from strength to strength in the years that followed. The Barbarians were not slow to recognise the contribution of individuals towards the collective renaissance at Welford Road and regularly selected Tigers for other staging posts in the Club's year. Not only the internationals but also the great club servants were honoured. Thus, when Brian Hall, a Leicester captain who played over 300 games for the club, was invited to join the Easter tour in 1981, John Reason in the *Daily Telegraph* was quick to applaud all concerned. He wrote:

> For Brian Philip Hall, born Newark, 30 December 1946, his presence in a Barbarians tour party will mean a great deal, little of which has to do with ambition. Ambition is about playing in internationals and proud advancement. For Hall, and his friends, selection for the Barbarians will represent the seal of approval, the recognition of seasons of hard slog, the soothing balm for the disappointments, the knocks and, he says with a grin, the disruptions to his domestic life.

Leicester won four games in a row from 1981, culminating in a spectacular 90-metre try by speedy wing Barry Evans to conclude a 35–11 victory in 1984. That was really a case of giving the Barbarians a dose of their own medicine. But the Club responded with two hard-fought victories in as many years before contributing fully to a record 78-points extravaganza in

The cover of the 1998 match programme
is a suitable reminder that the Christmas-
time match at Leicester was always played
in the best of spirits.
(© Barbarian Archive)

1987. Leicester took the honours by 48–30, but
the Baa-Baas had sensational runners of their
own, with a marvellous climax provided by the
Welsh fly-half Jonathan Davies, who set off on
an arcing run of 70 metres before touching
down under the Tigers' posts. As the
Barbarians' selectors cast their net further
afield, other stars entranced the local fans.
Australia's David Campese came in 1988 and,
inevitably, scored the final try in a 36–19
triumph. He was back again the following year,
this time in a 16–32 defeat, but dropped out in
controversial circumstances in 1991, citing
poor communication from the Club committee
about his travel arrangements from Italy, where
he was playing club rugby. There were no

reported problems elsewhere on the European
mainland and four French backs – Serge
Blanco, Philippe Sella and the brothers Lafond,
Jean-Baptiste and Jean-Marc – did turn up and
displayed their rich array of skills in a 29–21
victory.

As every season went by, there was
breathless entertainment for the unfailing
capacity crowds but, at some stage, there was
the faint ringing of what eventually became
alarm bells. When, many people wondered, did
running rugby and try feasts tip over into
matches that lacked a certain competitive edge?
Alickadoos of old might well have raised the
point in 1993 when the Tigers posted a half-
century of points against the Barbarians for the
first time (51–14). Or again in 1995 when the
match finished 51–25 in favour of the home
side. Invitation teams of individuals, however
gifted, were finding it more difficult than ever
to challenge club outfits who had perfected
unit skills and who knew each other's ways
inside out. Allied to the difficulties of player
availability and a crowded league calendar, the
future of the traditional fixture was questioned
seriously for the first time. Ironically, too, the
1996 game never took place not because of any
administrative expediency but because of bad
weather. And, another irony, when the match
was eventually played in February 1997, the
Barbarians still attracted a midweek evening
crowd of over 12,000 and won comfortably
38–22. The Leicester coach at that time was the
Australian Bob Dwyer, later to fulfil a similar
role on several Barbarian tours. His view was
clear: 'It'll be a shame if these matches ever go.
The players love being involved. You only had
to see the faces of some of our youngsters when
they were told they had been selected. The
boys love playing for the Baa-Baas, too, but

we've got to get the match back to Christmas again.' But the Christmas mould was broken. The fixture was played again in March of the 1997–98 season with, ominously, the Barbarians running away with the match to the tune of 73–19 and the Tongan fly-half Siua Taumalolo setting an individual record of 33 points.

The Christmas tradition received a temporary reprise the following December and the Barbarians celebrated with another good win. They had also lost none of their sense of perspective, with it being reported that the team and committee had enjoyed an evening at Leicester City Football Club followed by a curry. The next two meetings, however, were in a new location altogether, as the Barbarians accepted an invitation to play at Twickenham every early summer against England's champion club. Almost inevitably that turned out to be Leicester, but such was the strength of the Barbarians' assembled teams on those occasions that new records were being set. The effect of the Baa-Baas' second win, by 85–10, in June 2000, was to send the organisers of the Sanyo Challenge Match back to the drawing board and they eventually decreed that, in future seasons, the Barbarians would not play the champion club but England itself. In its way it was the ultimate compliment. As for the fixture against Leicester in the more familiar surroundings of Welford Road, it refused to die and in March 2003, and again 12 months later, the old traditions continued.

As old traditions go with the Barbarians, however, the Mobbs Memorial Match against the East Midlands at Northampton has a special niche of its own. Rarely in any sport is there an example of an annual match that is played in memory of one person that has

Andy Marinos carries the ball against Leicester in 2004 with Neil Jenkins (left) providing support.
(© Getty Images)

survived for over 80 years. Testimonial matches for individuals are commonplace and are worthy occasions in their own right. Mostly, though, they are one-off games, often attracting a lot of publicity, and soon forgotten. The Mobbs Memorial Match is something altogether different. By March 2004 it had been staged 77 times, and if the resolve of the respective officials of the East Midlands Rugby Union and the Barbarian Football Club has any relevance, it will reach the landmark 100 games in due course. The fixture also entails more than its 80 minutes of rugby. Every year, usually on the first Thursday in March, those same officials from both sides assemble in the mid-afternoon at Abingdon Square in the centre of Northampton for a brief wreath-laying ceremony, a minute's silence and the playing of the Last Post. The focus of their attention is Edgar Robert Mobbs, who, in his short life, achieved such eminence

Edgar Mobbs played for and against the Barbarians before being killed at the age of 35 in 1917. (© Barbarian Archive)

as a sportsman and army man that a bronze bust resting on a 20-ft high Portland stone pedestal was commissioned in 1921. As a soldier his career was remarkable but tragic. Being deemed too old at the age of 32 to be awarded a commission when war broke out in 1914, Mobbs joined as a private but soon enlisted 264 volunteers to form a Company of the Northamptonshire Regiment. They became popularly known as 'The Battalion of Sportsmen and Soldiers', with Lieutenant-Colonel E.R. Mobbs DSO as their commander. Though badly wounded at Guillemont in the summer of 1916, he returned to lead the battalion again later the same year. But in July 1917 he was shot through the neck and died at the Ypres Salient in an attack on a German machine-gun post. As a sportsman Edgar Mobbs was equally distinguished, with nearly

250 games for Northampton, 7 caps and the captaincy of England, and 10 appearances for the Barbarians. He also had a burgeoning career in the administrative area of the game and was already the East Midlands' representative on the Rugby Football Union and a Barbarian committeeman when war broke out. His last games were for the Club, captaining the sides that played twice at Leicester and then near Aldershot against the RAMC and at Cardiff Arms Park against Wales in the early months of 1915. Then he went to serve his country and made the ultimate sacrifice. In his definitive history of the East Midlands Rugby Union, published in 1997, Peter Eads wrote:

> Edgar Mobbs was a wing three-quarter of genius. He was 6 ft 1 in., weighed 14 st. and was nearly an even-timer of 100 yards. He ran with a high step, could swerve at speed and had a violent hand-off. All this made him a very hard man to bring down, especially as he ran for the line with great determination . . . His technical skill and superb physique were only part of the qualities which have ensured his name lives on. He played with intense enjoyment and with an inspiring will to win. This made him a perfect captain. It was often said that for Mobbs a match was never lost until the final whistle was blown and he was at his superb best when his side was ten points down at half-time. Then he played with his full genius, and drew from his team more than they knew how to give.

Edgar Mobbs was undoubtedly perfect Barbarians material. If he had lived, he may well have become another of the marvellous alickadoos who have served the Club so well over the years. In his courageous death he generated another priceless tradition for the game. The first Mobbs Memorial Match was played at Franklin's Gardens, Northampton, on 10 February 1921. The Barbarians scored five tries against the opposition's four in a 19–14 victory. Two of the conversions were kicked by H.B.T. 'Teddy' Wakelam, later the pre-eminent BBC radio sports commentator of the inter-war years. Unfortunately, the great tradition was almost over before it had begun when the match was cancelled in 1922 because of a heavy frost. In 1923, however, it began a run that continued uninterrupted until the outbreak of war in the autumn of 1939. At first the Barbarians were successful, winning seven and drawing one of the nine matches between 1921 and 1930. The matches were often high-scoring affairs by the standards of the day: five tries in a 15–3 win in 1924; another five plus three conversions two years later (21–7); and a record six tries and a 22–6 result under Douglas Prentice's leadership in 1930. In 1927 the teams agreed to try out a new laws experiment of not kicking the ball direct to touch outside the defending team's 25-yard line. As it turned out, this made no discernible difference to the try count – the Barbarians won the match 24–11 with four tries to three – though both sides could claim they were 40 years ahead of their time. That particular amendment to the laws eventually came into force in 1968.

There was a reversal of fortunes in the early 1930s and it was not surprising. In those years, the East Midlands were one of the most formidable county teams in England. Having been semi-finalists in the then-prestigious County Championship in 1933, they were crowned champions the following year. More significantly, they combined with neighbouring Leicestershire, a separate entity in the county system, on 14 November 1931 – in later years such temporary combinations were known as Midlands Counties (East) – and shocked the rugby community by beating the Springboks 30–21. It was the South Africans' only defeat in a 26-match tour of the British Isles that included a 'Grand Slam' over England, Scotland, Ireland and Wales. In the Mobbs Memorial Matches the East Midlands won five times between 1931 and 1937, though their two defeats were heavy ones by over 30 points. The second of these, on 7 March 1935, was, for the Barbarians at least, another highlight in a notable season in which they won all eight games in great style. At Northampton they were captained by P.E. 'Pop' Dunkley, an England international back-row forward, who claimed one of their eight tries in a 32–8 triumph.

When the post-war Mobbs Memorial Matches resumed in February 1946, it was the turn of the Barbarians to put together a winning four-match sequence. The 1938 British Isles scrum-half Haydn Tanner led the side and, partnered by Bleddyn Williams at half-back, put on a display of running rugby that resulted in six tries and a 20–6 win. In the following year the match was postponed because of frost in early March and its eventual staging at Bedford the next month is another classic example of the lengths players were prepared to go to when called up by the Barbarians. Its new date was Wednesday 9 April 1947 – immediately after the four-match Easter tour of Wales that had concluded the previous day at Newport. Elaborate travel plans were put in place to get the players from South

Wales to the East Midlands. Twelve of them had been in action for the Club over the Bank Holiday weekend and four of them had played against Newport 24 hours earlier. Bleddyn Williams went one better than that in what was for him a busy Easter: on Good Friday he played at fly-half for the Barbarians at Penarth; on the Saturday he was centre for Cardiff against them; and on the Tuesday he was back at fly-half again for the Club against Newport. He was also on the winning side each time. Incredibly, he had also helped Cardiff beat the Harlequins on Easter Monday. Now he was travelling with the rest of the Baa-Baas for the match at Bedford, his fifth game in six days. The official itinerary for the day speaks for itself:

> 8.00 a.m. – breakfast at the Esplanade Hotel, Penarth
> 9.00 a.m. – charabanc leaves for Cardiff
> 10.15 a.m. – leave Cardiff station; lunch on train
> 1.30 p.m. – arrive Paddington
> 2.40 p.m. – leave St Pancras
> 3.51 p.m. – arrive Bedford station
> 5.15 p.m. – match v. East Midlands

And, of course, the Barbarians won. Led by the Australian-born English international flanker B.H. 'Jaika' Travers, they scored five tries against two from the East Midlands in a 20–8 result. It had been quite a long weekend.

Over the next few years the matches at Northampton and Bedford continued to attract big crowds to watch the top international players in both sides. The East Midlands had great players of their own, such as Don White, a legendary figurehead of the sport in the area, who captained them in nine Mobbs Matches.

Ron Jacobs, who succeeded him for another four, went on to become the most-capped England prop and there were several other England representatives, like Lewis Cannell, John Hyde and Vic Leadbetter. Dick Hawkes, a durable lock forward, never quite made it to the full international arena but left such a good impression after several appearances against the Baa-Baas that he was selected to play for them against the All Blacks at Cardiff Arms Park in 1954. In the same pack were White and Jacobs, further testimony to the quality of rugby in the East Midlands. The Barbarians, in turn, were led by the likes of Jackie Kyle, John Kendall-Carpenter, Haydn Tanner and Jack Matthews, and the quality of their sides is reflected in the impressive record of 14 victories in the 16 post-war matches up to 1961. Obviously, a home victory became an occasion to celebrate, and that happened in 1950 and again in 1953, both by narrow margins of 5–3 and 8–5. These were noticeably low-scoring affairs but in no way suggested a paucity of back play. In *The Times* O.L. Owen reported the 1953 match at Bedford to be 'fast and often astonishing' and it was a fascinating contest between the powerful home pack led by White and the attacking ambitions of the Club's backs, spearheaded by Jackie Kyle at fly-half. Outside the Irishman in the three-quarter line were four gifted runners – England's W.P.C. Davies and Jeff Butterfield, and the Cardiff and Wales duo of Alun Thomas and Haydn Morris. All of them were selected for the British Isles tour of South Africa two years later. But in this match all they could manufacture was a late try for the Bath wing-forward Alec Lewis, and by then the game was won and lost. As if to further illustrate that the quality of the rugby is not always reflected the scoreline, when the

Baa-Baas returned to winning ways with a comfortable 26–8 win, including six tries, in 1954, the same correspondent in *The Times* commented that the game 'was disappointing, with little of the brilliant play which one associates with the two sides and with this particular match'. Normal standards were resumed in subsequent years. Saluting the match and the Barbarians' 25–11 victory in 1956, J.P. Jordan pointed out in the *Daily Telegraph*: 'Such a spate of scoring [seven tries to three in favour of the Club] may lead one to suppose that tackling was at a discount. Far from it; the defences were beaten through brilliant passing that left the attackers with the man over.' Or, as someone once said, the object of the game is for 14 men to run and pass the ball for the 15th to run clear and score.

The East Midlands enjoyed more success in the 1960s with five good wins. A new breed of Midlands forwards were now challenging the illustrious visitors. Budge Rogers, D.L. 'Piggy' Powell and Bob Taylor had preserved the legacy left by White, Jacobs, Hawkes and their teammates, and were doing so with no little success. Taylor, a fine back-row forward who captained England, played Test rugby for the British Isles and became chairman of the Match's organising committee in later years, was instrumental in snatching an honourable draw from the jaws of defeat in 1967. With his side trailing 9–14 in the dying moments and defending yet another attack with Barry John at the helm, he snapped up a loose ball and, as David Frost reported in *The Guardian*, 'charged into the blustering wind from his own half of the field and put [Keith] Savage on the right wing over for a try, which K.J. Taylor converted'. The 14–all draw was the first such result since 1929 and has not been repeated

since. John and his Wales half-back partner, Billy Hullin, had further cause to rue that particular match. The previous month they had occupied the roles for their country against Scotland at Murrayfield and the selectors were about to announce the team for the next international against Ireland. Hullin, with a doleful smile on his face, still recalls, 'We went onto the field at Northampton as the resident Wales half-backs; when we came off it 80 minutes later we had been dropped!' Hopefully, the so-called 'Big Five', meeting 100 miles away in Cardiff, were not influenced by events at the Mobbs Memorial Match.

Hullin's tongue-in-cheek remark about his international demise – he ended his career as a 'one-cap wonder' but also as a notable Barbarian who captained the Club five times in nine appearances – gives a clue as to how important the match was in the British season. At a time when the International Championship was spread over ten weekends from January to April each year, the selectors of the four home countries would often be seen at Bedford or Northampton running the rule over prospective changes for their next match. In 1971 the occasion was even more significant. Not only was it the 50th anniversary of the first Mobbs Memorial Match, but also officials and selectors of the imminent British Isles tour to Australasia turned up to look at likely candidates. They must have liked what they saw. John Dawes captained the Barbarians that day and, four months later, found himself captaining the Lions to a historic first-ever series win in New Zealand. With him in the Midlands and the southern hemisphere were six others – Bob Hiller, Sean Lynch, Stack Stevens, Gordon Brown, Derek Quinnell and Peter Dixon. The Bedford wing Jeremy Janion,

playing for the Baa-Baas, would have been an eighth Lion in the team but was forced to withdraw after originally being selected. The Barbarians won the anniversary match 18–14.

Such attention from international observers, complimentary though it may have been, was always secondary in Barbarians' minds to the main purpose of the exercise, which was for the annual match to continue the great traditions of the Club in commemorating Edgar Mobbs. There were no signs of the fixture losing its importance throughout the 1970s and 1980s, though there was no denying the fact that the tries and the points were mushrooming almost year by year. The Barbarians passed the 50-points barrier in 1977, scoring 11 tries on an almost waterlogged Franklin's Gardens pitch. Phil Bennett scored three of them and, with a penalty goal and four conversions, finished with a personal tally of twenty-three points. Neither team nor individual records lasted long as the Barbarians posted 50 points-plus a dozen times in the next 25 years. Along the way an Irish wing, Simon Geoghegan, scored four tries in 1993 (when the final score was East Midlands 59, Barbarians 77) and an Irish prop, Gary Halpin, claimed a hat-trick two years later in a relatively modest 56–19 scoreline. There were other winners, too. With Scottish Amicable donating £300 to youth rugby for every try scored, the 1993 game alone set them back £3,900. But as the game entered the new millennium, the points avalanche entered uncharted territory. In 2000 the Ebbw Vale fly-half Shaun Connor contributed 34 points as the Barbarians won 99–54 and, almost inevitably, the century watershed was finally passed in 2004 when the final score was 104–10 in favour of the Club. The growing disparity in the teams was almost entirely due to the unavailability of

The great Irish flanker Fergus Slattery played 18 times for the Club and was captain against the East Midlands at Northampton in 1979.
(© Barbarian Archive)

the professional tier of players from Northampton and the county selectors' unavoidable policy of calling on players from the local junior clubs such as Bedford Athletic, Old Northamptonians and Kettering. At the same time, the Club achieved a delicate balance of international players, mostly not of the current generation, alongside aspiring youngsters and loyal servants of clubs such as Henley, Exeter Chiefs, Wharfedale and the universities of Oxford and Cambridge. Happily, the results were not entirely predictable: in 2001 the East Midlands reached a landmark of their own in a 62–12 victory.

Whatever the misgivings about runaway wins for either side, the Barbarians rarely miss opportunities to mark special achievements or welcome back old friends. In 1989 there was a notable 'first' when the three Milne brothers from Heriots FP in Scotland, David, Kenny and Iain, formed the front row of the pack. Seven years later, in the first season of the professional era, the committee invited Jonathan Davies on his return from rugby league to team up again with his former Wales colleague Robert Jones at half-back. It was also the 75th anniversary of the Mobbs Memorial Match. The rugby world may have been changing, but the Barbarians retained their knack of doing the little things rather well. Edgar Mobbs would have approved.

If the matches against Leicester and the East Midlands rightly remain the staple diet of the Barbarians' calendar in England, it is equally true that many other clubs throughout the country have benefited from visits by the Club. These have invariably been linked with anniversaries of their own, sometimes to celebrate their seventy-fifth season or, more often in the last three decades of the twentieth century, their centenaries. Fittingly, Blackheath were the first to reach the landmark in 1959. The club with which Carpmael, Hughie Glyn Hughes, Emile de Lissa and Jack Haigh Smith were so closely connected had a special place in Barbarians' hearts. In 1934 the clubs met on the occasion of Blackheath's 75th birthday. The Barbarians had won what Jock Wemyss reported to be 'an extraordinary game' by 16 points to 13 thanks to a last-minute try by Wilson Shaw. Twenty-five years later the centenary match was staged under floodlights at the White City Stadium in London. By then it was calculated that 275 Blackheath members had played for the Barbarians – and the Club pulled out all the stops in their latest selection.

A unique event – the Milne Brothers, Iain, Kenny and David, formed the Barbarians' front row in the Mobbs Memorial Match of 1989. (© Adam Robson Collection)

All 15 players had toured South Africa nine months before so the match doubled up as a gala reunion for some of the most celebrated names of the era, such as Tony O'Reilly, Rhys Williams, Andy Mulligan, Ronnie Dawson, David Marques and Ron Jacobs. Also present were government ministers and the high commissioners of Canada, Australia, South Africa and Rhodesia. *The Times* reported: 'The Barbarians were in effervescent mood, flitting about all over the place both fore and aft . . . and they clearly enjoyed the experience.' The fact that Blackheath held an 8–3 lead at half-time added to the excitement but, by the end, not only had O'Reilly and Marques scored tries, but the double British Lion Malcolm Thomas had stolen the headlines with a hat-trick of touchdowns in his side's 21–8 victory. It was a great night for both clubs.

Next to Blackheath the universities of Oxford and Cambridge have the strongest Barbarian links, going back to the last decade of the nineteenth century. From Percy

Carpmael in 1890 right down to Micky Steele-Bodger and Geoff Windsor-Lewis in the modern day, the Light Blues' influence and leadership in the Club has been crucial. Seven Oxford men played for the Barbarians in the inaugural season of 1890–91 and Frank Evershed was elected to the first committee. In the post-war years it was always the case that the committee would have Oxford and Cambridge representatives. So, as their centenary landmarks were reached, it was inevitable that the Barbarians would provide the opposition for the celebration matches that accompanied them. Oxford were first up on 2 December 1969 and two strong teams were assembled at Iffley Road. The University fielded a Past and Present XV under the captaincy of the All Blacks scrum-half Chris Laidlaw. Other distinguished old Blues included England's newly appointed captain, Bob Hiller, at full-back and the Welsh lock Mike Roberts. There was also a sensible balance to the team, with ten undergraduates included. Billy Hullin led the Barbarians' line-up of 13 current and future internationals but they were handicapped from late in the first half by a rib injury to Barry John. Reduced to 14 men, the Club moved J.P.R. Williams to fly-half and the Northampton flanker Brian West to full-back. What Williams may have lacked in tactical nous in his unfamiliar position, he more than made up for with his customary courage. In *The Times* U.A. Titley commented, 'Any position comes alike to the enthusiastic Williams, who had a splendid afternoon, both attack and defence, where he clutched the ball to his stomach in suicidal falls as a man does his sword in committing hara-kiri.' With both wings – Ireland's Alan Duggan and the uncapped Llanelli club man Andy Hill –

scoring tries, the Barbarians led 13–8 at the interval. Laidlaw had created a try for the University centre Doug Boyle in reply and then, after the break, scored one himself. With another try coming from Andy Morgan, and Hiller kicking a second conversion, the Barbarians' 14 men had ground to make up at 13–16 with time running out. They did so when Duggan went on another of his weaving runs and their second uncapped player, the Rosslyn Park lock Geoff Bayles, was on hand to dive over and level the scores. Hill kicked his third conversion of the match to go with his first-half penalty goal and the Club had narrowly won the match 18–16.

Cambridge University's centenary arrived three years later on 25 October 1972 at Grange Road and, again, the special match would involve a Past and Present XV against the Barbarians. The presence of nine British Lions of various vintages in the Club's line-up, not to mention the brilliant Frenchman Pierre Villepreux at full-back, might have suggested another victory in the offing but, far from it, the Light Blues, under the guiding hand of the illustrious Michael Gibson at fly-half, coasted to a 37–14 triumph on their special day. As at Oxford, injuries caused some disruption. The Baa-Baas' centre, Jeremy Janion, missed all of the second half because of a displaced rib cartilage and Gibson departed the scene for the final 15 minutes with a muscular spasm in his back. By then, however, the Irishman had long since guided his former university to a famous win built on 7 tries and a surfeit of lineout possession supplied by the 21-year-old number 8 Bob Wilkinson. A little over three months later the youngster would attract even more attention playing in his more accustomed position of lock as the only uncapped player in

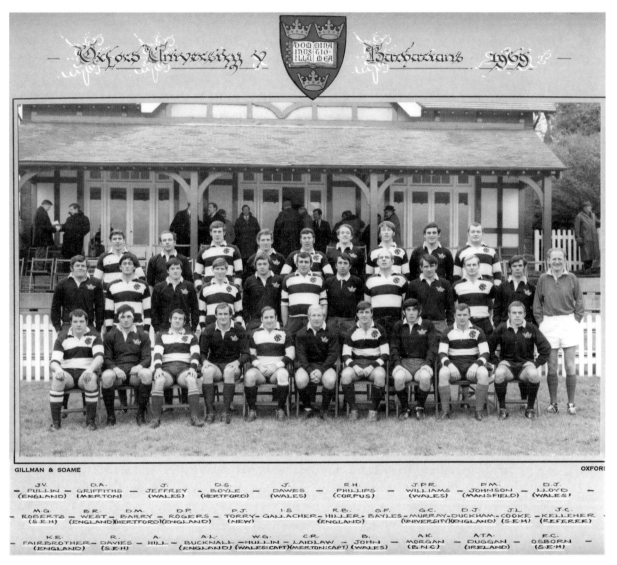

GILLMAN & SOAME
OXFOR[D]

| | J.V. PULLIN (ENGLAND) | D.A. GRIFFITHS (MERTON) | J. JEFFREY (WALES) | D.S. BOYLE (HERTFORD) | J. DAWES (WALES) | R.H. PHILLIPS (CORPUS) | J.P.R. WILLIAMS (WALES) | P.M. JOHNSON (MANSFIELD) | D.J. LLOYD (WALES) | |

| M.G. ROBERTS (S.E.H) | B.R. WEST (ENGLAND) | D.M. BARRY (HERTFORD) | D.P. ROGERS (ENGLAND) | P.J. TORRY (NEW) | I.S. GALLACHER | G.F. HILLER (ENGLAND) | R.B. BAYLES | G.C. MURRAY-DUCKHAM (UNIVERSITY) | D.J. COOKE (ENGLAND) | J.L. (S.E.H) | J.C. KELLEHER (REFEREE) |

| K.E. FAIRBROTHER (ENGLAND) | R. DAVIES (S.E.H) | A. HILL | A.L. BUCKNALL (ENGLAND) | W.G. HULLIN (WALES:CAPT) | C.R. LAIDLAW (MERTON:CAPT) | B. JOHN (WALES) | A.K. MORGAN (B.N.C) | A.T.A. DUGGAN (IRELAND) | E.C. OSBORN (S.E.H) | |

The centenary of Oxford University was marked with a special match at Iffley Road in 1969.

(© Barbarian Archive)

the Barbarians team that played the All Blacks at Cardiff Arms Park.

Respecting traditional rivals and responding to the invitations of long-established friends were not the only criteria when the Barbarians played matches against the English clubs. The first member of the Wasps club to play for the Club was as recent as 1934, when a back-row forward, N. Compton, was selected against East Midlands. Indeed, he was the only pre-war Wasp Barbarian. But after 1945 there were several great names to receive the call, including Ted Woodward, Richard Sharp and a Wasp who became a respected Barbarian

Scottish fly-half Graham Shiel makes a break against Bath in 1994 with close support from Neil Back (left) and Richard Cockerill. (© Kevin Stewart)

alickadoo, Peter Yarranton. Their centenary match was played in April 1967 and the Barbarians were seen at their best in a 36–8 win. Other fixtures at the time were arranged outside England, with centenary games in Dublin for the Wanderers in 1970 and in Wales for Neath (1971) and Llanelli (1972). In England, meanwhile, the anniversaries came around at regular intervals, with Coventry in 1973 and Moseley a year later. The oldest of all opponents, Hartlepool Rovers, were visited again in October 1979 and, across in the North-west, the Waterloo club received a visit in 1982. In the match programme for the latter, an unnamed Waterloo official wrote, 'The greatest playing honour that can be bestowed upon a rugby club is the award of a match against a national side or the Barbarians. Thus it is tonight that Waterloo is honoured more deeply than it could ever have dared to hope. This match marks the club's centenary and

represents an accolade. Accolades are never sought; they have to be earned – and even then, not consciously.' With their respects duly paid, the men of Waterloo, unbeaten in ten games to date that season, then went out and beat a star-studded Barbarians combination that included three All Blacks – Graham Mourie, Murray Mexted and Gary Knight – in their pack by 24 points to 14.

More often than not, though, the Barbarians won such matches with something to spare. In September 1983 they travelled to Redruth to share in the Cornwall county side's 100th birthday. It was an occasion of particular poignancy for Vic Roberts, a Barbarian player for ten years after the war, a committeeman since 1956 and a future vice-president, but also a proud man of Cornwall to the core who had led the county side for a decade. For him it was a reunion of all the Cornish players who had played for the Barbarians and an opportunity for his home county, in turn, to make presentations to the Club's officers. On the field of play the Barbarians won the match 32–7; off it, yet more friends were made. Another visit was made to the South-west ten years later, when the Barbarians notched up a big win (59–14) over Exeter, a club that had last been played in 1908. In 1985 London Welsh were beaten 27–24 at Twickenham, and at Bristol in 1987 there was a 20–all draw. The final centenary celebration of that period was in 1994 when Bath beat the Barbarians 23–18. By the time of the new millennium the clubs were already contacting the Barbarians with preliminary plans for their next landmark anniversaries in their 125th years. The first of them to do so was Coventry, who played and beat the Barbarians 68–40 on 23 February 2000. In one sense it was a score that again reflected the changing nature of the game in general and of the types of free-scoring matches that the Barbarians were increasingly part of. In another respect, however, the old values were preserved. In his welcome message, Coventry's chairman, Keith Fairbrother, wrote, 'In these days of professional rugby the Barbarians represent the true ethos of rugby union. As a former Barbarian myself I know the traditions of the past rugby greats will be upheld by all the players on the field this evening . . . Here at Coventry we welcome all [of them] selected by the Barbarians. To give up your time in these days of ever-increasing commitments associated in the game of rugby union, on behalf of the Coventry club, I thank you.'

Over a century after Percy Carpmael and his fellow Barbarians had begun their travels around England, the bonds between the Barbarian Football Club and the town, city, university and county clubs in every corner of the land remained as strong as ever.

IV

EASTER
IN
WALES

'Players are asked to be in bed by 11 p.m. on the night prior to playing; and not to play more than nine holes of golf on the morning of a match.'

– Easter Tour Itinerary 1938 (or any year)

On 5 April 1901 the Barbarian Football Club began a new venture that was to last 95 years and become as much a part of the British rugby calendar as the international matches between the home nations and the visits from southern hemisphere countries. The Easter tour of South Wales (and, for a while, the West Country) was born. Today, such an expedition, encompassing four matches in five days, sundry social activities and a day or more on a golf course, all undertaken by the biggest names in the sport, would be unthinkable. For the Barbarians at the turn of the last century, it seemed the most natural next step in the Club's development. As the editor of the Cardiff match programme

wrote in 1930, 'There is a magic about the Barbarians which has the power to draw players from nowhere. It would seem as if the officials had merely to press a button and about 20 internationals from all over the British Isles appear on the spot to join their one great sporting event of the season – the annual tour to South Wales.'

Micky Steele-Bodger admits with a mixture of nostalgia and wistful regret that he was 'terribly attached' to the whole concept and experience of the Bank Holiday weekend in Wales and to the starting point at Penarth in particular. It is easy to understand why.

A get-together that stretched from the

Thursday afternoon to the following Tuesday evening or even Wednesday morning and was based at an Edwardian seaside resort was an obvious attraction for players and officials alike. The Esplanade Hotel in Penarth proved to be the perfect headquarters until its closure in 1971. Indeed, it is tempting to conclude that the fate of the hotel marked the beginning of the end of the tour itself. Not that the accommodation and recreational sides were the only ideal aspects of the enterprise. The matches themselves, in their regular format after 1925, seemed to be perfectly constructed: what some may regard as a gentle opener against Penarth (though that was far from the case in the early days in particular); the full glare of publicity and expectation for the Cardiff match on Easter Saturday; another stiff test at Swansea after the rigours of a golfing Sunday; and the final hurdle at Newport on the Tuesday, when the local team would be keen to emulate or exceed whatever their Welsh rivals had achieved in the previous few days. It might be reasonable to suppose, too, that the last leg of the tour might be the point at which the players were literally on their last legs and that reinforcements would be sent for. That was increasingly the case in later years, but for most of the time the Easter tour party was a self-contained unit in which comradeship and self-support were quickly established and any shortages in particular positions were covered from within.

The tone for what was to follow was invariably set at Penarth on the Thursday evening. As the weekend unfolded, anything might happen inside or outside the Esplanade Hotel. Haydn Mainwaring recalls returning in the early hours one Easter to find four or five sheep in the foyer and to be told by the

Alickadoos and players are photographed outside the Club's spiritual home at the Esplanade Hotel in Penarth at the start of the Easter tour of 1928.
(© Barbarian Archive)

England forward Alan Ashcroft, 'That's nothing, there's a horse in the Brigadier's [Glyn Hughes'] bedroom!' Micky Steele-Bodger's veterinary skills were obviously called on from time to time. At first, though, there was a formality to the proceedings. A team dinner, the distribution of ties, scarves and blazer badges to new Barbarians, and the announcement of the first team of the weekend provided the perfect launch pad. And for several seasons at the start, the Penarth club team would fully test the mettle of the tourists on the Athletic Field the next afternoon. The Seasiders were not a team to be trifled with. They often included former players from the Cardiff club and elsewhere – in the 1900s such luminaries as Reggie Gibbs, Willie Llewellyn, Ralph Thomas and Louis Dyke were to be found among the Good Friday opposition. Though the Barbarians began the series with three straight wins, the hosts cancelled those out with their own hat-trick between 1904 and

1906. It was apparent from the outset that the new fixture was destined to be a great success. As well as the large crowds, even the weather conditions seemed ideal for year after year. In 1907 it was reported that 'the day was beautifully fine' and two years later 'the heat was sweltering when play opened'. The visit of the Barbarians became a social occasion in its own right. In 1907 the *South Wales Daily News* reported, 'A blazing sun, June-like in its splendour, and a dry, dusty ground were conditions absolutely unfitted for football [but] it was a holiday crowd, numbering quite 7,000, attracted from Cardiff and the populous suburbs of the city and a large contingent from Barry.' Much later, in the 1920s, the *Penarth Times* observed, 'A brilliant sunshine poured down on what closely resembled a miniature Ascot. Magnificent dresses were to be seen everywhere, whilst the gentlemen, not be outdone, made a brave show with their plus fours and sandies.' On the field of play the rugby on offer was a fine spectacle, too, though the Barbarians' first defeat in 1904 coincided with a bad patch in the Club's playing performances. In that season it lost all seven games played, including, of course, an Easter 'whitewash'. Results eventually improved but there was the first drawn match in the series in 1910. Reporting that game, 'Pendragon', a prominent correspondent of the time, wrote: 'There must have been at least 4,000 people in attendance, and at an average of only sixpence per head that would produce £100, which ought to be sufficient to put the Penarth club's finances right for the remainder of the season.' In the game itself a star-studded Barbarians team failed to score a try, their ten points coming from three of their internationals – a penalty goal by Doug Lambert, a drop goal by

Henry Vassall and, as allowed at the time, a goal from a mark by their captain, Khaki Roberts. Penarth responded with two converted tries and were generally commended for 'playing good football'.

The Barbarians continued to struggle for several seasons, losing the three games immediately before the First World War and the first after it in 1920, when the Club again lost all six of their season's fixtures. After another drawn match the following year the tide finally turned. Beginning in 1923 the spectators saw tries scored at an unprecedented rate: five in 1923, six the year after that and seven in 1926. It is not difficult to see why. The usual array of stars were captained by the likes of Scotland's Dan Drysdale and Ireland's Ernie Crawford, and both of them played in the 1924 match when the XV included seven members of the British Isles team about to leave on a tour to South Africa, plus Hughie Glyn Hughes and Jock Wemyss. Yet, even in that match, the Seasiders stretched their illustrious opponents to the limit before going down narrowly 9–11. But, from 1922 to 1954, the locals lost 27 consecutive matches to the Club and, for much of that time, there seemed little prospect of their fortunes ever being reversed. In the years immediately after the Second World War the Barbarians passed 30 points when posting big wins in 1947 (36–10), with Cyril Holmes scoring a record five tries, and in 1952 (36–3). A look at the team in what might be described as 'Holmes' match' gives some indication of what Penarth were increasingly up against: the Cardiff and Wales stars Frank Trott, Jack Matthews, Bleddyn Williams and Haydn Tanner behind the scrum, and seven capped players in the pack, including the future vice-president Vic Roberts. The games, nevertheless, remained competitive – it is notable that penalty kicks at goal continued to be taken – and well supported.

Sooner or later Penarth were sure to record a historic victory, and the great day finally dawned in 1960. The Barbarians had four future Club alickadoos in their line-up – Geoff Windsor-Lewis, Haydn Mainwaring, Mike Weston and the captain for the day, Adam Robson – but they may all have sensed the portents were not good from the beginning. The previous year the Barbarians had scraped a fortunate 6–all draw. Now the rain poured down. *The Times* reported that, 'A brave band of the 6th Battalion, Welch Regiment, tunefully sloshed about before the start, but the usual goat had not left his stable, or wherever it is that goats live.' The Barbarians rather naively attempted to play their traditional ball-in-hand rugby ('as though larks were singing in high summer' continued *The Times*) and suffered accordingly. And Penarth had an inspirational leader of their own: Bernard 'Slogger' Templeman. For years the diminutive, pocket-battleship scrum-half had been a thorn in the side of the Baa-Baas, regularly scoring tries and dropping goals. They had already recognised his worth by selecting him for the Mobbs Memorial Match a month earlier, but this time he was to plot their defeat. Though the Barbarians scored first through a captain's try by Robson, which was converted by Mainwaring, Templeman was soon up to his tricks. Using the conditions to perfection, his teasing kicks kept his side camped in the visitors' 25, and when they didn't have the ball, the men of Penarth tackled like demons. Their reward came when one of Templeman's henchmen in the back row, David Walkey, snapped up a fluffed clearance kick and dived

over. His captain converted with a fine kick. The Barbarians took the lead again early in the second half when Windsor-Lewis went over – the committeemen of the future were obviously in fine fettle – but an 8–5 lead was always under threat from the wily Slogger. Sure enough, with time running out, the Barbarians were again forced into error near their own line and another back-rower, Ken Roberts, dived over near the posts. From that angle, the hero of the afternoon had no difficulty in kicking the winning conversion. David had beaten Goliath again after a 40-year interval. The Barbarians forgave but didn't forget. Four days later, having lost at Cardiff and Swansea as well that Easter, and about to face a Newport team that had not lost at home all season, they sent out an SOS to Slogger. The call was answered. He dropped a typically improvised goal to give the Baa-Baas a lead they never lost and the Rodney Parade ground record fell. The following Easter the unlikely hero was back in Penarth colours, scoring another 13 of his side's 22 points, but this time in a 4-point defeat. He continued to be a figurehead at the Penarth club for several years. Bernard Templeman died in November 1992 at the age of 56. In his obituary the *South Wales Echo* recorded, 'Slogger became a Barbarian in 1960 and wore the tie with immense and enduring pride.'

The Barbarians regained the winning habit for the remainder of the 1960s. Andy Mulligan led them to a 10-try haul in the 39–3 victory in 1962. Times had changed rapidly since the great deeds of two years earlier. Penarth's forwards were unable to win any possession and Mulligan had a field day supplying a back division that had Richard Sharp at fly-half and two more British Isles backs of that year, John Willcox and the uncapped RAF centre, H.J.C.

The Easter tour party of 1970 is led in the middle of the front row by the president, Hughie Glyn Hughes, and two subsequent presidents, Herbert Waddell and Micky Steele-Bodger.

(© Barbarian Archive)

Brown. The floodgates opened after 1969 with the Baa-Baas passing forty points three times in four years – but, as if to show they should never be written off, Penarth won again in the fourth year of that sequence. In 1971, in a match again played in wet conditions, it was a case of history repeating itself from the Templeman era. The local side had several new recruits from the bigger clubs in Wales and they chased and harried a disjointed Barbarians outfit. They took the lead four times, were caught four times, but in injury time Wally Carter kicked his third penalty goal to settle the result at 15–12.

Such afternoons were something for the Penarth club to savour because their defeats, when they came, were threatening to be landslides. In 1974, under David Duckham's captaincy, the Baa-Baas won 73–10. Worse was

to follow four years later, when the visitors led 68–nil midway through the second half and went on to win 84–12. One press report described the match as a 'merry massacre', but there were sadder undertones as, for the first time, the future of the fixture as a meaningful contest was questioned. In the *Western Mail* the veteran writer J.B.G. Thomas concluded:

There may be two points of view concerning one-sided matches, as one may argue that the Barbarians could have eased up, while others argue that leading internationals in the Barbarians team are expected to play 80 minutes throughout any match and entertain the spectators. When the ball and side is running well, it is difficult to ease up, and most of the crowd thoroughly enjoyed it.

The centre of attention was the Wales and British Isles captain Phil Bennett. He kicked 10 conversions in 11 attempts, orchestrated several of his team's 15 tries and offered what the *Daily Telegraph* described as 'a selection from his repertoire that had the crowd laughing and cheering . . . his twists and turns, the stunning sidesteps and the perfectly timed passes'. Another 80-pointer followed in 1982, ironically at a time when the Barbarian committee were already experiencing difficulties with player availability every Easter. Penarth had made the best case for preserving the old traditions with two more victories in 1976 and 1980, the latter a remarkable performance against a side that again had Bennett at fly-half in partnership with the French captain Jacques Fouroux. Not even a Barbarians pack that contained the English lock Paul Ackford and Lions' back-row men John O'Driscoll and Andy Ripley could contain the hosts as they recorded their biggest ever win (29–22) and, appropriately, in their centenary season. But the tide of change was going against them. By the spring of 1985 the Barbarian committee had reluctantly decided that the following Easter's match would be the last in the series. The traditional Newport fixture on the Tuesday had already been switched to the autumn in 1983. The president, Herbert Waddell, had the thankless task of informing Penarth's officials. He wrote:

> It is all very sad [but] I can assure you that the decision had only been reached after much discussion and heart-searching over a long time . . . it was not related to Penarth's playing record nor to any grievance with your club with whom we have always enjoyed the most

friendly relationship. The decision was to do with the pressure of modern rugby which puts a heavy burden on the best players who, in the main, are the ones we need on tour so as to ensure that we can not only fulfil our obligations to our host clubs by playing an exciting and attacking rugby and attracting good gates, but can also help to bring on the less experienced players in our party.

There can be no doubt that the president was speaking from the heart. He had been an integral part of every Easter tour since 1924 as player and then committeeman. Writing in the commemorative match programme on 28 March 1986 he revealed:

> If ever a rugby club, or to be more precise a whole town, has commanded a deep and lasting affection from the players of a visiting side then that can truly be said of the Penarth–Barbarian connection.

The crowds turned out in great numbers for the final game. At least 5,000 of them packed the touch-lines and grandstand of the old ground. Before the kick-off the band of the 3rd Battalion of the Royal Regiment of Wales played the music and the Penarth president, Frank Wilson, presented Herbert Waddell with an inscribed plate. In the game itself Penarth scored two tries by centre Huw Rees and flanker Nick Wall; John Davies, an ex-Cardiff full-back, converted both and added a penalty goal. For the Barbarians the uncapped Irish hooker Willie Burns left an indelible mark with a hat-trick of tries, with other touchdowns coming from English internationals John

Palmer and Fran Clough and the Welsh trio of Mark Douglas, Phil May and Mark Titley, while Stuart Barnes kicked a penalty goal. The honour of captaincy in this historic match was handed to Gareth Davies. Appropriately, he also recorded the last points when he kicked his second conversion. The Barbarians had won the 74th and final game of the series by 39 points to 15. The memories would live on. Over the years eight members of the Penarth club had been invited to play for the Barbarians. The chairman in 1986, Kevin Bush, wrote in his farewell message:

> Yes, Penarth does mourn its great loss, but that in no way overshadows the great debt we owe the world's greatest and most exclusive rugby club. They have done as much to put, and keep, Penarth on the sporting map as anyone or anything, and for that we are eternally grateful.

He added:

> The way we have had with the Baa-Baas over the past 85 years has been more than jolly, it has been fantastic. Although it won't be continuing in the foreseeable future, we all harbour hopes at Penarth that some day the Baa-Baas will come home to roost again. There will always be a warm and special welcome for them at Penarth and wherever they go they have our best wishes.

Where they went, for the next ten years at least, was to their other familiar hunting grounds in Wales. Cardiff and Swansea

It was a sad day, but the Penarth club did everyone proud with a splendid souvenir programme for the last Good Friday match in 1986. (© Barbarian Archive)

remained on the Easter itinerary and Newport had found a new slot in the autumn. Adjustments were being made all around but that was nothing new in the broader scheme of things. Both Cardiff and Newport had originally been Christmas fixtures for the Barbarians in the 1890s. Indeed, the capital-city club had benefited from visits at both Christmas and Easter between 1899 and 1921. It was always likely that, as the Barbarians' commitments in Wales were streamlined, the matches at Cardiff Arms Park would survive the longest, and this proved to be the case. The first game was played in the Barbarians' first season on 31 March 1891; the last on 6 April 1996. In that time, 113 matches were played, with the Club winning 37 and drawing 5. That Cardiff won the other 71 fixtures says something about the strength of their sides over a long period of time and also why it was a match that both clubs were keen to sustain for as long as possible. Their determination was understandable.

A Cardiff man, Ralph Sweet-Escott, had played in the first Barbarians team against Hartlepool Rovers in 1890. Another, Hugh Ingledew, was an original member of the Club, while a third, Philip Hancock, had played for Cardiff in the 1880s before joining Blackheath and Carpmael's Southern Nomads and serving as a Barbarians player and committeeman in 1890–91. As luck would have it, Sweet-Escott and Ingledew also played for Cardiff in the first game of 1891 when the Barbarians were beaten 7–3. The pattern of home victories was to continue most of the time up to the First World War, by which stage the Blue and Blacks had won 31 and drawn one of the 38 games played. There were several high-scoring performances among the many home triumphs, including 41–3 on Boxing Day 1904 and a painful double (for the Barbarians, at least) of 38–nil and 35–nil at Easter and Christmas of 1906. There was no particular disgrace in losing so heavily to a club side that was itself enjoying a golden era. In four seasons from September 1905 Cardiff lost only 11 times in 125 matches, beat the Springboks and Wallabies, and went down to the legendary 1905 All Blacks only after conceding a late try. Yet the Barbarians never gave up hope of ever subduing their high-flying opponents, even after a salutary experience in December 1909 when the home

side defied the near-monsoon weather to run in ten unconverted tries without reply. So bad were the conditions that even attempts to convert tries under the posts proved fruitless. The Baa-Baas could console themselves that the Welsh club that afternoon fielded gifted runners and playmakers such as Percy Bush, Reggie Gibbs, Billy Spiller, Louis Dyke, Bobby Williams and their captain, Johnnie L. Williams, who was to score 17 tries in as many games for Wales. Remarkably, the Barbarians returned three months later for the Easter fixture and beat a Cardiff team containing eleven of the Christmas marvels, with something to spare. Admittedly, it was a much stronger Club combination with only one player, the Richmond and England forward Dyne Smith, surviving from the earlier game. Now the Baa-Baas contained a dozen internationals and were captained by the mercurial Harlequin Adrian Stoop at fly-half, with three more 'Quins – his brother Frederick, John Birkett and Douglas Lambert – in the outside-backs. The local critics soon realised that a different game was in prospect. In the *South Wales Daily News* Pendragon wrote:

> On this occasion the tourists had undoubtedly made a special effort to beat Cardiff by whipping up a team of extraordinary strength. When the Barbarians came to Cardiff at Christmas, they were beaten by the huge score of ten tries to nil; but it was obvious that they intended that the disaster should not be repeated today, for their team – on paper – was capable of swamping the Cardiffians. However, we have had many previous experiences of how these teams of brilliant individualists crack up

before the combined play of our best Welsh clubs, and supporters of the Blue and Blacks quite expected that that would happen today.

In the event the Barbarians didn't crack up and the threatened victory did happen. The tone was set by Fred Stoop when he intercepted a home attack and raced into the Cardiff half to give Birkett the scoring pass. Lambert converted this try but not the second, again from an interception; that was finished off by another Harlequin, the forward H.E. Ward. After that the Barbarians never looked back. Though Cardiff reduced the arrears to 8–5 at the interval after a try by Billy Jenkins that Louis Dyke converted, the second half belonged to the Baa-Baas. A penalty try was awarded when Lambert was obstructed chasing a missed drop goal and Birkett claimed his second try after more brilliant back play. Khaki Roberts converted the penalty try to complete a notable victory at 16–5.

There was another long wait for the next victory over Cardiff but when it arrived in 1921, it heralded the beginning of the Club's ascendancy in the inter-war years. The boot was now very much on the other foot, with three more wins in the 1920s and five in succession from 1931. The Barbarians were now in a golden period of their own, with a total of twenty-one consecutive wins against the four Welsh clubs, including five all-conquering Easters that finally ended at the Arms Park in 1936. After the Second World War the results were more evenly balanced, even though Cardiff were now in their second golden era. In 1947–48, under the captaincy of Haydn Tanner, they were beaten only twice in 41 matches, though the Barbarians ran them

Between 1899 and 1920 the Club played Cardiff at Christmas as well as Easter.
(© Barbarian Archive)

close in front of a 35,000-strong crowd. It was truly a clash of the great names of the era: Billy Cleaver and Tanner at half-back for Cardiff against Ireland's Grand Slam winners Jackie Kyle and Ernie Strathdee; Jack Matthews and Bleddyn Williams ruling the roost in the Welsh club's midfield; and Rees Stephens, Frank Coutts, Des O'Brien, Bill McKay and Jimmy McCarthy starring in a powerhouse Barbarians pack. It was the cast list that typically made the fixture the highlight of the post-international spring calendar for many years. The 1948 match was duly won by Cardiff 13–3, with Cleaver and Matthews scoring the only tries of the game. Throughout the next eight years the matches were shared four each before a real landmark occurred in 1957: the Barbarians won by 40 points to nil. In the *Sunday Times* the distinguished former Barbarians, Wales and British Isles full-back Vivian Jenkins began his match report:

> No, dear reader, this is not a misprint. The Barbarians, unless my powers of observation have deserted me, actually did beat a team bearing the name of Cardiff, and at Cardiff Arms Park, too, by the score recorded above – five goals and five tries to an abysmal nothing.

It was Cardiff's biggest defeat in 80 years, and the shock waves it sent out were obvious. Three of their star backs – Cliff Morgan, Gordon Wells and Gareth Griffiths – were admittedly members of the Barbarians tour party that Easter and were about to leave with them for the Club's ground-breaking tour to Canada. There was a gentleman's agreement, however, that they were available for Cardiff if required. In the event they didn't play and could only sit in the stand and watch as a particularly strong Barbarians back division scored the majority of their side's ten tries. The Scotland and British Isles wing and captain for the day, Arthur Smith, claimed a hat-trick and Tony O'Reilly and Peter Thompson scored two each. Others came from Ricky Winn, Andy Mulligan and the Gloucester prop George Hastings. The tourists led 16–nil at half-time but, as *The Times* reported, it was in the second half that they ran riot: 'Every man jack of them was bang in the picture, with forwards and backs dovetailing with bewildering speed and accuracy, and with the focus of attack often changing several times in a matter of seconds.'

By the end the conversions were being attempted by England's hooker Eric Evans. It was certainly a red-letter day for the Barbarians and one that caused much shaking of heads among the Arms Park faithful.

The Barbarians won another comprehensive victory in 1959, although on that occasion by a more modest 21 points without reply (Mulligan and Hastings were again among the scorers), but such results and one-sided affairs were generally the exception to the rule. Crowds in excess of 20,000 invariably turned up at the old Cardiff Arms Park every Easter Saturday in the knowledge that they were virtually guaranteed free-flowing rugby by the biggest names in the British game. There were very few summer tours undertaken by the individual countries before the late 1960s and then they were only irregular; the Lions only went abroad every three or four years. Even when they did, it was still the case that most of the summer tourists would still be available for the Barbarians at Easter. In the big 1959 win, ten of that summer's Lions played against Cardiff a few short weeks before they left for Australia and New Zealand – though they eventually became nine after the unfortunate Peter Robbins broke a leg three days later at Newport and was forced to withdraw from the British squad.

When the Cardiff club moved to its smaller ground alongside the rebuilt National Stadium after 1970, the fans still flocked in to fill its 16,000 capacity and the high-quality entertainment continued. The first Easter fixture there could not have had a more auspicious start, as 58 points were scored with the Barbarians narrowly shading the match 30–28. An unusual feature on the score sheet was the three drop goals – two for Cardiff by Gareth Edwards and Robin

The packed grandstands and terraces watch Andy Ripley in rampaging form against Cardiff in 1975.
(© Huw Evans Agency)

Williams and one for the Baa-Baas by Phil Bennett. The latter caused great consternation among the alickadoos and Bennett admitted years later that he and his scrum-half and captain Roger Young were hauled before the committee to give an explanation. He recalled, 'Roger got straight to the point, saying the Baa-Baas had been a soft touch for too long and sometimes the odd drop goal was needed to win a match. There was no arguing against that as we had pipped Cardiff by a couple of points after a cracking game but one in which their full-back, Robin Williams, had been kicking penalties from all around the park. They accepted Roger's point.' There were obviously no hard feelings because, 48 hours later, Bennett trumped his Arms Park effort by dropping another two goals as Swansea were beaten 24–8. And, as if to underline the great fly-half's point, six years later in 1976 Cardiff staged a remarkable

comeback from 28 points down to win 29–28 thanks to a final score in injury time – a drop goal by Gareth Edwards.

The 100th game between the sides was played on 2 April 1983 and, with a great sense of style as well as occasion, it ended as a 32–all draw. This was another era when Cardiff were at their strongest, with a team that regularly won cup finals and what were then still unofficial leagues. They had power and pace in every department with a pack built around an all-international front row of Jeff Whitefoot, Alan Phillips and Ian Eidman and the lineout skills of Robert Norster. Gareth Davies and Terry Holmes controlled games from half-back, Mark Ring worked his magic in midfield, and Adrian Hadley was the ultimate scoring threat on the wing. In this game, however, they met their match in the Barbarians' secret weapon. Danie Gerber was a South African centre who, because of his country's isolation from international sport, was relatively unknown in Europe. That situation changed in the course of ten days in April 1983. The Barbarians invited him to come with his fellow countryman Errol Tobias to play against Scotland at Murrayfield and then stay on for the Easter tour. Both were in the team at Cardiff. So were the formidable England trio of David Cooke, Peter Winterbottom and Dean Richards in the back row, and Steve Bainbridge, about to become a Lion himself, and Pontypool's John Perkins at lock. And it was Gerber who shone out in a match of many heroes. In the *Daily Telegraph* John Mason reported:

> Though Danie Gerber, the South African centre who scored four of the Barbarians' six tries, gave the season's

outstanding performance in midfield, there were home-grown skills in profusion to admire in this Easter parade of rugby talent. The Cardiff crowd, knowledgeable and sympathetic, royally saluted the speed and strength of the forceful Gerber . . . As well as the resounding applause for [him] and his fellow Springbok, Errol Tobias, the outside-half, there were rousing receptions, too, for Terry Holmes, Bob Norster and Adrian Hadley.

Hadley stole everyone's thunder in the third minute of injury time as he plunged over in the corner for the try that levelled the scores. It seemed only right that Gareth Davies, for once, should miss the conversion. It was the perfect ending to what was already established as one of the Barbarians' most treasured fixtures in their year. But even Easter Saturday at the Arms Park would eventually be under threat. In the following year Cardiff raced away to a record 52–16 victory. They fielded 11 of the previous year's side and were even stronger thanks to the return of their captain, John Scott. The Barbarians, on paper at least, looked a capable side, with Jeff Squire opposite Scott, and two other fine back-rowers in John Jeffrey and Gary Rees. The second row of John Fidler and the captain Bill Cuthbertson were streetwise customers, too, but, to the Baa-Baas' consternation, the pack as a unit proved unable to secure any worthwhile possession throughout the match. Instead, Davies and Holmes at half-back controlled the play as their side racked up ten tries, six of them converted by the fly-half. The game was sufficiently one-sided for questions to be asked about the viability of even this venerable Easter

Martin Offiah, the Rosslyn Park wing, scores a try at the Arms Park in 1987 despite the attentions of Mark Ring. (© Huw Evans Agency)

institution. Twelve months earlier, on the Monday after the drawn match, the Barbarians had gone down to Swansea by 6–58 – the biggest defeat in their history. Now Cardiff had almost matched that. In the *Sunday Times* Stephen Jones wrote:

> The only poor devils who did not enjoy their afternoon tremendously were the Barbarians team. The trill of the final whistle would have been as attractive to them as the sweetest concerto. They finished only just the right side of humiliation. The increasing pressure of the European rugby season has taken heavy toll of the Barbarians' Easter tour. It is too much to expect that players who have spilled blood in a variety of important causes almost weekly will achieve the same level of commitment on a bone-hard ground in a festival

atmosphere against the major Welsh clubs.

Barbarians down the years would beg to differ with that conclusion. Matches were always meant to be hard. One-sided victories, whether for or against, were always few and far between. Players eagerly welcomed a Barbarians calling card partly for the *craic* but mainly for the honour. While Jones was right to highlight the increasing demands of clubs and competitions, two bad results in Wales couldn't sweep away nearly a century of not only tradition but also goodwill, expectation and achievement. The Barbarians were far from down and out. Though Arms Park victories were hard to come by (they always had been),

Mike Teague of Gloucester on the charge against Cardiff in 1990.
(© Huw Evans Agency)

they won four in a row from 1991, culminating in a points half-century of their own in the 1994 match. The side included, at hooker, Yves Kummer, the first Dutchman to play for the Club, and he celebrated in fine style with a spectacular try-scoring dive under the posts. That was the signal for 100 rugby fans from Holland to spontaneously sing their national anthem. Before the end they were at it again after the Oxford University captain, Chad Lion-Cachet, scored the last of the team's eight tries. He was about to receive a Dutch passport the following week. Also in the tour party that weekend was a third Dutch forward, George De Vries, and his debut came 48 hours later against Swansea. The Cardiff result was something to savour and a reminder to everyone never to write the Barbarians off. But the record victory had a sting in its tail. The following year the Barbarians scored well again – 33 points – but conceded 75. The Club had Alain Penaud, Denis Charvet and a young Richard Hill in their ranks and were not entirely without stars but the days of gifted individuals outwitting well-organised club teams were virtually at an end. The former sprint-hurdler Nigel Walker scored three of Cardiff's eleven tries and now the writing was on the wall for the fixture's future. The Barbarians' proud history could not be compromised by such a result and the time had come to take stock.

On 6 April 1996 Cardiff v. Barbarians on Easter Saturday came to an end. Neither club particularly wanted that to happen, but leagues and the professional game that had emerged seven months before were proving insurmountable obstacles. Cardiff had an important league game two days later that, if won, would confirm them as champions of Wales. Against the Barbarians they selected 13 reserves plus scrum-half Andy Moore and Walker, who this time scored two tries. The Club still had Charvet and other quality performers such as Agustin Pichot, John Gallagher and Iain Morrison. But this was not a cast list to compare with Jackie Kyle v. Cliff Morgan or Gareth Edwards v. Roger Young. Fortunately this final game was more competitive, with Cardiff winning 49–43 because they converted all seven of their tries. The Baa-Baas matched them try for try but could only convert four. The result was never the priority, the performance and the upholding of standards were. As with Penarth and the other Welsh clubs, communication and contact would continue via dinners and golf tournaments, but for the time being, at least, the final whistle had been blown.

Fifty miles to the west the Easter parade at Swansea had already suffered the same fate after 82 matches stretching back to 1901. The story of their Barbarian connections was remarkably similar to that of Cardiff's. The significant difference was that they came off marginally worse in their playing record against the Club, winning 40 times but losing on 41 occasions. That was another source of pride for the Barbarians because Swansea could never be taken lightly. Like Cardiff, they had a golden era in the 1900s during which they beat the Springboks and Wallabies. Where Cardiff had Gwyn Nicholls, Rhys Gabe and Percy Bush, Swansea had W.J. Bancroft, Billy Trew and Dickie Owen. They also shared with Cardiff the right to stage international matches and their St Helen's ground regularly attracted 20,000 attendances for the Easter fixture. At first the Barbarians found victories at St Helen's elusive. To judge by some reports, Swansea were often charged with extra responsibilities after Cardiff

in particular had been beaten by the tourists. Thus, in 1910 the *South Wales Daily News* reported, 'Swansea restored the prestige of Welsh rugby on Easter Monday by triumphantly reversing the verdict in favour of the Saxon [*sic*] at Cardiff.' Scots such as Jim Mackenzie and Andrew Lindsay, and the Irish full-back S.H. Beattie, had been in the victorious team but there was still a tendency in Wales, despite all evidence to the contrary, to regard the Barbarians as essentially English. They were even referred to as 'the pick of the England rugby union team'. They had won 16–5 at the Arms Park but were to leave St Helen's pointless for the sixth time in eight visits, after a match not without incident. The newspaper continued:

> A very unpleasant incident [occurred]. Trew was placing the ball for Bancroft when a visiting forward dashed up and kicked violently at it. Then it was seen that Trew was laid out. He rolled over and over on the ground as if he had been kicked. After a few minutes, during which the crowd loudly called for the expulsion of the player who had charged so unfortunately, the game was resumed and Bancroft, by kicking a goal, elicited loud applause. The incident threatened to spoil the game.

It didn't spoil the result for the home side as they won 11–nil. The Barbarians continued to suffer in the seasons that followed, though at least in 1911 and 1912 they were in the lead at half-time, only to be overhauled even when, as in the latter game, 'they played sporting football and never gave up trying.'

However hard the rugby was on the field,

particularly after the social events of the Sunday, the West Wales fixture was another highlight of the Easter tour. It was not always played on the Monday – the first game, in 1901, was on the Tuesday and two years later it was a Saturday fixture. In the early days the committee were quite keen to rotate the weekend sequence. Indeed, for two years in 1906 and 1907, Swansea was left off the itinerary altogether and Devonport Albion and Exeter were added. After 1910, however, Easter Monday at Swansea became sacrosanct and a routine was built around a mid-morning departure from the Esp, a pleasant lunch on the Gower peninsula, a late-afternoon kick-off (usually 3.30 p.m.) and, after the usual post-match reception and gathering of old friends, a return journey to Penarth in time for further recreation and refreshments.

After 14 defeats and a nil–all draw in 1922 the Barbarians finally beat Swansea in 1923. They did so in style, scoring five tries in a 23–nil result. Ironically, the victorious captain was Douglas Marsden-Jones, who had been born in Swansea and educated at the local grammar school and university before leading London Welsh and playing for Blackheath. Hughie Glyn Hughes was also in the team but the star man was the Scottish full-back Dan Drysdale, who played against Swansea four times in five years. Though they lost the next three matches, there was a marked reversal of fortunes between 1927 and 1937 when they won ten of the eleven games played. Herbert Waddell and Ernie Crawford shared the goal-kicking duties in the record 27–9 win in 1927 and there was an even more significant result in April 1936. Earlier in that season Swansea had beaten the All Blacks 11–3. Ten of their team that day, including the precociously talented

teenage half-backs Willie Davies and Haydn Tanner, also turned out against the Barbarians. But the Club had stars of their own, notably an all-international back division. It was quite a line-up: at full-back, Vivian Jenkins of Wales; on the wings, Scotland's Ken Fyfe and England's Ted Unwin; Wilfred Wooller (Wales) and Robert Dick (Scotland) in the centre; and two more Scots, Wilson Shaw and Ross Logan, at half-back. Fyfe and Unwin scored five tries between them (Fyfe with three) and Jenkins converted two as the Baa-Baas romped to a 19–8 win. Swansea gained revenge in the final two games before the Second World War but after it the tourists were unbeaten in ten matches.

There were some impressive individual contributions during that period. In 1953 the 21-year-old Cardiff centre Gareth Griffiths scored two tries against the Baa-Baas on Easter Saturday but more than paid off the debt with a hat-trick on his Club debut at St Helen's two days later. The committee were suitably impressed and the following year selected him for the big game against the All Blacks. In 1955 the Irish lock Robin Thompson led the side to victory before leaving to perform a similar role for the Lions on tour in South Africa; in 1959 his fellow Irishman Ronnie Dawson emulated him in both respects.

Swansea's first post-war victory was in 1956 and it was a notable one because they outplayed another star-studded tourists' back division that included an all-Lions three-quarter line of Scotland's Arthur Smith and three Irishmen, Noel Henderson, Tony O'Reilly and Cecil Pedlow, and deservedly scored eight points without reply. In 1957 they rose to the occasion again and presumably could hardly contain their smiles as the Barbarians were

The tour group for Easter 1959 is another reminder of how strong the squads were at that time. It contained ten of the British Isles team about to tour Australasia. The committee in the second row (left to right) are R.J. Barr, E. Evans, A. Wemyss, H. Waddell, H.L. Glyn Hughes, M.R. Steele-Bodger, C.R. Hopwood, V.G. Roberts and C.R.A. Graves.

brought down to earth after their 40-point annihilation of Cardiff two days earlier. *The Times* praised their efforts:

> Swansea, at home, showed that they were respecters neither of persons nor reputations and knocked a nasty dent in the Barbarians' Easter record . . . nor was there the slightest suggestion of a fluke about it – a large and distinctly partisan crowd certainly got their money's worth.

Full-back Alun Prosser-Harries converted all three of Swansea's tries, scored by Brian Ford,

Bryan Richards and Glyn Davies. For the Barbarians Terry Davies converted tries by Gareth Griffiths and Peter Thompson. Even in such closely contested matches there was a relaxed holiday mood and room for much humour. In 1963 the Rugby Football Correspondent of *The Times*, presumably U.A. Titley, mused over why there were multiple changes to the team listed in the match programme: 'Of the 15 Barbarians names a full dozen were given incorrectly, which recalls Dr Goebbel's wartime theory, that if you are going to tell lies you should make sure of telling real whoppers.' The Barbarians still won the match 11–9, thanks to an injury-time try and conversion by their captain, John Willcox.

The Barbarians scored their highest points to date ten years later when, despite playing over half the game with 14 men, they won the 1973 fixture 35–9. Writing in *The Guardian*, Clem Thomas, who for so many years had led rousing Swansea packs and was also a distinguished Barbarian, said, 'Barbarian stock has never been higher than at the present time, and the renaissance in their fortunes was never more timely.' It was the first time 30 points had been scored by either side in 60 matches since 1901 – but the points dam was about to burst. Swansea won 37–25 in 1976 and passed the thirty-points mark three more times in the four matches after that. A good match ended 25–22 in the home club's favour in 1982 but nobody was quite prepared for what happened in the next match on 4 April 1983. Swansea's 58–6 triumph was the biggest defeat for the Barbarians in 93 years. Looking at their team on paper it is hard to see why. Their 11 internationals included the Springboks Danie Gerber and Errol Tobias, who had already made such an impression against Scotland and Cardiff, and seven Welshmen in the pack. Swansea at that time were on a high, regarded as the best club team in Britain in some quarters, but they could not have anticipated the swiftness of their opponents' capitulation. The Baa-Baas could only score two penalty goals through another capped player, Marcus Rose, and Swansea's ten tries included four by the wing Arthur Emyr.

After such a setback reputations needed to be restored and they were, swiftly, twelve months later, with a 40–13 revenge. With the Frenchman Didier Camberabero at fly-half the backs scored seven of the eight tries, two of them by Rory Underwood. Everyone could breathe a sigh of relief: the Barbarians' renowned refreshing attitude and winning ways were still alive and well. The pattern of close matches returned for a while in the rest of the 1980s, though there was no room for complacency. Another one-sided affair in 1992, won 55–12 by the tourists, was a reminder that perhaps an open mind should be kept about future plans. Cardiff and Swansea formed a two-match Easter tour from 1987 but in 1994 the St Helen's match, like the Newport fixture before it, was moved to the autumn. Swansea won their final Easter Monday match on 4 April 1994 by 41–31. The howling wind and storm conditions were surely a bad omen. Swansea fielded a reserve team but still beat a Barbarians line-up led by Gavin Hastings. The captain was not amused. He said, 'I probably won't be coming down on another Easter tour of Wales. I don't see that there is the incentive any more. The Barbarians give up their spare time expecting to play against the Swansea first team. If they want to keep the fixture they will have to do a lot more than they did today.' The Barbarian committee probably agreed with him but diplomatic relations were retained. Gordon Ferguson was presented with a plaque by the host club in recognition of his 40 years of service to the Barbarians. Six months later Fergie, the committee and the Barbarians returned for what was hopeed would be the start of a new tradition. Unfortunately it wasn't. An under-strength home side was again good enough to win the 82nd match in the series 39–17. Almost as a mark of respect for the great deeds of the past, both clubs reluctantly agreed to discontinue the fixture.

No one was sadder than Haydn Mainwaring, a modern Barbarian committeeman who went on four Easter tours as a player but who also played for Swansea against them. For men of his generation the non-appearance of the top players was baffling. He said, 'Playing for Swansea against the Barbarians was up alongside the club fixtures with Llanelli and Cardiff as the highlight of every season. Everyone wanted to be selected; there was never any question of being unavailable.' He was doubly sad because he had seen the other Welsh club from his playing days, Newport, lose their Easter slot on the tour and soon their own new autumn arrangement would be lost as well.

The Newport fixture had originated in April 1893, the third match of a typically demanding Easter tour that had encompassed Hartlepool Rovers and Huddersfield before an overnight trip to South Wales for the match at Rodney Parade. The match had been postponed from the previous December because of frost but the revised date against one of the strongest club sides in Britain was very ambitious. It was the Welsh club's final match of a 29-match season that had seen them remain undefeated for five months before losing twice to their great rivals Cardiff and again on their own northern tour to Oldham. The Barbarians were led by Percy Carpmael but the opposition had their own stars in the likes of Arthur Gould – the first prince of Welsh three-quarters – Arthur Boucher and Harry Packer. Carpmael scored the only try of the game but that was more than cancelled out by two four-point drop goals by the home side's wing, F.W. Cooper. Newport's victory set the pattern for many years to come. As with the Cardiff and Swansea fixtures in the early days, Barbarian victories were hard to come by. It was to take the Club 11 years and 14 attempts to finally achieve that elusive win.

Two Swansea defenders move in on Chris Oti in 1989. (© Huw Evans Agency)

That was on 27 December 1904, 24 hours after they had lost heavily to Cardiff. Ten of the team turned out again at Newport. Sidney Coopper, the Blackheath wing who was to play 21 times in Barbarian colours, scored one of the tries, and A.R. Thompson, a forward from Richmond, the other. Another Richmond club man, H.F.P. Hearson, converted both to complete a 10–6 victory. It was a day to savour as another long interlude of 22 years was to pass before the Barbarians beat Newport again. Along the way there were some heavy defeats: 21 points without reply in 1921, and 39 in 1920. Occasionally, the convincing scorelines may have flattered the hosts.

Reporting the latest home win at Christmas in 1913, the *Monmouthshire Evening Post* acknowledged that the match was 'bright, fast, open, vigorous and good-tempered, but Newport's superiority was rather over-rewarded by a win of 14 points to nil'. But it

was not until 1926 that the pattern of results finally took a turn for the better. At first it was a modest improvement, with single-point victories in that year and again three years later. As the golden period of Easter tours unfolded in the 1930s, Newport felt the full force of the Barbarians' resurgence. Five straight wins for the tourists included the 23–3 result in 1935 that extended their undefeated run in Wales to an unprecedented 21 matches. In the middle of this period they had also played a one-off fixture against Newport and District, a memorial match for a former Newport player and official, Walter Martin, and won 16–10. That was in October 1933. Six months later they completed a season's double at Rodney Parade when they won in a manner that typified their never-say-die attitude at that time. With five minutes left to play the Barbarians were trailing by three points and it seemed as if their long unbeaten run in Wales was about to end. Newport had performed heroics with only 14 men for most of the game but, as *The Times* reported, 'the Barbarians made a brilliant recovery and pulled the game out of the fire.' Several players handled the ball before the Edinburgh Wanderer Idwal Rees crossed for a try at the corner. A brilliant conversion from the touch-line by the prop John Allan established an 8–6 lead and then the Club rubbed salt in Newport's wounds with another try in injury time from another forward, the England international John Dicks. The long period of success finally ended in 1937 when scrum-half Jim Hawkins kicked a drop goal and scored a try in Newport's 7–3 win.

After the Second World War, Newport regained the ascendancy but there were also good days for the Barbarians. A feature of the 1946 match was the inclusion of two members of the New Zealand Forces team, the Kiwis, who had recently completed a 33-match tour of Europe. Fred Allen was honoured with the captaincy while the wing Bill Meates, having already scored on his previous appearances against Penarth and Cardiff, completed a notable weekend with another try against Newport, but this time in a 6–11 defeat. The next match was notable for the captaincy of Micky Steele-Bodger and, alongside him in the back row, the future vice-president Vic Roberts. Four tries were scored in a 19–3 victory but, as the 1950s dawned, a new era of brilliant Newport backs posed a fresh challenge for the visitors. The Olympic sprinter and record cap-holder Ken Jones was the main strikeforce (he also scored a hat-trick of tries for the Baa-Baas at Leicester in 1953) and alongside him were creative players such as Malcolm Thomas and Roy Burnett. The first of only three victories in the decade came in 1953 when the team was captained by the 1950 Lion Jack Matthews. Dr Jack had retired from first-class rugby a year earlier but took a particular delight as a Cardiff man in putting on his boots again to beat his club's arch-rivals. Despite perfect conditions the home side's backs were strangely misfiring as a unit and the visitors took full, if unspectacular, advantage. Jones did score his customary try, chasing a Burnett kick, and the fly-half also dropped a goal. The only score of the first half had been a penalty goal for the Barbarians by John Robins and it was the final moments of the match before he struck again, converting the Oxford University full-back C.J. Saunders' try to ensure an 8–6 win. Ironically, the rare win had been achieved by a side not particularly full of household names or players in prime form. As well as

Matthews coming out of retirement, the Harrogate and England full-back Ian King had been drafted in as a stop-gap fly-half, and there was little fluency in the play. Yet, when the Barbarians returned with a side containing 13 internationals in 1954, they proved no match for the Black and Ambers. In front of a 20,000 crowd, scrum-half Onllwyn Brace, renowned for his scissors pass and unorthodox play, orchestrated several fine moves. Three tries were scored and Brace dropped a typically audacious goal in a 14–3 home win. There was exactly the same scoreline in 1956 when the 50th match was played between the sides. Again the tourists were packed with stars – 15 past, present or future internationals and a three-quarter line of Tony O'Reilly, Cecil Pedlow, Tommy McClung and Peter Thompson – but Newport outscored them by three tries to one. Malcolm Thomas, Des Greenslade and Colin Evans, a very different type of scrum-half to Brace, claimed the tries, and full-back Norman Morgan converted one and kicked a penalty goal. Thompson claimed the Baa-Baas' only points. The outstanding forward that day was the England flanker Peter Robbins, but three years later the corresponding match was to end in tragedy for him.

Before then, in 1957, there was another Barbarian victory. Although playing without the ball for long periods, the side, captained by Vic Roberts, took their chances well. The Scotland wing Arthur Smith put them ahead with an opportunist try early in the second half. But when Burnett replied with one of his own for Newport and Norman Morgan converted from the touch-line, it looked as if the tourists were again about to be denied. But, in the dying moments, Smith was in full stride again and linked on his inside for Ricky Winn

to claim the decisive try. Haydn Mainwaring, playing at full-back, emulated his opposite number with a touch-line conversion of his own.

Three facts stand out from the match of 1959: the Barbarians won convincingly 15–5; Peter Robbins captained the side; and Robbins broke a leg. The latter accident is what the match will mostly be remembered for, because, only days before, the wing-forward had been selected for a Lions tour. The match report in *The Times* neatly summed up everyone's reaction:

> Not only was this a personal tragedy after the comebacks Robbins has made, but it was also a nasty blow for the British team who are to tour the Antipodes, for in spite of the marvels of modern science nature calls the tune in the long run and the chances of a timely recovery appear to be slender. But all his friends will clutch to any hope and wish him the speediest recovery.

Robbins never did become a Lion and for him it was a case of lightning striking twice – two years earlier he had been forced to withdraw from the Barbarians tour to Canada after injuring himself in a swimming pool at Penarth.

As for the match itself, the Cambridge Blue Mike Wade scored a hat-trick of tries and George Hastings converted all three. A back-to-back win followed in 1960, this time under the captaincy of Haydn Mainwaring. He now doubles up as a Barbarian committeeman and avid Newport fan but when he applied for club membership at Rodney Parade, he was told by the secretary, 'We will have to check you out;

The tour party to Wales in 1973. It was the 60th anniversary of Hughie Glyn Hughes' first visit to Wales and the Club won all four matches against Penarth, Cardiff, Swansea and Newport.
(© Barbarian Archive)

you helped the Baa-Baas to beat us.' The 1960 Easter party was notable for its lack of Scottish players. In a foretaste of the problem that was to beset the Club in later years, Scotland were about to go on the first overseas tour by a home country, as opposed to a Lions tour, and several leading players were unavailable. The topsy-turvy results continued in the 1960s: three home wins followed by a record-equalling 23–3 triumph for the Barbarians in 1964. Echoes of Peter Robbins' misfortunes could be heard in 1968 when the Gloucester and England full-back Don Rutherford broke an arm. To compound Barbarian woes, Newport recorded a 26–11 win, their biggest points total since 1920. In *The Guardian* Christopher Ford reported, 'Towards the end Newport were playing daredevil rugby and only a few forward passes and knocks on prevented a

score of almost embarrassing proportions.' But even bigger scores were only just around the corner for both sides.

Thankfully, it was the Barbarians who first took the points-scoring to new levels, and they did so with a great sense of style. Easter of 1973 marked the 60th anniversary of Brigadier Glyn Hughes' first visit to Wales. Only the Barbarians could then go out and win the final match of the weekend by registering 60 points. Appropriately, too, in the light of his own future elevation to the committee, the team at Newport was captained by John Spencer. He scored three of the twelve tries himself and was instrumental in awarding the final conversion from in front of the posts to the Coventry hooker John Gray. Having already succeeded three times, he was no slouch as a goal-kicker. This time, with a marvellous sense of history, he missed, and the president could nod with satisfaction at the 60 prominently displayed on the ground's scoreboard. It was the Barbarians' biggest ever score and, at 15–60, Newport's heaviest defeat. Though they conceded a hefty 46 points in 1975, Spencer again leading from the front with two of his side's nine tries, revenge was not long in coming. On 20 April 1976 Newport won 43–nil. It completed a miserable Easter for the Barbarians. A season that had started so well, with victories at Leicester and in the Mobbs Memorial Match, and the 19–7 defeat of the Wallabies at Cardiff Arms Park, had ended with a whitewash in Wales for the first time in the Club's 86-year history. There was another first in 1978 when a match was abandoned. With Newport leading by 13 points, the game was halted in the 68th minute because of a flooded pitch in the torrential rain. The records continued. The final Easter fixture was in 1982, when the Barbarians won 48–20. In the match programme it was noted that:

> Discussions took place between the committees of both clubs and agreement was reached that today's fixture would be the last during the Easter period. For the next three years the annual fixture will be played during mid-week at the start of the season with an evening kick-off.

The article went on to list the three dates that had already been decided. The omens were good for the new arrangement. Difficulties over recruiting enough good players for the long weekend in spring did not at first carry over to the autumn. On 28 September 1982 the Club fielded 13 internationals, though admittedly

Bill Gammell of Edinburgh Wanderers and Scotland scores a try against Newport in 1979. (© Huw Evans Agency)

none from England. But names such as Robert Norster of Wales, Nigel Carr of Ireland and the Scots John Rutherford and Jim Calder were there, suggesting that a solution had been found for the problem of player availability. The experiment survived for 14 years, a respectable time but one in which there was a repetition of the increasingly high scores and one-sided matches found elsewhere on the restructured calendar. There was another 60-pointer in favour of the Barbarians in 1988; a match of 15 tries in 1994 (won 54–45); and Neil Jenkins scored 24 points in the 59–28 win in 1995. The last game of all had the most points. The games at Penarth, Cardiff and Swansea had already fallen by the wayside but again, beforehand, the Newport match programme on

8 October 1996 was optimistic: 'the fixture must be preserved as it is part of our heritage and we are privileged to be the only Welsh club to retain its annual match with the Barbarians.' Wise words, but the match that evening wrote its own final chapter. A score of 86–33 in favour of the Barbarians defied all attempts to consider it a competitive exercise. Newport could not prevent a modest Barbarians side from running in fourteen tries, four of them by the Richmond centre Mike Hutton. The doubters had a field day. More importantly, the Barbarian committee was wise enough to accept that in a changing world they should not allow the Club's standards and reputation to slip. Better to call a halt with those factors intact. Regular fixtures against Welsh clubs ended that evening in 1996.

The future almost certainly means that the Barbarians will periodically return across the Severn to play anniversary matches or games to open new grounds. That, after all, is what happened in the not-too-distant past. Quite apart from the revered Easter tour, the Club had visited Neath in 1971 for that club's centenary and Llanelli twice, in 1965 (to open new facilities) and in 1972 for another 100th birthday. Each time, the matches were followed by calls for more regular visits. The first-class-rugby scene in Wales is now changing, but four regional sides are based at Cardiff, Newport, Llanelli and halfway between Neath and Swansea – all venues familiar to the Barbarians. Back in 1996, as the traditional fixtures petered out, Gerald Davies wrote, 'If Wales cannot find a place for them, then the Barbarians should find the welcome of friends elsewhere.' In the years that followed, the Club did just that and were greeted with open arms in rugby outposts as far apart as Japan and Portugal, Russia and Uruguay. There is no denying that the passing of the Easter tour is lamented by all involved, but it was a dignified withdrawal. It was a credit to the Barbarians and their hosts that it lasted as long as it did. In 1932 Emile de Lissa noted:

> I do not think our older members of 20 years or more ago . . . realise the present-day difficulties of collecting really first-class sides for the Easter tours. Owing to the great increase in the number of fixtures, many of the stronger London and other English clubs run their own Easter tours. Consequently the English field of selection has become very narrow and very different to the time when Carpmael conceived his idea of forming this Club.

Seen in that light, the 95-year history of the Easter tour was indeed a triumph.

NORTH OF THE BORDER AND ACROSS THE SEA

'I think that the Barbarians are a superb concept and that's why I play for them whenever I'm asked.'

— Gavin Hastings, 1995

Given the contribution of numerous individuals from Scotland and Ireland to its history and development, it is more than a little surprising that the Barbarian Football Club has ventured so rarely to Scotland or Ireland. Players and officials such as Herbert Waddell, Jock Wemyss, Adam Robson and, nowadays, John Jeffrey north of the border and Ernie Crawford, Ronnie Dawson, Syd Millar and Kevin Flynn across the Irish Sea have been part of the lifeblood of the Club on and off the field. Others, such as Douglas Elliot, Arthur Smith, Sandy Carmichael, Andy Irvine, Tony O'Reilly, Andy Mulligan, Michael Gibson and Fergus Slattery, are forever linked with some of its greatest deeds. Yet no fixtures were played in

Ireland before 1957 and, although they appeared in a handful of seven-a-side tournaments at Melrose, Langholm and Galashiels, Scotland did not see the Barbarians in a full-scale match until 1970. Part of the explanation probably lies in the reluctance of successive committees to spread the Club's annual commitments outside the perceived ideal number of six regular fixtures and the occasional match against a major touring team from overseas. For most of the last century that meant the Easter tour, Leicester at Christmas and the Mobbs Memorial Match in late winter, with the All Blacks, Springboks or Wallabies every third or fourth year. Certainly, the committee was well disposed to a Scottish

connection in particular but the stumbling block always seemed to be the self-imposed constraint of the sacred six. All approaches to expand the itinerary from whatever quarter were resisted with a gentle firmness. In November 1955, Herbert Waddell wrote to Jock Wemyss:

> If the Barbarians couldn't play Blackheath, who were largely responsible for founding the Club, why should they play anyone else? We have turned down Wales and innumerable others, Ireland, Llanelli, etc . . . if the Barbarians are going to play anybody I would rather it was Edinburgh Accies or Glasgow Accies than anyone else but it is a question of opening the gates . . . when we refused to Blackheath we really made it impossible for us to play anybody else. The Barbarians are a peculiar club and the committee have already agreed that six matches are enough . . . If we have to play too many games then we won't get the players and the honour becomes less.

As it happens a centenary match was played against Blackheath in 1959 and by then the Club had also relented and gone to Northern Ireland to play Ulster. The latter game was staged in honour of Ernie Crawford, who had won 30 caps for Ireland in the 1920s, had been a Barbarian committeeman since 1933 and, in the autumn of 1957, was beginning his 12-month term of office as president of the Irish Rugby Football Union. The match was played at Ravenhill, the Belfast ground that had only recently lost its status as an international venue but was still a worthy stage for the Barbarians'

first appearance in Ireland. Ulster were a strong provincial side in their own right – they had drawn with the All Blacks three years earlier – but for this fixture on 19 October 1957 they fielded a 'Select XV' that included the Dublin Wanderer Ronnie Kavanagh and several other guest players. The backbone of the side was undoubtedly made up of Ulstermen, none more illustrious than the captain, Jackie Kyle. The legendary fly-half had played many fine games for the Barbarians but was now approaching veteran status; later the same season he would play his 46th and final game for Ireland and retire as the world's most capped player in his position. Interestingly he found himself up against not one but two Barbarian fly-halfs in the course of a largely disappointing match. The Club started with Gordon Waddell, son of Herbert, in the pivot position but he switched places with centre Carwyn James early in the game. James, the Llanelli man who was later to achieve fame as the coach of the 1971 British Isles team that beat New Zealand, relished the opportunity to play in such a high-profile match. Though a fine footballer, his career had been overshadowed by that of the mercurial Cliff Morgan, and his two caps for Wales, one when Morgan was injured and the other as a centre, came later in the 1957–58 season. For the Barbarians he was to show his silky skills without ever quite making the backs outside him click. There were several alterations to the original selection – Tony O'Reilly, Peter Thompson and Dickie Jeeps were among the eminent internationals who did not make it to the starting line – but the Club still fielded a strong line-up under the captaincy of Scotland's Jim Greenwood. The number 8 didn't entirely endear himself to his countryman, Herbert Waddell. In another of his frequent letters to Wemyss he wrote, 'Instead of putting [Fenwick] Allison in charge of the backs as we had meant and forgot to tell him, he appointed [Ricky] Winn. Told the team not to be afraid to kick to touch! [But] he led the forwards well. Played well himself.'

It appears that Waddell Senior was not completely convinced of the merits of the fixture, concluding to Wemyss, 'Never seemed like a Barbarian match. Big hotel. Players arriving from time to time and going from time to time by plane. We were lost in the hotel.' As if that wasn't enough, he added, 'These extra games on Saturday at this time are very difficult indeed.' Unknowingly, Herbert Waddell was presaging more than one problem that would confront later Club committeemen. Hughie Glyn Hughes was also unconvinced about the merits of the fixture, with Wemyss again the recipient of the reservations: 'It never really felt like a Baa-Baas game either on or off the field.'

Yet, for the new audience in Belfast, the game was a success. A crowd of over 10,000 turned up and local reporter B.S. Nolan wrote in the *Sunday Independent*, 'It was a most exciting tussle and provided plenty of intelligent and enterprising football.' The Barbarians pack impressed him, especially 'two capital wing-forwards in the Englishman [Reg] Higgins and the Welsh livewire [Brian] Sparks . . . and the Welsh international [Russell] Robins ran, passed and handled with quite amazing smoothness and purpose for a second-row forward.' Despite these good individual performances it looked for most of the match as if the home side would prevail. After ten minutes the two centres, Richard Lee and David Hewitt, combined to send the left-wing Gordon Hamilton over for an unconverted try.

Within a couple of minutes the winger added a second, this time chasing a kick ahead. The only other score of the first half was a Barbarian try by the Blackheath wing, Wallace Gray. But Ulster pulled away again shortly after the restart when their international prop Jim Brennan chased another cross-kick for a try converted by Hewitt. Trailing 3–11 with barely a dozen minutes left to play, the Baa-Baas had to look to their laurels. Inspiration came when their other wing, J.C. Walker of Edinburgh Academicals, swerved beautifully in a run of 40 yards for a try in the corner. Then they drew level with another good try by Gordon Waddell, converted by Allison. It was left to Carwyn James to add the final touch, dropping a goal five minutes before the end for an unlikely 14–11 victory. The home crowd, to their credit, were reported to have given the visitors 'sustained applause'. Once again the Barbarians had won new friends.

Having enjoyed the north of the island, another 13 years would pass before they travelled to the Republic, but when they did a spectacular show was put on for a large Lansdowne Road gathering in Dublin. It was not, however, the first time the Club had encountered Dublin opposition. In December 1891 they had played hosts to a Dublin University side in a match at Blackheath. The Irish students were on a short tour of England and had beaten Cambridge University decisively a day earlier. They seemed a good side who, it was anticipated, 'were expected to make a sad example of the very scratch XV which the Barbarians mustered to meet them'. Those expectations didn't materialise, the Barbarians winning by a try and a goal to nil, and the *Morning Post* rather disdainfully concluded that: 'their ideas of modern tactics,

as is the case with most of the Irish teams that have paid us a visit, are quite rudimentary, and when, in imitation of their opponents, they did take to passing, it did them more harm than good.'

In Dublin in 1970 there were far more sophisticated skills on display. The occasion was the centenary of the Wanderers club and the Barbarians graced it by selecting an all-international line-up. In the backs, four stars of the Wales team of the era, J.P.R. Williams, Gerald Davies, Phil Bennett and Gareth Edwards, were joined by the England centre duo of John Spencer and David Duckham, plus Chris Wardlow on the wing. It was as strong a combination as any the Club had fielded in modern times apart from games against the major touring teams. The forwards were no slouches either, with two from each of the four home countries: Delme Thomas and Mervyn Davies of Wales; England's Keith Fairbrother and John Pullin; the Scots Peter Brown and Tom Elliot; and Ireland's Phil O'Callaghan and Mick Hipwell. The Club's selectors had done their hosts proud. The Lansdowne Road setting also proved equal to the occasion – 'The rich green turf would have graced a royal palace,' wrote Vivian Jenkins in the *Sunday Times* – and the Wanderers held their illustrious opponents until the final quarter. Under Spencer's captaincy the Baa-Baas took every opportunity to attack and by the end had scored seven scintillating tries. Williams and Edwards claimed two each, Duckham and Gerald Davies added brilliant efforts of their own, while the flanker Elliot ensured the forwards were also on the scoreboard. Williams converted three and added a penalty goal. For the Wanderers their captain and fly-half Kevin McGowan scored a try and prop John

The Club's first-ever game in Dublin was at Lansdowne Road in 1970 to celebrate the centenary of the Wanderers club. (© Barbarian Archive)

O'Gorman kicked two first-half penalty goals. The final score of 30–9 was a tribute to one of the Barbarians' vintage displays. An indelible impression had been left with the Dublin rugby community, but it would be another 21 years before the Club took their next team across to Ireland.

The two centenary games against the Constitution club in Cork and Old Wesley at Donnybrook in Dublin in September 1991 served to rekindle the notion of more visits to the Emerald Isle. In the next decade they travelled there more than at any other time in the Club's history. The decision to stage the end-of-tour match against the 1994 Springboks at Lansdowne Road was understandably described by the distinguished Irish journalist

Edmund Van Esbeck as an 'overdue compliment' and was to earn a special niche of its own in the story of the Club's epic series of matches against the major touring teams. Then, in 1996 and 2000, came the first matches against a full Ireland side, though, unlike similar fixtures against Wales at that time, they were not designated full internationals. That suited the Barbarians because both of them were notable for other factors. The match in May 2000 was to celebrate the 125th anniversary of the Irish Rugby Football Union (IRFU) but the forerunner in 1996 was, if anything, even more noteworthy. It was designated 'The Peace International' and its very staging reflected great credit on the IRFU and the Barbarian Football Club. For a quarter of a century Ireland had suffered what came to be known as 'the Troubles', essentially civil unrest based on republican and nationalist aspirations and their respective Catholic and Protestant allegiances. Northern Ireland and Ireland may be two distinct political states that also preserve separate sporting identities but one of the glorious exceptions to that rule is rugby union. In soccer there was Northern Ireland and Eire; in rugby there was simply Ireland. As the unrest showed few signs of sustainably abating in the mid-1990s – a politically negotiated ceasefire had broken down – the idea of staging a very special rugby match – more than a match, a statement of intent – was born. The project entailed the dovetailing of two charities, Cooperation Ireland and The Ireland Fund, to support a match between Ireland and the Barbarians. The two organisations had long since been widely recognised and praised for their work in the field of peace and reconciliation. The focus of both was to provide social, recreational and

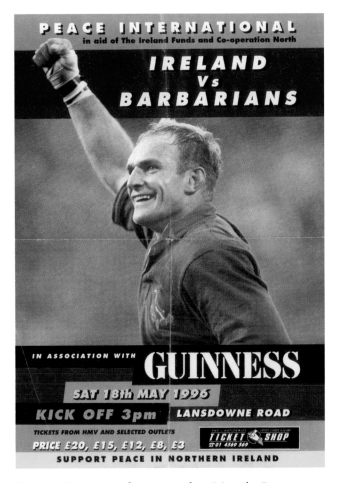

François Pienaar on the poster advertising the Peace International. (© Barbarian Archive)

educational support for children of all backgrounds and communities. To stage a major rugby match in support of their efforts was indeed a worthy aim. There were practical issues for the officials behind both teams to consider. The IRFU were proposing to approve, organise and stage the match within a timescale of barely five weeks. In that time it would need to be marketed and tickets sold, the infrastructure of stewarding and policing would need to be arranged, and there would need to be ongoing communication. They

decided it could be done. The Barbarians' main problem, once the principles were agreed, was ascertaining the availability of players – and they would need to be the top players for such a prestigious event. They, too, decided it could be done. Both parties had in-built advantages. In Ireland, rugby union enjoyed a unique position within the sporting culture: it encouraged participation irrespective of creed or political affiliation, and had maintained that approach throughout the difficult times of turbulence. The Barbarians had a similar apolitical reputation and, for this particular initiative, had the invaluable contribution of the former Springbok captain François Pienaar. The South African would be forever linked with the image of his country's World Cup triumph in 1995 when he had shared centre-stage at the final with the state president, Nelson Mandela.

There were other major personalities involved in the Peace International. The Ireland Fund had been created and chaired by Dr A.J.F. O'Reilly, the legendary Tony O'Reilly of Barbarians' and Lions' fame and now a successful businessman and newspaper magnate. The joint patrons of Cooperation Ireland were Her Majesty Queen Elizabeth and the president of Ireland, Mary Robinson. To turn the dream into reality, moreover, the Peace International had the advantage of the combined skills and commitment of two former Irish internationals, Hugo MacNeill and Trevor Ringland. MacNeill was a southern Catholic; Ringland a Protestant from the north. Working together they epitomised all that was best about rugby in Ireland. The omens were good but the result of their endeavour was far better than anyone might have dared hope for. Two days before the game Paul Hayward

flagged up in the *Daily Telegraph* what was in prospect:

> If you think rugby has been invaded by charlatans, head for Dublin this weekend and watch some of the world's best players lower their shoulders and give a mighty heave for the Irish peace movement in a historic match at Lansdowne Road. Then try saying the rugby boys have sold out. There will be no appearance money, no win bonuses and strictly no politics or sectarianism allowed.

On the day itself there was a poignant pre-match atmosphere. Immediately prior to the kick-off four youngsters between the ages of 11 and 15, all in their respective school uniforms, were quietly led onto the pitch. Two of them were from Northern Ireland, one from the south, one from Britain – all had parents, brothers or friends who had perished during the troubles. No anthems were played. Instead, a minute's silence followed their presentation to the players of both teams. The Barbarians number 8 and renowned competitor Dean Richards summed up the feelings of all of them: 'Rugby players are unemotional people, even at the best of times. But when those kids came on and we were introduced to them it brought home what it was all about. It was special, very special. Quite an emotional day. I'm very proud to have been part of it.'

Richards was only one of a complete team of world stars who had kept their promise to turn up. Even those who had initially accepted then reluctantly been forced to withdraw because of injuries travelled to Dublin. Pienaar was one of them, and Australia's David Campese and

England's Ben Clarke also came. There was still no shortage of stars fully involved in the action. Eric Rush had returned again from New Zealand. Philippe Sella, the world's most-capped player, was in the centre. England's record try-scorer Rory Underwood was on the wing. As well as Richards, the pack contained two Frenchmen, Laurent Cabannes and Olivier Brouzet, and the entire Leicester front row of Graham Rowntree, Richard Cockerill and Darren Garforth. In all, there were players from six countries, fifteen fully-fledged internationals, in the Barbarian squad, under the captaincy of the England centre Phil de Glanville. They were up against almost the same Ireland XV that had recently featured in the Six Nations matches and they were to prove far too strong for them. In perfect conditions, and in front of a 35,000 crowd, the Barbarians scored four converted tries in the first twenty minutes and never looked back, going on to win the match 70–38. Nine players shared the ten tries, all converted by the Bath full-back Jonathan Callard, with Ireland replying with six tries; but, as had always been intended, the result was incidental. The final words lay with Dean Richards, who said at the post-match press conference, 'No one was talking about money today, no one was talking about contracts. All of us, instead, talked about the occasion, about why we wanted to be here. Our game is changing, but one would hope that future players will never forget what good they can do by responding to a cause of this stature.'

The Peace International was another example of how the Barbarians were redefining part of their role in the new world of professional rugby. Good causes and special appeals would be regularly supported as they travelled to many far-flung outposts in the 1990s and into the new millennium.

Their next match in Ireland four years later reflected another development that quickly established itself in the Club's itinerary. The concept of an early summer tour around the British Isles saw the light of day in May 2000, with matches at Lansdowne Road, Murrayfield and Twickenham. Over the next five seasons fixtures against Scotland and England would become the norm, with Wales added to the brew in 2001 at the expense of Ireland. The absence of a match in Dublin from the rotation was something the Club regretted, but it was the consequence mainly of the ever-present imminence of a summer tour overseas. Of course, the other home countries also had such trips pending in early June of every year but Ireland, at least, was influenced by what had happened in the game of 28 May 2000. What had doubled up as a celebration of 125 years of rugby in Ireland and the first leg of the new Club tour was blighted for the hosts by a series of unfortunate injuries to key players. That was a great pity because both Ireland and the Barbarians had picked particularly strong sides. The game took place on the same weekend as the Heineken Cup final at Twickenham, in which Munster were involved, and only six days before a full-scale international between Argentina and Ireland in Buenos Aires. Even so, the only players missing from the home team were the Munster men, while the Club had assembled a notably celebrated squad for their three-match tour. In an all-international starting line-up at Lansdowne Road they had Jonah Lomu, arguably the biggest name in the world game at that time, on the wing, as well as the All Black Walter Little and the Springbok Pieter Muller together at centre; Argentina's

Ireland's top players have been regularly selected in the big games for the Club. Here, Malcolm O'Kelly, Andy Ward, Peter Clohessy and Brian O'Driscoll relax after the game against South Africa in 2000.
(© Getty Images)

Agustin Pichot partnering another Springbok, Hennie le Roux, at half-back; and a pack with a sprinkling of Wallabies, All Blacks and Springboks.

Though the Barbarians scored first through a second-minute try by hooker James Dalton and added another soon afterwards by Kenny Logan, by half-time Ireland had established a 20–10 lead. Guy Easterby, Justin Bishop and Shane Horgan shared three tries and skipper David Humphreys converted one and kicked a penalty goal. This was all the more commendable as two key players, full-back Girvan Dempsey and lock Jeremy Davidson, were both stretchered off injured in that time while the hottest Irish property of all, Brian O'Driscoll, tore a hamstring. After the interval Horgan left the field with a knee injury and replacement full-back Geordan Murphy was another casualty, with an ankle injury. The

visitors reduced the deficit shortly after the restart with a Pichot try converted by Logan but the hosts were proving remarkably resilient. Another try by Kevin Maggs, converted by Humphreys, restored their ten-point lead before two tries in the final quarter put the Club ahead. Both were scored by Springbok full-back Stefan Terblanche, the first converted by le Roux and the second by replacement Neil Jenkins – a further indication of the strength of the Baa-Baas' squad. Humphreys almost won the game for his side, kicking a goal to tie the visitors back to 31–30 only to miss another in injury time. The Barbarians were more than happy to play again in Dublin and to record a win. Sadly, Ireland had less to celebrate. Several players, including O'Driscoll, were forced to withdraw from their summer tour and this led to a reluctance to agree future fixtures at that stage of the season. It was no reflection on the Barbarians per se because, after all, the European match at Twickenham also accounted for another couple of Irish injuries. Ironically, several Irish players in the years that followed, O'Driscoll and his fellow casualty in 2000, Shane Horgan, among them, continued to turn out for the Barbarians against Scotland, England and Wales. But, after 2000, the Irish leg of the itinerary was put on hold. Fortunately, the trips to Scotland and elsewhere continued.

In many respects the fact that the Barbarians took so long to agree fixtures in Scotland is even more perplexing than the absence of Irish visits. No one could accuse Herbert Waddell and his fellow Scottish Barbarians on successive committees of giving their countrymen preferential treatment. When the long overdue journeys north of the Border finally saw the light of day, they proved to be

No trip to Scotland would be complete without an afternoon on a golf course, and at Gleneagles in 2000 Jason Leonard is on hand to advise Lawrence Dallaglio on the finer points of putting. (© Barbarian Archive)

different scale altogether. The 'Scottish XV' was in fact the full Scotland side that had won the Calcutta Cup game against England six weeks earlier. Though this was another example of a match understandably not deemed to be an official international, one side effect was to mitigate against the home side. In 1970 substitutes (as they were then called, rather than replacements) were only allowed in internationals and no dispensation was made for this game. As luck would have it, the Scottish XV were reduced to fourteen men from the fourth minute after wing Mike Smith departed the field with a facial injury. Late in the game, scrum-half Duncan Paterson suffered the same fate and the team played the final fifteen minutes with a two-man disadvantage. This proved an insurmountable handicap against another very strong Barbarians formation. David Duckham and John Spencer were again in the centre, and Phil Bennett and Gareth Edwards at half-back. Completing a formidable back division were J.P.R. Williams and the wings Alan Duggan of Ireland and England's Keith Fielding. The pack was equally strong, with eight capped players including John Pullin at hooker and three other future Lions – Ireland's Mick Hipwell and Fergus Slattery, and, from Wales, Mervyn Davies – forming a great back row.

Wind and rain failed to disrupt another flowing game in which the Scottish side played a full part. At first the play was scrappy with the only scores in the opening half-hour being two penalty goals for the home side by number 8 Peter Brown. With him in the pack was his brother, Gordon, and Norman Suddon, Frank Laidlaw and Sandy Carmichael in the front row, the 6 ft 10 in. Peter Stagg at lock, and flankers Tom Elliot and Rodger Arneil.

well worth the wait. With over 200 Scots having played for the Club, there was sure to be a warm reception. The first match was against a Scottish XV at Murrayfield on 9 May 1970 and the proceeds were in aid of the Commonwealth Games that were being held in Edinburgh later that summer. Two earlier visits had been made to Melrose in 1932 and 1965, but both of these were to participate in seven-a-side tournaments. The Murrayfield match was on a

A scrappy game in slippery conditions would suit their marauding instincts but the nature of the play changed after the Barbarians' first try. Inevitably, it was created by their brilliant backs, with Williams joining in an attack for Fielding to take full advantage of the overlap to race in for the touchdown. The full-back converted and in first-half injury time the Baa-Baas took the lead. As the tempo of the match increased, more and more attacks were mounted and it was Duckham who finally side-stepped over in classic fashion for an 8–6 interval lead. He was to score again early in the second half, bamboozling half-a-dozen would-be tacklers, to cap an impressive individual performance. In *The Scotsman* Norman Mair wrote, 'The English believe Duckham to be the best centre in the world. The French might have something to say about that but, my word, he was wickedly quick and elusive on Saturday.' Barbarian matches were to provide the perfect stage for the Coventry centre to display his many skills for several seasons to come. Duckham's second try was quickly followed by another couple from Spencer and the Irish lock Mick Molloy. Williams converted all three and within a space of seven minutes the Baa-Baas had stretched their lead to 23–6. Edwards then fully exploited the gaps on the fringes of a scrum for a typically opportunist try but the biggest cheer of the afternoon came when Gordon Brown thundered through the defence from a cross-kick and Elliot was on hand to touch down. Peter Brown converted to reduce the arrears to 11–28 but the Baa-Baas backs had one more trick up their sleeves. Again it was Duckham who did the damage, linking with Fielding before the Welsh prop Barry Llewelyn raced under the posts for Williams to convert. At the very end Peter

Brown kicked two more penalty goals but the Barbarians were comfortable winners by 33 to 17.

Murrayfield and the Scottish Rugby Union welcomed the Barbarians again in March 1983, this time for a special match to celebrate the official opening of the East Stand at the stadium. It was the day that the Club unveiled the exquisite skills of the Springbok centre Danie Gerber to northern-hemisphere eyes. He stole the show, scoring two of his side's five tries in a 26–13 victory over another full-strength Scotland team. More than that, he gave an impressive all-round display – one critic said that 'he looked strong enough to knock over the posts' – and created several scoring opportunities for his teammates. With him at centre was his country's first non-white Springbok, Errol Tobias, with a third South African, Hennie Bekker, in the pack. Fergus Slattery captained a side of five nationalities but the Scots, buoyant after a rare Calcutta Cup victory at Twickenham, were understandably the tighter unit in the opening stages. All they had to show for their territorial dominance, however, was a penalty goal by Peter Dods. After Bekker charged over from a tapped penalty for the opening try, the Barbarians were eventually firing on all fronts. Jean-Baptiste Lafond, at that stage yet to be capped by France, gathered a loose ball in his own 22 and shook off several tacklers en route to a fine try. The 8–3 lead was reduced to a single point after the interval, after John Rutherford had touched down for the Scots, but on the restart the Barbarians took control. England wing John Carleton, after a defensive muddle, and Gerber, after a break by Terry Holmes, scored tries that were both converted by Gareth Davies. Rutherford scored his second try and

Dods' conversion gave the home side some hope at 13–20, but Gerber had the last word, dummying through the defence for a try converted by Davies.

There was more success for the Barbarians when they returned to Scotland less than a fortnight later for two seven-a-side tournaments. After disappointingly losing to Royal High School in the first round of the Melrose Centenary Sevens on 9 April, they quickly made amends the following day when they beat the Cooptimists 32–10 in the final of the Edinburgh Charity Sevens at Murrayfield. Their next visit to the home of Scottish rugby was during the extended centenary celebrations of 1991, and then in 1996 another special match was arranged. The occasion and the reason for it that day was fit to rank alongside the Peace International in Dublin three months earlier. The noble cause in Edinburgh on 17 August 1996 was the Dunblane Fund in aid of the victims of the horrific shooting at the primary school in the Scottish town in March of that year. Sixteen pupils had been killed and many more of the school and the community mentally scarred. The aim of the Dunblane Fund was to help those bereaved and injured in the tragedy to create a lasting memorial and to help the wider community. A match that attracted a crowd well in excess of 30,000 would obviously generate much-needed income for the cause and, as the Scottish Rugby Union's chief executive Bill Hogg noted, it was also arranged as a mark of respect for everyone in Dunblane. The Barbarian committee had immediately accepted the invitation to provide the opposition to the Scotland team and, even in high summer, had again secured the services of several major players under the captaincy of

Gavin Hastings. The Leicester front row of Rowntree, Cockerill and Garforth again played, as they had in Dublin, while the gifted Argentinian scrum-half Agustin Pichot, then five days short of his twenty-second birthday, was making his second appearance for the Club. He had played against Cardiff the previous Easter and a mutual respect and admiration soon evolved between him and the Club. On his return to South America after the Scotland match, he wasted no time in writing to Micky Steele-Bodger: 'I am very proud of being part of the Barbarians family and more of being your friend.'

The Club itself had much to be proud of after the Dunblane International, as it was officially known. Praising its participation, David Hands wrote in *The Times*:

> Rugby union needs to re-establish its values . . . and the Barbarians were [at Murrayfield] to jog the memory. One hopes that they always will be. The response by players from eight countries to appear in the famous Barbarian shirt without recompense was heartening, their attitude refreshing, their victory deserved.

The victory, almost incidental in the circumstances, was by 48–45, thanks to a late try by the Ireland lock-forward Paddy Johns. Earlier, Gavin Hastings' two tries for the Barbarians had been matched by two by his brother Scott for the opposition. A happy note on an afternoon tinged with great sadness.

With the development of the summer tour in May 2000 the Barbarians returned to Scotland on an annual basis. They were certainly making up for lost time and their stock north of the border remains high to this day. There have also been four visits to play club sides. The first, in October 1976, was to celebrate the centenary of the Melrose club. The match was played on a Monday evening and the big crowd witnessed a typically flamboyant Barbarians performance. With Phil Bennett as captain it was never likely to be anything else, but what was also a crowd-pleaser was the inclusion in the team of eight Scottish internationals, including Andy Irvine, Ian McGeechan and Sandy Carmichael. Rather ignoring the basics up front, the Baa-Baas tried to run the ball from everywhere from the outset. As is often the case, the lack of a forward platform made such a tactic unsuccessful and, uncharacteristically, Bennett opted for a couple of penalty goals and Irvine chipped in with an outrageous drop goal. With the scoreboard at last ticking over, the tries soon followed. Mike Biggar, another Scottish Barbarian, scored the first and then everyone felt better with a textbook length-of-the-field try. Irvine started the attack near his own line and Rosslyn Park wing Dave McKay finished it off at the other end. Right on the half-time whistle Melrose hit back with a try by wing Mike Bleasdale. In the second half it was always likely that the visitors' pace would prove decisive but at least the hosts had the satisfaction of two more tries from Bleasdale and Finlay Calder, playing at prop. For the Barbarians, J.J. Williams scored two tries, and Alan Tomes, Garry Adey and Andy Irvine added others for a 47–17 win.

In 1988 the Barbarians went to western Scotland for the first time to play Glasgow Academicals in the Herbert Waddell Memorial Match. All surviving Scottish Barbarians were invited to attend the match and the dinner that followed. At the New Anniesland ground the scenario was very similar to that at Melrose 12 years before. The team included three leading Scots – Matt Duncan, Iain Paxton and Finlay Calder, now in his more familiar position of flanker – plus a pair of brilliant Welsh half-backs in Jonathan Davies and Robert Jones, England's captain Will Carling and the Ireland lock and future Club committeeman Donal Lenihan, who led the side. What was different was that the Accies had strengthened their side with three guest players, the Edinburgh full-back Chris Spence and two capped Scots, Keith Robertson and Derek White. Belying his reported pre-match quip at the joint teams photograph, when he turned to a fellow Scot in the famous hoops of the Barbarians and whispered, 'You wouldn't like to swap jerseys, would you?', White made an outstanding contribution to the Accies' efforts. Far from being swept away by the visiting team that had fly-half Davies putting on a virtuoso display, the Accies held their own for long periods and were still in touch at 22–28 midway through the second half. Their five tries in a thirteen-try match were scored by Ian Jarvie (two), Ray Pirrie, Andrew Garry and Walter Malcolm, a gallant effort worthy of Herbert Waddell himself. The headline grabber, though, was Paxton, who, from the number 8 position, helped himself to four tries despite suffering from tennis elbow. The other Baa-Baas tries were shared by Davies, Calder, Duncan and Welsh prop David Young, four of them in the final quarter, as they pulled away for another comfortable victory by 48 to 28. The official dinner, at which a vote of thanks was proposed by Alan Waddell, son of Herbert, was a fitting end to an important day for both the Glasgow Academicals and the Barbarians. As Bill McMurtrie observed in the *Glasgow Herald*, it

The Glasgow Academicals and Barbarians teams at the Herbert Waddell Memorial Match in 1988.
(© Barbarian Archive)

was one that the former president of both clubs would have enjoyed.

The Barbarians recognised another worthy cause in Scotland in September 1995 when they played the Stirling County club in support of the Princess Royal Trust for Carers. There were several other beneficiaries, with the 14 tries scored at £300 each under the Scottish Amicable sponsorship agreement raising a healthy £4,200 for youth rugby. With the Princess Royal also in attendance at Forthbank Stadium it was truly a Royal occasion for the 5,000 crowd. The Barbarians, captained again by Gavin Hastings, won the match 57–34 but Stirling County had international stars of their own in Kenny Logan and Ian Jardine. Logan was one of their try-scorers despite the handicap of a suspected broken finger, with other tries going to Matt McGrandles, Gus Turner, Mark McKenzie and Murray Fraser. Hastings converted five of his side's nine tries, scored by Rob Subbiani (two), Niall Woods, Cammy Little, Simon Shaw, Iain Morrison,

Canadian flanker Al Charron and Scottish half-backs Gregor Townsend and Bryan Redpath, and afterwards he was as positive as ever about the role of the Club in the new professional age: 'The Barbarians, as a concept, will survive if the players want it to. At the end of the day it is up to them. Personally, I think that the Barbarians are a superb concept and that's why I play for them whenever I'm asked.'

The Princess Royal Trust for Carers was again a beneficiary in April 2001 when the Barbarians' next visit was to honour 100 years of rugby in the south of Scotland. As in 1976 the Greenyards in Melrose was the venue, but the opposition this time was not the local club but a combined selection: the Border League, under the coaching eye of the redoubtable Jim Telfer. For the first time the Barbarians included a Swiss international, Alain Studer from the Oyonnax club, and awarded the captaincy to the Edinburgh Reivers fly-half Graham Shiel. Also included in the team and replacements were six Fijians who had played

The captain, Shaun Longstaff, holds the Cup with the Barbarian squad after defeating the Fijian team Nawaka in the final of the Melrose Sevens in 2001.
(© Barbarian Archive)

draw (in 1991) against Scotland at Murrayfield and victories over Melrose, Glasgow Academicals and Stirling County between 1976 and 1995, they were not expected to succumb to the Border League. This seemed even more improbable after the Club scored the first two tries to establish a 12–nil lead in as many minutes. Wales full-back Matt Cardey claimed the first and Manchester wing Phil Graham the second, but by half-time they trailed 12–26. It was a complete turnaround and though prop Jock Bryce and Studer scored two more in the second half it was not enough and the Border League ran out winners by 31–24. Local commentators regarded this result as further evidence of the need for a third professional team in Scotland, following the examples set in Glasgow and Edinburgh.

The Barbarians had no such agenda. For them the Club's existence and priorities remained as before: to accept as many invitations to play rugby matches as was practically possible and to continue to spread its ethos as it had always done. To those ends the incorporation of Ireland and Scotland into the Club's travels after 1957 had been another success story.

for their own club, Nawaka, against the Barbarians in the final of the Melrose Sevens 48 hours earlier. The Baa-Baas had won that tie 38–19 to complete a good day as sevens champions. Against the Border League they were less successful, losing in fact for the first time ever in Scotland. After three wins and a

SPREADING THEIR WINGS

'We have received a great welcome wherever we have been and that is the essence of all rugby tours.'
— H.L. Glyn Hughes, 1969

With its reputation in the British Isles long since established it was inevitable that, sooner or later, the Barbarian Football Club would give serious consideration to playing matches overseas. Indeed, in the first 65 years or so of its existence the Club had only travelled to France outside the British mainland, to Paris in 1899 and 1908 for fixtures against Stade Français and Racing Club de France, and to Le Havre in 1900. By the late 1950s the time was ripe for the Barbarians to spread their wings. The only major tours overseas from the British Isles had been by the Lions, and they only numbered two in the first decade after the Second World War; and occasionally by teams drawn from Oxford and Cambridge Universities. Ireland had gone to Argentina in

1952 but tours to the southern hemisphere by the individual home countries did not become established until well into the 1960s. From time to time tentative invitations had been received suggesting first-ever visits to far-flung reaches of the rugby empire and, in the late spring of 1957, a pioneering tour finally took place. It was to Canada, at that time still a developing rugby community, and when Hughie Glyn Hughes took the team there as Club president and tour manager, he explained, 'It could have easily either been Australia, South Africa or New Zealand for our tour but Canada just asked us first. The other countries just talked about it. We were overwhelmed by the invitation and glad to accept it.'

A tour to South Africa would follow within

The team photograph for the tour to Canada in 1957 was taken before departure from home. It includes Peter Robbins, who was forced to withdraw injured and was replaced by Tom Reid. Back row: C.R. Jacobs, D.G.S. Baker, P.H. Thompson, A. Robson, T.J. Davies, A.A. Mulligan; second row: G.M. Griffiths, P.G.D. Robbins, E.J.S. Michie, R.W.D. Marques, R.H. Williams, A.J.F. O'Reilly, G.W. Hastings, G.T. Wells; front row: R. Roe, E. Evans, J.E. Woodward, H.L. Glyn Hughes (president), C.I. Morgan, J.T. Greenwood, A.F. Dorward.
(© Barbarian Archive)

a year but in April 1957 the Canadian venture was very much the focus of attention. It was planned with typical thoroughness throughout the 1956–57 British season, with prospective players regularly monitored and several seen at closer quarters in the traditional Club fixtures. In his official report on the tour Glyn Hughes outlined the principles behind team selection: 'Opportunity was taken of honouring players who had given good service to the game, their country, county and the Barbarians, and also those who, for one reason or another, had been unable to participate in any British Isles tour.' These were laudable aims and they were reflected in the final composition of the party. As it happened, nine of the team had toured South Africa with the Lions two years earlier, among them two of the most charismatic players of their generation, Cliff Morgan and Tony O'Reilly, but they and most of their teammates were also established Barbarians and their presence was important because another aim was to popularise rugby union in Canada. Though six matches were to be played in eighteen days, only twenty players were taken, so another factor in selection became the ability to play in more than one position. On this and succeeding overseas tours, and, indeed, when the Barbarians played the All Blacks, Springboks and Wallabies at Cardiff or Twickenham, the president and committee always emphasised to the players that they were representing a club side and were not the Lions under another name. It was an ethos that everyone happily accepted, though, almost inevitably from time to time, the media in particular would attempt to draw comparisons both home and abroad between 'Barbarians' and 'Lions'. Refreshingly, wherever the Barbarians went in Canada, they were invariably described by the local press as 'the greatest rugger club in the world'.

The tour received the full support of the Four Home Unions Tours Committee and the provinces of Ontario, British Columbia and Quebec, who between them shared all travel costs. In addition the hosts provided accommodation and hospitality and everything was considered to be of a high standard. Under the regulations of the time, each player was given out-of-pocket remuneration of £3 10s. 0d. (£3.50) per week but, with the benefit of hindsight, even Brigadier Glyn Hughes, a jealous protector of the amateur ethos, admitted that the sum 'owing to the cost of living in Canada and America cannot possibly compare with the same amount in this country'. Not that the players complained. In a marvellous article in the *Toronto Daily Star*, headlined 'Don't Touch Lucre, Mates, It Spoils the Blinking Game', local reporter Jim Hunt drew favourable comparisons with the insidious influence of professional sport in Canada. After interviewing the Barbarians' England international lock, David Marques, he reported:

> Marquis [*sic*] got down to brass tacks to explain why he doesn't feel the

Canadian game can hold a candle to rugger . . . It's not the equipment our gladiators wear that bothers the Barbarians. It's not the substitutions or the times out we permit that worry them, although they think the game could do without both. It's the money that is the root of all evil. The Barbarians can't understand how Jackie Parker [a grid-iron footballer] can pocket a $20,000 pay cheque and still go all-out on the grid-iron.

The reporter then touched upon what the Barbarians stood for:

> Actually they may have something. We've travelled, talked and dealt with a lot of athletic teams but we've yet to see a happier group than the Barbarians. Unlike our teams they don't spend hours practising. They get together after dinner on Friday, run a little on Saturday, and then have a whale of a party afterwards. That's the reward of an amateur sport.

In more ways than one the Barbarians were to be great ambassadors for the rugby union game during their three weeks in Canada.

All the Canada-bound players had also been on the Easter tour of South Wales that immediately preceded the transatlantic flight. For the time it was an impressively ambitious itinerary. Having played Newport on Tuesday 23 April, the party travelled by train to Paddington station in London the following morning, then transferred to Heathrow airport in time for a cocktail party (they were, after all, the Barbarians), before boarding an overnight

The team arrive at Toronto in style with Arthur Dorward (third from left) wearing a kilt.
(© Adam Robson Collection)

flight via Glasgow and Goose Bay in Greenland to Montreal and then Toronto. Forty-eight hours later they would be playing their first game against the Ontario All-Stars.

No tour captain had been appointed, the traditional procedure being to select a different captain for each match. He, in turn, would assist the manager in team selection for the relevant game. For the tour opener at the East York Stadium in Toronto the honour went to the Sale hooker Eric Evans, who had led England throughout the recently completed International Championship matches. That side had won the Grand Slam – a good omen. The Barbarians team that took the field on 27 April was, in its way, equally strong. At full-back was the Llanelli and Wales star Terry Davies. The wings were Peter Thompson and Tony O'Reilly, both regular try-scorers for the Barbarians at home, with the Cardiff centres

Gareth Griffiths and Gordon Wells inside them. Cliff Morgan partnered Ireland's Andy Mulligan at half-back, completing a back division fit to take on any opposition. George Hastings and Ron Jacobs joined Evans in an all-England front row, Rhys Williams packed down with Marques behind them, and the back row had Tom Reid at number 8 with Adam Robson and Jim Greenwood in the wing-forward positions. The latter three were to play as a unit in all six games on tour. It was no surprise that this combination proved far too strong for the local opposition, the Ontario All-Stars. A sell-out crowd of 5,500 watched the game start in brilliant afternoon sunshine before a torrential downpour early in the second half made conditions treacherous. Among them was the celebrated scrum-half of the 1930s and 1940s, Haydn Tanner. The local press sought his opinion and he said:

> The Barbarians were very unorthodox in their movements and switched the direction of the attack in bewildering fashion. One lesson should have been learned by this display – a missed tackle against such good handlers of the ball means only one thing. Time and time again Ontario midfield players missed their opposite number and the result was a try.

That was certainly the case. The visitors led 23–nil at half-time and went on to win the match 47–3. Three backs shared the twelve tries – O'Reilly (five), Thompson (four) and Wells (three); Hastings, the goal-kicking prop, converted three and Terry Davies one, plus a penalty goal. Ian Nichol, a reserve wing for Scotland in 1953, scored a try for the All-Stars, but it was the Barbarians who won all the praise. Having got to grips with the notion of amateurism, the *Star*'s reporter, Jim Hunt, went to the game and was suitably impressed, by Cliff Morgan in particular: 'He is a dandy . . . his sleight of hand and dipsy-doodle running is the key to the success of the Barbarians, drawing in the defence and setting the backs for their touchdown – oops, sorry, it's a try in this game.'

The Ontario team included a character of its own in the prop Rex Richards, who had won a cap for Wales against France in 1956. Known as Tarzan because of his penchant for wearing a loincloth when he was a performer with an aqua-diving show, he later left Canada, went to Hollywood and acted in *The Wild Women of Wonga*, voted one of the worst films ever made. Richards and his fellow All-Stars found themselves in the deep end again three days later when they played the second match against the tourists.

This time the game was played under floodlights at the same East York Stadium, but the hosts fared no better in front of another capacity crowd. The five Barbarians who had watched the first game played a full part. True to the pre-tour expectations about the need for utility, the England fly-half Doug Baker played at full-back. In more familiar positions were Ted Woodward on the wing, Arthur Dorward at scrum-half, Robin Roe at hooker and captain, and Ernie Michie in the second row. The pattern of the game was very much as before, the Baa-Baas moving the ball at every opportunity and the home defence eventually missing tackles for nine tries to be scored in a 52–nil victory. Any doubts about whether the tourists were taking the match seriously can be dispelled by the fact that George Hastings

Tony O'Reilly and Eric Evans (seated) at the heart of the action in Canada.
(© Adam Robson Collection)

kicked no fewer than five penalty goals. He also converted five of the tries, including one by himself, for a personal haul of twenty-eight points, surely a record for a prop forward. The other try-scorers were Peter Thompson and Gordon Wells with two each, and four of the new boys, Woodward, Baker, Dorward and Roe.

The first leg of the tour was now completed and the following day, 1 May, the team flew west via Winnipeg, Saskatoon and Edmonton to Vancouver, where two of the three matches against British Columbia would be played. These were expected to be the toughest games of the tour but all the party were still committed to a full range of social activities and official engagements, never losing sight of the need to promote the game and its virtues everywhere they went. Over the course of the two-and-a-half weeks in Canada the players visited a dozen schools, the parliament buildings in Toronto, the mayors and aldermen of Vancouver and Montreal, several official banquets and civic receptions, industrial plants and aircraft factories. These events were something from which the hosts and the guests benefited equally. A typical example is that of the Welsh centre Gareth Griffiths, who had already established a fine reputation when flown out to join the British Isles tour to South Africa two years earlier. At the time, he was forging a career for himself as a teacher, but in later years he went in another direction. He is particularly complimentary about his experiences as a Barbarian in Canada: 'I had much to thank the Barbarians for, off the field as on it. We all had to take turns as duty officer for a day and when it was my turn we had to meet the Canadian prime minister and we also visited an aircraft factory. It was there that I met the personnel manager who spoke about his job and I became very interested. It set me off on a new career path in later years. When I returned to Wales, I enrolled for a management course at Cardiff Technical College. What I also soon realised was that by simply being in the company of someone like Hughie Glyn Hughes for any length of time, as on such a tour, I had already received valuable management training.'

For Griffiths and all the team Brigadier H.L. Glyn Hughes was not so much a former army officer as a fatherly figure who guided them in the right direction. He also had a light touch that was particularly appreciated by the new contacts he made on the trip, whether they were government officials, rugby alickadoos or pressmen. The rugby was serious but there was always time to share a joke or indulge in a bit of badinage. In Toronto there had been one such moment when he was asked about the merits of American footballers wearing radios in their helmets so as to communicate with their coaches. Hughie was aghast: 'I'd jam the signals,' he chortled. 'But doesn't the idea of a radio in a helmet take away the individual's initiative in a game? He doesn't think for himself. He does what he's told.' Quite.

He soon built up a similar rapport with the media in Vancouver. At the first press conference there he was asked whether it was true that no one might play for the Barbarians who had been penalised on the field. 'That is simply not true,' he said. 'You can be penalised unjustly, you know.'

The matches against British Columbia were more serious affairs, beginning with the first game on 4 May. It was staged at the Empire Stadium in Vancouver where, three years earlier, England's Roger Bannister had defeated his great Australian rival John Landy in the 'Mile of the Century' at the Empire Games. That had been a close race and the Baa-Baas were to encounter equally strong resistance from the rugby men of the province. The captaincy this time was handed to Jim Greenwood, and Doug Baker continued at full-back in place of Terry Davies, still nursing a shoulder injury sustained in the first game in Toronto. Otherwise, it was the same team that had played that first afternoon against the Ontario All-Stars. The leading figure in the British Columbia side was Max Howell, a centre who had toured Europe with the 1947–48 Wallabies. Other, less-well-known teammates were to prove equally formidable opponents. At half-time the Baa-Baas led narrowly at 6–3. Tony O'Reilly had scored the only try of the half and George Hastings had kicked a 40-yard penalty goal; in reply, outstanding full-back Neil Henderson had also kicked a penalty. The Barbarians' attempts at open play were getting nowhere, partly because of a well-organised Canadian defence but also because of the narrowness of the pitch. There was a feeling that the dimensions had been unnecessarily limited, particularly in a large athletics stadium, and that this was a ploy to hamper the Barbarians' backs. A more pressing concern emerged soon after half-time when Ron Jacobs was accidentally injured in a collision. After several minutes' delay he was stretchered off to Vancouver General Hospital, where he was to remain for several weeks. He had dislocated a hip and this only served to make the rest of the team feel at their lowest point of the tour, even after winning the match. It had not been easy. Another Henderson penalty goal had levelled the scores and, with 14 men, the Barbarians were stretched to the limit. But fitness and pace told in the final 15 minutes. Marques, Griffiths and Morgan scored tries and Baker converted twice for a 19–6 victory. Once they had shaken off their concerns for Ron Jacobs, everyone realised it had been a good win in difficult circumstances. In *The Province*, local reporter Bill Dunford wrote: 'The game accomplished what it set out to do – sell rugby. New fans enthused over the adroit handling, fakes [dummies] and reverses of the Barbarians who, incidentally, never once fumbled a loose ball. They gathered in bounding balls like infielders.' The tourists still had two more fixtures against British Columbia selections in the next week, and they might well have been wondering what else was in store for them.

They needn't have worried. Despite the inclusion of the former Scotland and British Isles prop Graham Budge in their pack, the next British Columbia combination was significantly weaker. Twelve changes had been made, while the Barbarians, with only two props in the original squad, were forced after Ron Jacobs' injury to move Robin Roe from hooker to the side of the front row. He was to continue there for the rest of the tour. Elsewhere in the side Davies returned at full-back, O'Reilly, the day after his 21st birthday, moved into the centre alongside Griffiths, Dorward played at scrum-half, and Michie replaced Marques at lock. Ted Woodward captained the side from left-wing. The match was played at Macdonald Park in Victoria, a pitch that, for the first time on the tour, did not have a running track around it. The Baa-Baas enjoyed the compactness of the arena, with 3,200 spectators packed in and on top of the touch-lines. Once again the backs scored the majority of the eleven tries, O'Reilly leading the way with four, followed by Griffiths with three and one each for Woodward, Thompson, Michie and Robson. Terry Davies converted four and kicked two penalty goals, while Hastings converted two on the way to a final score of 51–8. The home side did well to hold the stars to 3–all after a quarter of an hour thanks to a penalty goal by hooker Stu Smith. They were behind 3–17 at the interval and had the satisfaction of a try by wing John Newton, converted by Smith for an eight-points total that was the highest scored against the visitors in all six matches.

As expected, the last game on the west coast was another tough proposition. It was again played at the Empire Stadium, this time in the afternoon but, to the Barbarians' consternation, the pitch was even narrower than before. The local side contained 13 of the team that had done so well in the earlier match, while Cliff

No tour was complete without a team sing-song and in Canada Cliff Morgan was always ready to tinkle the ivories. (© Adam Robson Collection)

Vancouver Sun wrote, 'The wizards of British rugby, the fabulous and fantastic Barbarians, make their farewell appearance here Saturday afternoon.'

Another good crowd came to watch the game and again the home side, thanks to a penalty goal by Neil Henderson, were holding their own at half-time. In fact, they led for most of the first period until O'Reilly crossed for his eleventh try of the tour. British Columbia were continuing with the tactic of keeping an extra player out of the forwards and in the backs that had been relatively successful a week earlier. The pattern of the game, however, repeated itself, with the Barbarians finally breaking through in the closing stages. Cliff Morgan scored two tries, Gordon Wells one, and Terry Davies kicked a penalty goal and a conversion for a final score of 17–3. The only disappointments were two more injuries to Wells, with a broken toe, and Dorward, with a bruised foot. More juggling of positions would be needed for the sixth and final match against Quebec in Montreal.

Adam Robson was appointed captain – 'A very great honour, indeed, one which I never thought I'd ever attain,' he later wrote to Jock Wemyss – and Arthur Dorward (long since called 'Art' in the local press) was converted into a wing. He wasn't to regret it. So the last XV of a memorable tour read: Davies; Dorward, Griffiths, O'Reilly, Thompson; Morgan, Mulligan; Hastings, Evans, Roe, Michie, Williams, Greenwood, Reid, Robson (captain). Among the crowd, this time numbering around 3,000, at a rain-soaked Westmount Athletic Grounds were two former Barbarians domiciled in Canada, Leslie Haslett, an international lock from the Blackheath club in the 1920s, and Tiny Bethell, another Blackheath man of more recent vintage: 1947.

Morgan took over the captaincy of the tourists. With Marques, Woodward and Baker joining Jacobs on the injured list there were only sixteen players left to choose from for this match and the final game three days later against Quebec. Andy Mulligan was the odd man out, with O'Reilly returning to the wing and Wells coming in at centre.

On their return to Vancouver from Victoria the squad had gone to watch a baseball game between San Francisco Seals and Vancouver Mounties and, according to local reports, had 'walked away scratching their heads and wondering what it was all about'. However baffled they may have been by some of their new experiences, the Barbarians continued to entertain their hosts. In its preview for the second game at the Empire Stadium the

This largely new audience again drew favourable comparisons with their more familiar American football. Not for the first time over the course of the three weeks in Canada, a local newspaper attempted to explain some of the intricacies of rugby union. In this case the scrum came under scrutiny. The *Montreal Gazette* explained:

> The scrum represented a tug-of-war in reverse. Players from both sides faced each other in a circle, and, bracing shoulders together, each team attempted to push the other one backwards. In the meantime another player stood to one side and at an opportune moment tossed the ball into the midst of their feet.

Not, perhaps, an analysis worthy of a coaching manual but undeniably explanatory for the lay person.

The poor conditions proved no handicap for the final flourish of the tour. Dorward scored a try within five minutes of the start. He was to take to his new position literally like a duck to water – Robson likened the conditions to Mansfield Park, Hawick, in a Scottish mid-winter. He went on to complete a hat-trick with two second-half touchdowns. By then the Barbarians were out of sight. Thompson and O'Reilly both scored twice in the first period, with another try coming from Griffiths. Davies kicked two conversions. At that point it was 22–3, with Quebec's sole points coming from yet another penalty goal by a front-row forward, Cyril Fagan. As well as Dorward's two second-half tries, Thompson also completed his hat-trick, Terry Davies and Robson both touched down, and Davies and Hastings kicked a conversion each. The final score was 41–3.

The Barbarians had completed their first trip overseas unbeaten in six matches. Equally importantly, they had been winners off the field, too. Wherever they went, the hospitality was lavish, the public reaction supportive, and the willingness to learn more about the game and the Barbarians encouraging. Hughie Glyn Hughes reported back to his committee that, as a direct result of the tour, three schools in Toronto had declared their intention to take up rugby union in the following autumn, while, in Montreal, one new club had already been formed, several new players, Canadian by birth, had joined other clubs and another two schools were showing an interest in taking up the game. Ever the pragmatist (and traditionalist), Hughie did have one caution: 'Certainly have pre-match entertainment, but allow nothing at half-time which prolongs the interval. Teams should not be permitted to leave the ground. There should be no flirting with any form of substitution.'

The president's overwhelming conclusion, though, was positive. His official report stated:

> As far as can be judged from our short stay and also the many letters since received by members of the team from officials and friends, the tour was of value and proved a success in stimulating enthusiasm for the game and in its missionary effort to widen recruitment to it.

Neatly understated, perhaps. Within a year the Barbarians would travel overseas again, but this time to a rugby stronghold. The Canadian trip undeniably had a missionary element to it; no trip to South Africa could be considered in that context. The five-game tour of May 1958,

The team that toured South Africa in 1958 was another strong unit containing some of the biggest names in the game. Back row: A.A. Mulligan, S.H. Wilcock, R.H. Davies, R.H. Williams, R.W.D. Marques, W.R. Evans, A.J.F. O'Reilly, A. Ashcroft, G.T. Wells; second row: N.S. Bruce, R.W.T. Chisholm, T.J. Davies, A.R. Dawson, G.H. Waddell, H.J. Morgan, B.J. Jones, R.E.G. Jeeps, H.F. McLeod; front row: G.W. Hastings, M.C. Thomas, J.T. Greenwood, H. Waddell (vice-president), H.L. Glyn Hughes (president), C.I. Morgan, A.R. Smith, A.C. Pedlow, C.R. Jacobs.
(© Barbarian Archive)

plus another fixture on the way home, against East Africa, was always going to pose new challenges. This time the matches would be played at some of the most famous grounds in the world, such as Ellis Park, Newlands and Loftus Versfeld, and against players of the calibre of Johan Claassen, Doug Hopwood and Tommy Gentles. There would be no need to 'educate' the local fans or the media in the intricacies of the game. From the outset the interest in the tour was huge. The crowds of 60,000 for both matches at Ellis Park in Johannesburg were the biggest ever for non-Test matches in the country. Fans were reported to be travelling to Cape Town from

vast distances to see the game against Western Province, while, at the other end of the scale, the final match in Nairobi attracted unprecedented coverage. There were two simple explanations for all of this: firstly, the reputation of the Barbarians was enough in itself to make the tour a financial and sporting success; and secondly, the British Isles tour to South Africa three years before had created an enormous groundswell of goodwill towards British rugby and its leading players. The latter would have benefits but also posed unwanted distractions for the Barbarians. This tour vies with the legendary match against the All Blacks in 1973 as the time when the Club had the greatest difficulty in persuading those on the periphery of the game that the Barbarians were not born-again Lions. In 1958 it was a bit of a Catch-22 situation because it was inevitable that several of the 1955 Lions would travel with the Club. All of South Africa wanted to see the likes of Cliff Morgan and Tony O'Reilly again and they were not to be disappointed. At a pre-tour meeting Morgan reputedly told his fellow Barbarians: 'When we go to schools, to business breakfasts or any social gatherings we will invariably be asked three questions – what do you think of our country, what do you think of our rugby and why does O'Reilly wear short shorts? The answer to the last is that he needs free movement to run and it also attracts the females.'

As well as eight of the 1955 Lions squad (plus another nine destined to tour Australasia in 1959) the Club's selectors invited two uncapped players to tour: the Oxford student Steve Wilcock in the pack and the Newport centre Brian Jones. Ten of the team, including Ron Jacobs – happily recovered from his dislocated hip – had toured Canada in 1957. What they didn't do was attempt to complete a tour with only twenty players as they had in Canada. Twenty-five players travelled to South Africa, with Hughie Glyn Hughes as manager and Herbert Waddell his assistant. The beginning was inauspicious. Their flight from London via Khartoum and Benghazi was delayed for 18 hours because of mechanical problems. Yet their 5 a.m. arrival at Jan Smuts Airport in Johannesburg still attracted a big crowd and Glyn Hughes' immediate announcement of the team to play Transvaal 48 hours later only served to increase the expectations. To no one's surprise, Cliff Morgan

would be captain, with Dickie Jeeps, his Test-match partner three years earlier, at scrum-half. O'Reilly and Arthur Smith were on the wings, Gordon Wells and Jones at centre, and Terry Davies at full-back. The pack was equally strong: Hugh McLeod, Ronnie Dawson and George Hastings in the front row, Rhys Williams and Roddie Evans at lock, and a back row of R.H. Davies, Alan Ashcroft and Jim Greenwood. The London Welsh wing-forward Robin Davies was to be one of the success stories of the tour. Herbert Waddell later wrote to Jock Wemyss, 'I would say the outstanding success relative to excellent form was Robin Davies, who was simply tremendous. I have never seen anyone run so often at top speed.'

The attention of the South Africans, though,

Transvaal Rugby Football Union (Inc.)
Transvaal Rugby Voetball Unie (Ing.)

BARBARIANS

ELLIS PARK
SAT., 10 MAY/MEI, 1958

TRANSVAAL

Souvenir Programme   Aandenkingsprogram

The 1958 tour received the best possible start when the match against Transvaal attracted a crowd of 60,000 to Ellis Park in Johannesburg. (© Barbarian Archive)

The 1958 team arrives in Johannesburg, complete with Alan Ashcroft and his guitar (far left). (© Barbarian Archive)

was firmly fixed on his countryman at fly-half. 'Cliff Morgan,' reported the *Rand Daily Mail*, 'is to world rugby what Rock Hudson is to the film world.' The fact that Morgan had already announced that the forthcoming fortnight would mark his swansong as a player and that he would retire immediately after it at the early age of 28 only increased the attention and publicity he would receive. There was never any doubt that great hordes of fans would turn up at Ellis Park on the Saturday afternoon, just as it seemed preordained that the Barbarians' first appearance in South Africa would prove memorable. 'This match will go into the fabled book of rugby as one of the greatest ever games seen at Transvaal headquarters,' reported the Johannesburg *Sunday Times* the following day. The cause of the excitement was simple: 10 tries shared equally between the sides in a 17–all draw. More than that, the tourists came back from six points down with barely a dozen

minutes left to play and the handicap of Wells hobbling on the wing with an ankle injury from early in the match. The home side had set the early pace with tries by Joe Kaminer and Jan Prinsloo, the second converted by Jannie Buys, inside the first quarter of an hour. With Wells off the field for treatment on his injured ankle, the Baa-Baas opened their account when Smith finished off Morgan's clean break and kick ahead. Ten minutes later Terry Davies came into the line and Smith was sent on a 30-yard dash for his second try. Then it was Transvaal's turn as Kaminer scored again after a great combination with his co-centre Jeremy Nel. Before half-time O'Reilly scored a typical try after brushing aside several attempted tackles. Davies' conversion levelled the scores at 11–all but Transvaal again pulled away in the third quarter with tries by Mannetjies Gericke and Martin Pelser. The final tries were worthy of the great game that had unfolded. First a limping Wells linked with O'Reilly inside his own 25 and the Irishman interpassed with Smith before accelerating away for the try. There was even better to come with only eight minutes left to play. Again the Barbarians counter-attacked from near their own line, this time through a magnificent solo effort by Arthur Smith. The Scottish wing, who was to captain the Lions in 1962 but die tragically at the age of 42, was the silkiest of runners and he showed all his skill as he beat the Transvaal full-back Buys with an inward swerve and then swung back to the right on an arcing run that was too much for the covering defence and resulted in a try that saved the game. The foremost South African writer Reg Sweet reported:

> There is a corner at Ellis Park that must now belong forever to the Baa-Baas. Here it was that Arthur Smith set the final seal on Saturday upon a match that ranked with the finest this vast stadium has seen, gained an acclamation unheard since the great days of the Lions, and earned a 17–all draw with the Transvaal in a finish pulsating with all that is best in rugby union football.

The tour had received the best possible start. Four days later attention turned to Olën Park in Potchefstroom, where the euphoria off the field and legerdemain on it was to prove less apparent. The Western Transvaal side were fêted as having the strongest pack in South Africa, a not inconsiderable compliment in the land of the giant forwards. At its centre was Johan Claassen, a fixture in the Springboks' engine room for the previous three seasons and already hotly tipped to be the next captain.

Directly opposite him as Barbarians captain was David Marques and they were to have their own private tussle. As well as Marques, all nine players who had missed the first game were drafted in to his side: Robin Chisholm at full-back; Cecil Pedlow and Malcolm Thomas in the centre; Gordon Waddell and Andy Mulligan at half-back; and in the pack Ron Jacobs and Norman Bruce in the front row and Steve Wilcock and Haydn Morgan at the back. Though the Westerns had promised to enter into what they called the 'Barbarian spirit' and play expansive rugby, the temptation to rely on their tried and trusted ways proved too great. As well as Claassen, their pack included, at prop, Fanie Kuhn, who was to tour Europe with Avril Malan's Springboks two years later, and Dick Putter, who rejoiced in the mantle of 'Iron Man of South African Rugby'. When the latter scored the opening try in the fourth minute, appropriately chasing a high punt by his captain, and full-back Meyer converted, the writing was already on the wall. The Barbarians' only score came six minutes later, when Greenwood scored a scrappy try that rather typified the rest of the match. Two quick scores just after half-time, when Meyer dropped a goal and Claassen dived over from a clean catch in a lineout, closed the scoring at 11–3. There was disappointment all round for the tourists, not necessarily because they had lost, but, more importantly, there had been a lack of fluency in their play. To cap it all, O'Reilly had sustained mild concussion and Smith had damaged an ankle.

The tour, however, still had several great days ahead of it. Western Province, the reigning Currie Cup champions, were the next opponents and Cliff Morgan was again handed the Barbarians captaincy. In Cape Town preparations were well in hand for another big crowd and a gala occasion. The city's traffic department was reported to be working overtime to control the expected increase in vehicles as thousands of people converged on Newlands from the outlying districts. On the eve of the match against Western Province a special dinner was held at the St James' Hotel for the old Barbarians, among them Ossie Newton-Thompson, Clive van Ryneveld and Tuppy Owen-Smith. Five hundred boys greeted Tony O'Reilly, recovered from his concussion, when he visited the famous rugby academy of Christian Brothers' College. They presented him with a pair of the school's rugby stockings. He told them, 'If I am fit enough to play tomorrow, I will wear these stockings.' He played. But other injuries were taking their toll. Cecil Pedlow was not expected to be fit again for the remainder of the tour, while Arthur Smith would only play in an emergency. Gordon Wells played with his ankle heavily strapped and back-rower Steve Wilcock was chosen as a wing. And still a 40,000 Newlands crowd saw an enthralling game, according to an eyewitness, 'of brawn, speed, quick wits, enterprise and good humour'. Two penalty goals by wing Swys Coetzee put Western Province six points ahead before O'Reilly linked with George Hastings and Wilcock galloped over for what he could proudly call a winger's try. In a fluent second half there was no score until the 40th minute. Then Brian Jones collected a loose ball in his own half, linked with Alan Ashcroft, who transferred to O'Reilly, who completed an 80-yard dash to the distant Western Province goal line. Terry Davies converted to ensure what seemed to be a famous victory. It was not to be. Eight minutes of injury time were played and at the very end the ball was slipped to the home side's fly-half, Lance Nel, who dropped a goal to snatch a 9–8 victory.

A draw and two defeats in three matches was a disappointment for the Barbarians and the remaining two matches in South Africa seemed to hold little prospect of an upturn in fortunes. A midweek fixture back on the high veld in Pretoria awaited them. There was every indication that Northern Transvaal would pose the same problems and adopt the same tactics as had Western Transvaal seven days earlier. The Barbarians chose their next team wisely. There were still emergency selections behind the scrum, with Terry Davies at centre, but there was a strong pack, with Hastings and McLeod propping Norman Bruce, the Welsh locks Rhys Williams and Roddie Evans, and Wilcock back in a more familiar role as number 8, with Robin Davies and Haydn Morgan as the wing-forwards. Significantly, the great warrior Rhys Williams was appointed captain. His team talk was simple: 'We must win this one!' His team responded magnificently. There was still no shortage of passing movements but there was a realisation too that there were times when plugging the touch-lines was a sensible option. In the *Rand Daily Mail*, Norman Canale observed, 'One got the impression that Williams would kick the culprits in the seat of their rugby shorts if they repeated the rash tactics [of Potchefstroom].' The Barbarians kept their heads despite an early setback. Losing possession in an attack, they had to turn and watch as Northerns' wing Andre Ferreira raced 60 yards for a breakaway try. Cutting out the frills, they dominated possession and midway through the half a clever cross-kick by Gordon Waddell was collected by Malcolm Thomas, who sent Haydn Morgan over for their first try.

Terry Davies converted and five minutes later did so again after O'Reilly touched down from another kick ahead, this time by Brian Jones. A long-distance penalty goal by Davies completed an excellent half and a 13–3 lead for the tourists. The only scores of the second period were by the home side, with a try by Louis Schmidt and a drop goal by Andre du Plessis, both in injury time. By then, the Barbarians knew that a significant victory was theirs.

The South African leg of the tour ended where it had begun, at Ellis Park in Johannesburg. Another 60,000 crowd greeted them and the opposition was even tougher. In what was a Combined Transvaal XV nine of the home province's players in the tour opener were joined by six others from the Northern, Eastern and Western provinces. Predictably, Western Transvaal provided three of the pack, including the captain, Claassen, and 'Iron Man' Putter. The Barbarians were boosted by the return to fitness of Arthur Smith and he was a popular choice as captain. With Malcolm Thomas and Brian Jones at centre, Terry Davies was able to revert to full-back. Morgan, of course, played at fly-half with Mulligan as his partner. Equally inevitably, O'Reilly was on the left wing and he was to be centre stage in a dramatic incident. The forwards had come through the tour remarkably unscathed and the pack combination was a good one: Hastings, Dawson and McLeod in the front row, Rhys Williams and Roddie Evans an outstanding lock pairing, and a back-row unit of Robin Davies, Ashcroft and Greenwood.

Two tries by Jones and O'Reilly in the first 20 minutes set the scene for a thrilling match. Neither was converted and this was to prove crucial in the final analysis. O'Reilly's try in particular attracted a lot of comment. Having crossed the goal line near the corner flag, he was heading for the goalposts and an easier conversion when he collided with a press photographer who had encroached on the in-goal area. 'Press Man Robs The Barbarians' was one headline the following day. By half-time the lead had been lost. The number 8 Piet Bartman and centre Norman Bridger both scored tries that were converted by Jannie Buys. It was regained when Jones finished off a Morgan break and Hastings converted. As the excitement mounted, the lead changed hands again when Jan Prinsloo ran around behind the posts for Buys to convert. At 11–15 the Barbarians were far from beaten. Alan Ashcroft scored with a spectacular dive ('as if fired from a circus cannon' said the local *Sunday Express*) and Hastings converted. Even when left-wing Dippies Dippenaar put the combined side 18–16 up with an unconverted try, there was time left for the tourists to mount further attacks. At the very end Malcolm Thomas cleverly beat the full-back but failed to find Robin Davies inside him with a pass for what would have been the match-winning try. It was a breathtaking conclusion to another ground-breaking tour – and there was one more staging post in Nairobi.

The game against East Africa was always likely to be far more relaxed after the intensity of Johannesburg and points south, more reminiscent, if anything, of the matches in Canada the year before. The opposition was not likely to be strong but the Barbarians again chose an impressive side. Cecil Pedlow had recovered from injury and was able to play his first game in a fortnight. Both scrum-halfs were injured so Gordon Waddell filled the vacancy. The last captaincy of the tour went to Jim

Greenwood. The Baa-Baas won the match comfortably by 52 points to 12. O'Reilly scored seven tries, Brian Jones three, and Pedlow, Thomas, Waddell and McLeod scored the others. The conversion attempts were shared around with mixed results. Thomas managed two and Morgan, Jones and Hughie McLeod one each.

The game was memorable for another reason: Cliff Morgan played his last game of rugby. The South African media had confirmed his retirement ahead of the Transvaal match the previous weekend. Reg Sweet wrote:

> Away in the dark and slaggy corners of the Rhondda Valley, in rugby-fevered Cardiff and at Ellis Park the lights will be doused tomorrow on the career of one of the great figures of the modern game. Cliff Morgan will make his final appearance and rugby will have lost a character.

But Cliff had one last trick up his sleeve. The curtain came down not at Ellis Park but in the more modest surroundings of the Ngong Road ground in Nairobi. Somehow, it was fitting, for what he had always believed was that rugby was only a sport, only a recreation, not to be taken too seriously and the small village matches were as relevant as those played in the great international arenas. The Barbarians and Cliff Morgan and all they both stood for were hewn from the same rock.

The trips to Canada in 1957 and South Africa in 1958 had earned themselves a special place in Barbarian folklore. Both countries would be visited again and those tours too would be successful. A little of the magic of those first visits might have been missing but

nevertheless they were worthy ventures in their own right. There was quite a long interval between them. Eleven years between the South African trips and all of nineteen between the first and second tours to Canada. A great deal had changed in both cases. The 1969 tour of South Africa coincided with a Wales tour to New Zealand and Australia. That meant that the likes of J.P.R. Williams, Gerald Davies, Gareth Edwards and the rest of the Welsh superstars could not go with the Barbarians. That was of little consequence to the Club because they still had many big names and loyal Barbarians to make their own tour another notable success. There were new English stars emerging: David Duckham and Rodney Webb in the backs; John Pullin, Bob Taylor and the long-serving Budge Rogers in the forwards. Ireland provided Alan Duggan and Barry McGann, Scotland Alistair Biggar, Frank Laidlaw and Rodger Arneil, and Wales could still offer Billy Hullin, John O'Shea, Bill Morris, John Jeffery and the uncapped Stuart Gallacher. It was a strong tour party of 23 players that set off for Johannesburg in early May of 1969. Hughie Glyn Hughes was again the manager, this time with the assistance of the recently appointed secretary Geoffrey Windsor-Lewis and the treasurer, Gordon Ferguson. In addition Herbert Waddell travelled as a guest of the South African Rugby Board, of which he was also a vice-president. As in 1958 six matches were to be played – five in South Africa and then one in Rhodesia. Ellis Park and Newlands would again host fixtures and a significant addition was another famous international ground at King's Park in Durban. The invitation had come from the SARB, and Danie Craven and the other officials warmly welcomed the Brigadier and his party when they arrived at Johannesburg, again the starting point for the tour.

The opposition at Ellis Park this time was not Transvaal but the Quaggas, an invitation club set up only a dozen years before and on the same lines as the Barbarians (they were later to amalgamate with the South African Barbarians). As such they were able to draw on players from all over the Republic, the most distinguished of whom were scrum-half Piet Uys, who had toured Britain with the Springboks, and the world-class flanker Jan Ellis. They were no match, however, for an inspired Barbarians team. McGann and Hullin teamed up at half-back, with Duggan, Duckham, Biggar and Webb proving a potent threat outside them. The uncapped Irishman Barry O'Driscoll was at full-back. In the pack was the captain for the day, Bob Taylor, and two others who had toured South Africa with the Lions the previous year, O'Shea and Arneil. Two Scots in the front row were Laidlaw and Norman Suddon. Morris and Gallacher formed another Welsh second row, and joining Taylor and Arneil at the back was Mick Hipwell. Understandably the Baa-Baas took their time to find their feet, the Quaggas scoring first through a try by wing Rodney Bryant. The tourists were level at half-time thanks to a drop goal by McGann. In the second half it was one-way traffic as the Baa-Baas scored 26 points without reply. Six tries came at regular intervals from Webb (two), Duggan, Biggar, Hipwell and, at the very end, a captain's effort by Taylor; McGann converted four. The crowd of 30,000 may only have been half the size of that in 1958 but the impression made was equally impressive. Reg Sweet, still surveying the South African scene for *The Star*, particularly admired the backs: 'Duckham

carved numerous openings through a defence which crumpled badly,' and 'Webb is a superlative runner of tremendous power . . . it would be premature, indeed unfair, to label Webb here and now as the most thrustful winger we have seen since the days of O'Reilly, the "darlin' bhoy" of the '50s, but on this showing he could very easily qualify.' The 29–3 final score was an excellent start and Glyn Hughes was quick to praise the team's efforts. He told the press, 'The team's morale has been greatly raised as a result of this win. It means that the eight who did not play and who may all be included in the team to play against Natal provided they are fit are raring to go and anxious to do as well as those they will replace.'

True to his word, the eight players in question – Chris Saville, Colin Telfer and Nigel Starmer-Smith behind the scrum and Keith Fairbrother, John Pullin, Geoff Bayles, John Jeffery and the captain, Budge Rogers, in the pack – were selected to play against Natal at King's Park the following Wednesday. The provincial side would be more cohesive than the scratch Quaggas combination and were reputed to be weak up front, compensating by playing on their wits. They seemed to be ideal opponents for a game of Barbarians-type rugby, even without their talisman captain, Tommy Bedford, who withdrew injured 24 hours before the game. In difficult conditions caused by a strong wind they proved to be what Glyn Hughes later called 'a tigerish team which tackled like demons'. Natal had started as underdogs, were behind at half-time, but won the match 16–14 thanks to their superior goal-kicking allied to their watertight defence. The Barbarians had not used the strong wind at their backs to the best advantage in the first half, falling behind to a try by Andy Donovan, converted by Malcolm Swanby. They had edged ahead at the interval thanks to a penalty goal by Saville and a clever try by Duckham. Against the elements in the second half the Barbarians put on a virtuoso display of handling and switch moves. Swanby kicked a monster penalty goal from halfway and although Rogers regained the lead with a try 15 minutes from the end it was not enough. In the swirling wind the number 8 Richard Steyn dropped on a loose ball for another try for Natal and acting captain Rodney Gould added another. Swanby's conversion stretched the lead to 16–9 and the game was won and lost. Even then the Barbarians finished strongly when Duckham provided the inspiration for a second try for Rogers, converted by Saville.

It had been another great game. Percy Owen, who was covering the tour for Associated Newspapers, wrote: 'More than 15,000 people in Durban have sore throats today. It's nothing serious but that's what you get from watching the Barbarians in action.' Unfortunately, though, the disappointment of defeat was magnified by an injury to Rodney Webb, a torn hamstring, which meant he would be unable to play again on tour.

For the next game at Port Elizabeth the Blackheath utility back Chris Saville was drafted in as a wing. The opponents were the South African Barbarians, the nine-year-old offspring of the parent Club, and as it was the first match between the two it naturally attracted a great deal of attention. Glyn Hughes, Herbert Waddell and the others felt it would be the highlight of the tour but events, mainly in the shape of the referee, conspired against it. Yet all the omens were good. The hosts had again chosen a balance of experienced Springboks, such as Piet Visagie

and Gawie Carelse, and promising provincial and club players, among whom Billy Wepener of UCT (University of Cape Town) was considered to be a scrum-half on the verge of top honours. No one had speculated in advance about the quality of the referee, Jannie van Wyk. In the immediate aftermath of an unsatisfactory game that the visitors lost 11–23, all Hughie Glyn Hughes would say when pressed about the many penalties, 12 of them in kickable positions, that were awarded against his side was a terse 'no comment'. Later, in his tour report, he confided to the rest of the committee that the refereeing was 'quite incomprehensible'. His South African counterparts, clearly embarrassed by a game full of promise that had ended as a disappointment, were less diplomatic. At a post-match reception, Boet Erasmus, after whom the stadium in Port Elizabeth was named, memorably said, 'This was a case of forgetting the game and getting on with the whistle.' The press were positively queuing up to add their own insights. Reg Sweet said, 'The persistent shrill of the whistle was like a mother-in-law with all the grouses in the world'; Percy Owen concluded that, 'Jan van Wyk had difficulty in applying basic laws of the game, let alone the advantage law'; while John Reason, the only British journalist covering the tour, wrote, 'This was another saga in the sad, sad story of one-sided refereeing in South Africa.' The Barbarian management were not comfortable with the latter sweeping generalisation. Glyn Hughes subsequently reported, 'With one exception, we had no real complaints against the refereeing.' At Port Elizabeth, unfortunately, the scrummaging had come under the referee's microscope. Time and time again penalties were awarded against the Barbarians for 'not straight' put-ins and, if not that, 'foot up' by the front row. Scrum-half and captain Billy Hullin, returning to the ground where two years earlier he had led his Cardiff club side to a famous victory over Eastern Province, was at his wit's end. At the time, he too maintained a diplomatic silence. Now he is prepared to say that what happened was far from satisfactory: 'I was being whistled up at every third scrum and if I asked the referee what it was for he would take us back another ten yards. There was never any attempt to offer an explanation.' Hullin deserved better. He was a good Barbarian in every sense and captained the Club five times in nine appearances over the years. His brief international career had been overshadowed by that of Gareth Edwards but he was a top-notch scrum-half. He also appreciated touring with the Club. 'It was a great experience,' he said, 'not least because eminent leaders like Hughie and Herbert talked to us as men and treated us as such. They took an interest in our own lives away from the game and as I was in banking and Herbert was a stockbroker we hit off an instant rapport.'

The Barbarians paid dearly for the lack of such a rapport with officialdom on the pitch at Boet Erasmus stadium. The defeat could have been heavier but the South African Barbarians missed at least ten kicks at goal. As it was, Koos Meiring scored two tries, his fellow wing Willie Stapelberg another, with a fourth coming from Gert Nortje. In an otherwise undistinguished kicking display, Chris Luther succeeded with three penalty goals and a conversion. For the Barbarians, O'Shea and Gallacher scored tries, Saville converted one and McGann kicked a penalty goal. Many of the fans in the 25,000 crowd may have felt short-changed by the quality of the rugby they had seen but with a week and two matches left in South Africa there was every chance that reputations would be restored and appetites satisfied.

The next game was at Newlands against the Southern Universities, traditionally a strong outfit who warranted regular fixtures against international touring teams. They were particularly threatening in the back division where, even in the absence of Jannie Engelbrecht, they could still field four current or future Springboks in Ian McCallum, Eben Olivier, Jackie Snyman and Andrew van der Watt. For the Barbarians, Bob Taylor was again captain but the continued absence of Rodney Webb meant that Duckham played on the wing and McGann in the centre.

Another 25,000 crowd turned up for the game on a Wednesday afternoon. The fare was better than at Port Elizabeth but still not reaching the heights of the early matches. The situation was almost a rerun of that against Northern Transvaal in 1958 with the Barbarians, for all their emphasis on performance and style of play, quietly realising that a win was needed at this stage. Unfortunately, they were less successful than their predecessors. Although the pack performed well and Hullin was having a fine game snapping at their heels, they were ten points down at half-time and couldn't quite overhaul the Universities after that. To their credit the home team played particularly well in the opening quarter. Right-wing Hennie de Vos and number 8 Steve Hillock scored tries that were converted by McCallum. The full-back also kicked two penalty goals. In reply McGann kicked a penalty goal and Hullin broke from a five-yard scrum for a try. The second half was more to the Barbarians' liking

as the play became looser but it was the back row of Taylor, Arneil and Jeffery rather than the backs that made the inroads. Both Taylor, early in the half, and Jeffery, at the very end, scored tries but McGann could only convert the first and the Universities held on for an 18–16 victory.

Three consecutive defeats were undeniably a disappointment and a strong South African Country Districts team awaited them in Potchefstroom. The management was putting a brave face on the situation even though the injury list was lengthening by the day. Before every game since Durban, Webb had been given a fitness test in the forlorn hope of a quick recovery to his hamstring; in addition, Duckham and Biggar were carrying leg injuries. As they prepared for the final game in South Africa, there was speculation that an SOS would be sent for a replacement wing, possibly the Springbok Syd Nomis, but more probably the 1968 Lion Keith Savage, who had recently emigrated to South Africa. Commendably, Glyn Hughes and the management team sorted out their problems from within. The reward was the best performance of the tour and a fine win. There were some familiar names among the Districts team: Mannetjies Roux, the scourge of many opposing centres over the years with his dynamic (and occasionally late) tackling; Piet Visagie and Dawie de Villiers at half-back; and Hannes Marais and Jan Ellis in the pack. A capacity 16,000 crowd was at Olën Park, confidently expecting a home victory. The Barbarians, captained by Frank Laidlaw, rose to the occasion magnificently. Even without Budge Rogers, who needed hospital treatment after leaving the field with concussion at half-time, the pack dominated possession and the backs at last clicked into

gear. The game was also a personal triumph for scrum-half Nigel Starmer-Smith, at that stage uncapped by England. No one was more pleased than neutral South Africans who were beginning to wonder whether the Baa-Baas were losing their aura. In the *Sunday Tribune* Reg Sweet reported: 'Gone were those muffed passes of earlier matches; gone the costly failures to make the tackle. In their place was the old black-and-white Barbarian magic and it was a joy to see.'

Laidlaw's team dominated from first to last. They won the first seven lineouts and were soon putting points on the board. After two early penalty goals by McGann and one for the Districts by Visagie, Alan Duggan intercepted an attempted scissors move and streaked to the posts for a try converted by McGann. Great work by Starmer-Smith created a second try for Duggan and all the home side could reply with was another Visagie goal. The half-time lead of 14–6 was never threatened on the resumption as Biggar, Colin Telfer and Laidlaw added to the try tally. McGann converted two and Chris Saville one, plus a penalty goal. The shell-shocked Districts revived with tries from Kobus Koerts and Johnny Joubert, Visagie converted both and kicked another penalty, while Roux, his attacking instincts completely nullified, dropped a goal. The Barbarians had finished the South African leg of their tour in style. Hughie Glyn Hughes said, 'This must have been the strongest side we met during our tour in South Africa and we can be said to have ended it in a blaze of glory. Frank Laidlaw was an outstanding captain and his pre-match talk was really something.' Shades of Rhys Williams at Pretoria in 1958.

The tour was not quite over. Now came potentially the most controversial aspect of the whole trip – a match in Salisbury against Rhodesia. In 1969 the British government was imposing trade sanctions against their counterparts in Rhodesia and attempts were made to prevent a stopover in Salisbury. The Lions had played there the previous year and the Barbarians intended to follow suit. The Club's position was clearly stated by Hughie Glyn Hughes: 'The Barbarians are touring at the invitation of the South African Rugby Board to which the Rhodesian Rugby Union is affiliated as a constituent member. The fixtures and their venues are the prerogative of the host union – the SARB. The Barbarians remain emphatic that politics should be kept out of sport and feel that only good and help towards improved relations can result from this visit.' At the end of the tour he reaffirmed that they had.

On arrival at Salisbury the Rhodesian authorities left the British passports unstamped, in a cosmetic gesture of political protocol. During the two-day visit the Barbarians management were warmly received at Government House and everything proceeded without incident. The match itself was a great success. Still stretched to the limit of their playing resources behind the scrum, Barry McGann again turned out at centre while Barry O'Driscoll and Alan Duggan achieved the distinction of playing in all six games on the tour. The captaincy went to the Cardiff prop John O'Shea, another popular move. The life and soul of every party, 'Tess' O'Shea had been sent off playing for the 1968 Lions against Eastern Transvaal at Springs. The Barbarians tour was a chance for him to make amends and he did so, not least because he had gone out of his way to look up the referee from that match, Bert Woolley, and share a drink with him.

MASHONALAND RUGBY FOOTBALL BOARD
STAGES

RHODESIA versus **BARBARIANS**

WHIT MONDAY, 26th MAY, 1969
Police Ground · · Salisbury

*Souvenir Programme   With the Compliments of
The Mashonaland Rugby Football Board*

The final game of the 1969 tour was against Rhodesia. (© Barbarian Archive)

Barbarians, by nature, build bridges, and that's what they were doing in Salisbury. O'Shea couldn't quite emulate the example set by earlier captains on tour – Bob Taylor, Budge Rogers and Frank Laidlaw – by scoring a try but he was in the thick of the action when lock-forward Geoff Bayles dived over for the first try. McGann, having already kicked a penalty goal, converted and did so again when Duggan finished off a textbook move started by Taylor. The wing-forward scored himself before the interval, at which point the Barbarians led 16–11. Rhodesia had competed well, with tries by Ross Robertson and John Jones and five points from the boot of

Marthinus Martin. A converted try by Mick Hipwell early in the second half put the game out of Rhodesia's reach, though they finished strongly with two more tries for the centre Jones, both converted by Martin. Another McGann penalty goal was to prove the difference between the sides in a 24–21 win for the Barbarians.

The consensus was that the tour of 1969 had been another success for the Club and its players. Before they left Salisbury, Hughie Glyn Hughes said, 'All the games have been wonderful. As the tour has progressed, so our players have improved. We are playing much better rugby now than we were at the start. We have received a great welcome wherever we have been and that is the essence of all rugby tours.'

As every year went by, it became more difficult to organise further tours of five or six matches overseas, certainly with the top players on board, but in 1976, against all predictions, the Club did just that – and more. Nineteen years after the first-ever trip to Canada the wheel had turned full circle. Once again the Barbarians took with them a star-studded team – the cream, in fact, of British rugby. The only absentees were the Irish players involved in their country's tour of New Zealand and one or two of the Welsh superstars of the era. In the 25-man squad, nevertheless, were other leading lights of the Welsh team such as Bennett, Gravell, Fenwick, J.J. Williams and Wheel, while from Scotland there were Irvine, Lawson, Carmichael, Madsen, Tomes and Mike Biggar. The English contingent included Neary, Wheeler and John Watkins. This was a strong group by any standard and they were needed as the Barbarians set out on their longest-ever tour of eight matches in twenty-two days. It had not initially been planned as such. The original invitation had come from Bob Spray, chairman of the Canadian Rugby Union Tours Committee, and it had been for five matches in Canada. Less than a month before the tour began, the schedule had been increased to six matches. In the meantime the Club committee had already agreed to play two matches in Boston, where an American bicentennial tournament was being staged, en route to Vancouver. So five matches had become eight at quite a late stage. It was a demanding itinerary and Herbert Waddell, as tour manager, later reported, 'We would not like to play eight games in twenty-two days ever again on any short tour. Apart from anything else, we were lucky as regards injuries or we could have been in serious trouble.'

Rugby in Canada had moved on considerably since the 1950s. In 1976 there were 800 clubs with 3,000 teams and 30,000 players across the country, with the main centres in Ontario and British Columbia. On this trip there would be less need for the Barbarians to double up as missionaries spreading the game's gospel. The full Canadian side would be played in Toronto and an equally strong British Columbia team in Vancouver. However, the stopover in Boston was a throwback to the pioneering tour of 1957. Local reporters again tried to explain the intricacies of the game to their readers. The *Boston Globe* kept it simple:

> Rugby players are marvels of endurance, running virtually non-stop for 70 minutes [*sic*], except for a five-minute half-time, over a field slightly larger than a gridiron. They are rugged in the

tradition of [ice] hockey, with no provisions for substitutes and scant heed paid to limps and lumps. Each team fields 15 players.

But some of the stars of the sport were known to American watchers. One ex-pat was heard to exclaim on seeing Phil Bennett, 'My God, he's here: the Joe DiMaggio of rugby!'

Four English clubs – Fylde, Gosforth, Moseley and Rosslyn Park – were also in town for the tournament but the Barbarians would play two stand-alone fixtures, against New England on 29 May and a Californian touring team, Bay Area, two days later. They proved to be surprisingly competitive encounters. Apart from the merits of the opposition, the playing conditions were not ideal. The pitch was very narrow, barely fifty-five yards wide, and three games a day were played on it in hot weather; even though it was regularly watered, the clouds of dust were a continuing problem. The Cardiff prop Mike Knill summed up the situation after the first match: 'In the front row we were as busy as coal miners and we'll be suffering from dust poisoning if this continues.' Even so, the Barbarians gave a good account of themselves. The local fans, according to the *Globe*, 'admired their across-the-field laterals while whipping New England 40–12'. Roughly translated, that means Bennett, Andy Irvine and their teammates ran well and often. Seven tries were scored, beginning with J.J. Williams, Rosslyn Park wing Dave McKay and Harlequins back-rower Adrian Alexander in the first half, two converted by Bennett. Mike Darnforth kicked a penalty goal for the American side and did so again in the second period as well as converting a try by Collier. Andy Irvine crossed twice for the Barbarians, Williams also

scored a second try and a final score came from the Llanelli wing-forward Gareth Jenkins, all converted by Bennett.

The second game, against Bay Area, was less satisfactory. The Harlequins full-back Billy Bushell fractured a cheekbone and was out of the rest of the tour, Jenkins exacerbated a previous knee injury and would play only one more match, and Knill suffered badly bruised ribs. Only two replacements were allowed, so the team played the last ten minutes with fourteen men. It was hard luck on Bushell in particular as he was having an impressive all-round game as well as scoring twenty points from a try, two conversions and four penalty goals before he was removed to hospital. The management, realising that it was too early in the tour to proceed to Canada already one man short, drafted in a replacement, Brian Patrick, who was in Boston with the Gosforth club. Bay Area were beaten 28–7, the other tries being scored by Brynmor Williams and Dave McKay.

The following day the party flew to Vancouver to begin what promised to be the business end of the tour. The rugby community of British Columbia were still curious about what made the Barbarian Football Club tick, but Herbert Waddell was as clear as Hughie Glyn Hughes had been about what underpinned everything. He told the *Vancouver Sun*:

> We know what we are looking for when we invite a player to turn out for the Barbarians. He's got to be a chap with integrity, a chap willing to play open rugby. A Barbarian has never been ordered off the field or even warned by the referee. We permit no trickery – that is, players who feign injury and lie down, calling time, when his team is in trouble.

At the end of the tour the president was reassured that the right people had been chosen. He wrote:

> The team deserve the highest credit for their patience, discipline, punctuality and complete cooperation with the management throughout the tour. The Barbarian performance, thanks to a continuing attitude for improved play, greater teamwork and a virile spirit, was much better than we had envisaged and the team deserve the highest credit for producing at all times their very best rugby in the Barbarian tradition.

The match against British Columbia, played at Swangard Stadium on Thursday, 3 June, was a good example of all these virtues. The tour was still in its first week but it was already apparent that Phil Bennett was following in the twinkling footsteps of his fly-half predecessor Cliff Morgan as the main centre of attention. Barbarian rugby suited both of them to a tee. Having entranced the Americans in Boston, he received similar rave reviews in Vancouver. The *Sun* was in particularly lyrical mood: 'Bennett conducted an artistry of rhythm from the back-line, both jazzy and smooth-flowing attacks . . . the audacious fly-half with feet quick as a blink was omnipresent going both ways, his red Welsh socks ever conspicuous.' Others shone, too, including Bennett's Llanelli club colleague Ray Gravell and, of course, Andy Irvine. Home expectations of a famous win were blown away in the opening quarter. Bennett kicked two long-range penalty goals, sandwiched around a bustling try by Tony Neary that he also converted. Then Irvine glided 65 yards for an unconverted try that stretched the lead to 16

points without reply. Ro Hindson, a lock who had played for the President's XV against Ireland at Lansdowne Road in 1974, kicked a wide-angled penalty goal and scrum-half Preston Wiley kicked another. A 45-yarder by Bennett made it 19–6 to the Barbarians at half-time. Hindson added another nine points after the break, with a converted try and a penalty goal, but the Baa-Baas were in full flow by that time. Bennett kicked another penalty goal and added the extra points to tries by J.J. Williams and Peter Wheeler for a final score of 34–15.

The Barbarians left Vancouver with the feeling that their visit had been all too short. Herbert Waddell later recommended that on any future tour two matches should be played there – that had been the case in 1957, with a third at nearby Victoria. Ahead of them lay a couple of easier looking fixtures before the game against the national team. Edmonton had not been on the itinerary of the earlier tour but the area around it was considered to be a fast-developing nursery for rugby. The visit there was worthwhile but the opposition proved to be a disappointment. The Alberta team were found wanting in the set pieces, especially the scrums, where the Scottish hooker Duncan Madsen had a field day. There was also a certain naivety. The home scrum-half David Slater was bemused: 'Madsen was hooking with his nose. Whenever I went to throw [*sic*] the ball in, his head was about a foot off the ground. I might as well have just walked over and given it to their scrum-half.'

It is fair to assume, then, that the Barbarians dominated possession. It was put to good use. The match ended at 56–4, the first 50 of the tourists' points coming without reply. Dave McKay was to end the tour as top try-scorer, with a remarkable sixteen in only six matches

(Tony O'Reilly finished with thirteen in five matches in 1957) and here he snapped up three of them. J.J. Williams and Steve Fenwick scored two each with others coming from Irvine, Alan Lawson, Biggar and Geoff Wheel; Bennett converted six. Alberta's only score was a try by wing John Parton in the 65th minute.

Much the same happened at the next port of call in Regina. The hospitality was again warm and a record crowd of 5,500 was in attendance for the match against Saskatchewan at Taylor Field. Other records were set as well, for what they saw was not so much a contest as an exhibition. The 76–nil result went down in the record books as the Club's highest points score and biggest winning margin. As a stand-alone record it was to survive only eight days. McKay was continuing to add to his try haul with another five and Irvine, on the field as a replacement for fellow Scot Dave Shedden, ran in two. Other tries were scored by Fenwick, Wheeler and Knill. Brian Patrick was playing his first game since joining the team and celebrated with two tries and three conversions, and the Cardiff fly-half Gareth Davies also helped himself to a couple of tries as well as seven conversions. As preparation for the next match against All-Canada it was not ideal.

The running, free-flowing rugby of earlier matches temporarily came to a halt at York Stadium, Toronto, on 12 June. The Canadian team was steadily making its way up the pecking order of the second tier of rugby nations and was anxious to further enhance its standing. In later years, especially the 1990s, it did so by employing a pinpoint kicking game and a resolute defence. The Barbarians were to experience a foretaste of this. Although they won the game comfortably enough at 29–4,

they were far from pleased with the nature of the match. Geoff Windsor-Lewis, as the tour's assistant manager, pulled no punches. 'It was the worst game of the tour,' he said. 'It was the first time a team has come out against us with a totally negative attitude. They kept trying to kill the ball and with so many offences there was nothing the referee could do but give us penalty kicks.' In fact, Bennett kicked the first of his eventual four penalty goals after only thirty seconds of play. It set the scene for what followed – a match in which the referee awarded an incredible 35 penalties. The Barbarians had picked a side full of attacking intent. Irvine was at full-back, J.J. Williams, Gravell, Fenwick and McKay were the three-quarters, and Brynmor Williams was with

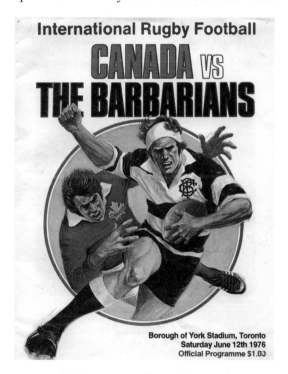

In 1976 the keynote match was against the Canadian national team, suitably commemorated with a colourful programme.
(© Barbarian Archive)

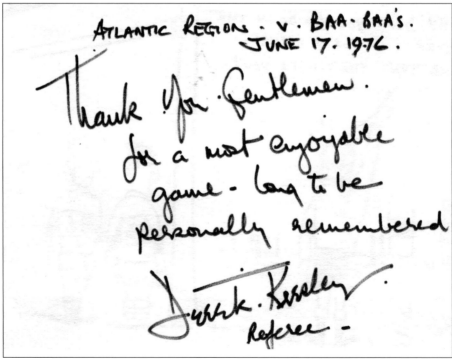

Some of the games in 1976 may have been one-sided but even the local referee for
the final game at Halifax could see the funny side. (© Barbarian Archive)

Bennett at half-back. The pack comprised Sandy Carmichael, Wheeler, Swansea prop Phil Llewellyn, Wheel and Alan Tomes at lock, and Biggar, Neary and the Leicester number 8 Garry Adey. It was a good team, well capable of countering whatever tactics the hosts employed. So it proved. As well as his first two penalty goals, Bennett converted one of two tries scored by McKay and Irvine dropped a goal to establish a nineteen-points lead before Canada registered their only score with a try by Spence McTavish. In the second half what should have been the showpiece game of the tour petered out, the only points coming from another brace of goals by Bennett and a try by Steve Fenwick. There was a sense of anticlimax as well as frustration. Fortunately, the team had two more matches in the next five days to rediscover their traditional brand of rugby and other facets of touring.

In Montreal several Barbarians conducted coaching clinics at local clubs and all the team visited the stadium that was to host the track and field events in the Olympic Games later that year. The match against Quebec was played at the Autostade ground, a Canadian football venue that had a narrow pitch. Nevertheless, some of the best running rugby of the tour produced thirteen tries, including another four for the insatiable McKay and two for J.J. Williams. Also among the try-scorers were centre David Cooke with two, Alan Lawson, Brian Patrick and John Watkins.

Capping them all was Gareth Davies, who finished with a personal tally of thirty-one points courtesy of two tries, a penalty goal and ten conversions. With Mike Alder kicking a penalty goal for the home side the Barbarians fell just short of their new record against Saskatchewan with a 75–3 win. Two days later in Halifax, however, they again ran up 76 points without reply. The final opposition of the tour was provided by the Atlantic All-Stars at the equally splendidly named Huskies Stadium at St Mary's University, Halifax. Despite the heavy rain the venue proved to be a delight, with a full-size pitch and an excellent playing surface. The Barbarians did it justice. The longer the game went on, the fewer scrums and lineouts there were, and they revelled in the broken play. Andy Irvine was at the top of his game, three times collecting loose balls and sprinting in for tries. Brynmor Williams also claimed a hat-trick, but J.J. Williams did even better with five, to finish with a tour tally of eleven. Other try-scorers were Shedden, Neary and Alexander; Bennett kicked four conversions and Irvine two. Bennett also scored two tries, including the last one of the match. It was a fitting end to the tour, coming as it did after a 40-yard run through the centre of the defence – and scored by the captain.

Between 1957 and 1976 the Barbarians played 26 matches in Canada, South Africa and the United States. Shorter tours to many other countries would follow.

VII

NEW HORIZONS AND NEW FRIENDS

'Playing for or against the Barbarians is the dream of any player.'

– Luis Pissarra, 2005

Luis Pissarra may not be a household name in the British Isles or, for that matter, in New Zealand, South Africa or Australia. He may not even be particularly well known among the wider sporting fraternity at home in his native Portugal. He is, however, a widely respected figure in the rugby community in Lisbon. Luis is a fine scrum-half and he is the captain of the Portuguese national team. He is also a Barbarian who has played with distinction for and against the Club. More than anything he is the classic example of how several aspects of the Barbarians' playing commitments have changed since the mid-1990s and of how those changes have benefited and inspired a much wider audience than ever before. In the dozen

or so years after 1992 the range of the Club's travels was astonishing. There were two- or three-match tours to Russia, Zimbabwe, Japan, Uruguay and Argentina; France and Italy were revisited; one-off games were played against the national teams of Germany and, in 2004, Portugal. Barbarian horizons were widened to a degree undreamt of barely a few years earlier. Invariably the visits and matches were tied in with a worthy cause: an anniversary or the simple aim of fostering the game in a developing rugby nation. Without exception the visits were successful not only for spreading the virtues of the Barbarians but also for the good of the sport in general.

Rugby clubs from Britain had visited Russia

before the Barbarians. Llanelli had done so as long ago as 1957. Few, if any, would have undertaken a two-match visit that involved a training session in St Petersburg before a long flight across to Siberia to play the first match there and then back to Moscow for the second game. That, broadly, is what twenty-three players and five committeemen of the Barbarians did in the space of eight days in the summer of 1992. The tour had only gone ahead with the permission of the Rugby Football Union, which, in turn, had received a recommendation from a specially convened delegation that had made a preliminary visit. The three-man delegation was made up of Dudley Wood, Albert Agar and M.R. Steele-Bodger. The president was fascinated by the tour. 'Our first match was at Krasnoyarsk in Siberia,' he said. 'It is what might be described as a boffin city but you'd be hard pushed to find it on a map. The hospitality was memorable. That match had 28 sponsors, which meant that 28 glasses of vodka had to be drunk, otherwise it would be disrespectful – and Barbarians are never disrespectful!' Somehow, Micky and his fellow committeemen survived the pace, though the opposition in the matches was surprisingly tough.

So were the travelling arrangements. The Aeroflot flight from Heathrow to St Petersburg was completed without incident and a training session was successfully undertaken there the following day. Not everything went quite so smoothly after that. The next day's planned flight across to Siberia was postponed for 24 hours when it was discovered that the private jet chartered for the journey didn't have enough fuel to get across the landmass. The delayed welcome in Krasnoyarsk was worth waiting for. When they did land, a day late, the

The official invitation card for the tour of Russia in 1992. (© Barbarian Archive)

party was met by an army band and the traditional fare of salt and bread. The new culture was well received by an appropriately cosmopolitan group of Barbarians, including three French backs – the Lafond brothers and Denis Charvet – and Japan's Maru Hayashi, plus several internationals from across Britain. The quality of the opposition was relatively unknown but, as Krasny Yar had been Russian club champions for two seasons, nothing was being taken for granted. The captaincy was given to the Moseley centre Ruory Maclean and with him in midfield were Charvet and the Harlequins fly-half David Pears. They promised to pose a potent attacking threat, even in the extreme heat. Yet the game was far from one-sided. After building up a 10–nil lead from early tries by Charvet and Jean-Marc Lafond, the first converted by Pears, the tourists were to find themselves trailing 10–21 early in the second half. The extraordinary turnaround repeated itself, with the Barbarians, having conceded 21 points without reply, then scoring 22 of their own for a final victory of 32–21.

A very collectable memento – the programme
for the match against Krasny Yar.
(© Barbarian Archive)

the Bolshoi Ballet and tours of the Kremlin and
Red Square. The opposition in the second
match was equally impressive. The first
internationals from the Soviet Union to play for
the Barbarians had been Igor Mironov and
Alexander Tikhonov, both members of the
Gagarin Academy side, who had been selected
against Cardiff and Swansea on the Easter tour
of 1990. The quality of their play on that
occasion, plus the standard shown by Krasny
Yar, left the tourists in no doubt that they were
in for a stern test against the CIS at the
Locomotiv Stadium. This proved to be the case.
The Bath and England flanker Andy Robinson
led a strong side containing a dozen capped
players and, as in the earlier game in Siberia,
they held the upper hand for most of the 80
minutes. Alex Moore and the Lafond brothers
shared three tries, the Swansea fly-half Aled
Williams converted one and kicked two
penalty goals and Jean-Baptiste Lafond also
dropped a goal. The Barbarians led 17–9 at
half-time but were up against opponents who
seemed to have made several substitutions
during the interval. Nevertheless, they were
holding on in the energy-sapping heat at 23–21
with only moments left to play when their
opponents unveiled a movement worthy of the
Barbarians themselves. Mounting an attack
from near their own line, the CIS took the Baa-
Baas by surprise for winger Voropaev to score
the winning try. The conversion by Bugrov was
academic but confirmed a famous 27–23
triumph that brought the partisan crowd to
their feet. The disappointment of defeat was, as
always, softened by the nature of the post-
match hospitality, notable for a banquet at
which the CIS rugby president proposed a toast
to 'the British Queen'. There could be only one
form of reply from Robinson and his men –

Lafond went on to complete a hat-trick of tries,
Pears and Hawick wing Alex Moore added
others, with Pears also kicking three more
conversions. With an attendance of over 5,000
the game had been a success in every respect.
Six of the Krasny Yar team were scheduled to
play for the national side against the Barbarians
in Moscow three days later.

In both Siberia and Moscow the team stayed
at hotels formerly used as premises by the KGB,
and Micky Steele-Bodger, having warned his
colleagues of the dangers of petty crime, duly
suffered the inconvenience and indignity of
losing his wallet to a pickpocket. But there
were many cultural delights to divert them,
including visits to the Moscow State Circus and

they sang 'God Save the Queen' and, for good measure, continued with 'Mae Hen Wlad Fy Nhadau', 'Flower of Scotland', and 'Molly Malone'. And, of course, the French trio contributed 'La Marseillaise' before, heroically, Maru Hayashi offered a solo rendition of the Japanese national anthem. Once again a Barbarian tour had featured a bit of everything.

The Russian adventure had been a pioneering tour in the true traditions of the Club. The next overseas trip, in 1994, was more a case of revisiting old friends. Much had changed in the 25 years since the Barbarians' previous visit to southern Africa. Rhodesia had become Zimbabwe and the capital city was now named Harare. Politically, the country was no longer regarded as *persona non grata* in Britain. The short stopover of 1969 was now replaced by a fully fledged three-match visit, regarded by then as the preferred length of a short tour. It also spread the matches across three separate venues and allowed for time to be spent at Victoria Falls, as well as the usual quota of local visits to schools and other organisations. The Zimbabwe Rugby Union had asked the Club to select a squad with a cross-section of experienced and young players and the party that flew out of Heathrow Airport on 25 May reflected that. The younger element included future stars of the world game such as Neil Back and Matt Dawson, while the Northampton and Scotland lock Neil Edwards was to prove the ideal captain.

Over the years the arrival of the Barbarians at various airports worldwide has been reported in many effusive ways. The *Bulawayo Chronicle* used its fair share of artistic licence when it concluded, 'The great British Barbarians, jam-packed with internationals and raring to give a good account of themselves,

The second game was against the CIS at the Locomotiv Stadium in Moscow.
(© Barbarian Archive)

flooded the arrival terminal at Bulawayo Airport yesterday afternoon looking as much at ease on foreign soil as the United States Army might on an invasion of the Vatican.' The allusion was, to say the least, perplexing; what the late Brigadier Glyn Hughes would have made of it is beyond imagining. Bulawayo was, in fact, the midway point of a tour that had started with a comfortable win over the Goshawks, themselves an invitation club on the Barbarians model, in Mutare. The final score of 53–9 included 7 tries, the first by Neil Back, and 23 points for Aled Williams who, with his fellow Welshmen Roger Bidgood and Nigel Meek, was the only survivor from the Russian tour two years earlier. The other try-scorers, apart from Williams, were Rhodri Jones, Cameron Glasgow, Simon Davies, Steve Hackney and Meek. In Bulawayo the Barbarians played against Matabeleland, their country's provincial champions, who were expected to do well. The match was played at

The tour party prior to the first game against the Goshawks in Zimbabwe in 1994.
(© Kevin Stewart)

the Hartsfield Ground, a historic venue that had been the scene of several matches against international touring teams, including the All Blacks, Wallabies and Lions. The Matabeleland players were not short of guts and determination, especially in defence, but failed to gain enough possession to mount a serious challenge. They did manage to score two tries in a 23–35 defeat, but these were no match for the Baa-Baas' unconverted tries by the Swansea wing Davies, Dawson, Derek Eves and Steve Burnhill. Fly-half Colin Stephens kicked four penalty goals and his replacement, Williams, added another.

The key game of the tour was against the national team of Zimbabwe, which was in the final stages of preparation for a World Cup qualifying tournament. It was billed as an 'international rugby friendly' and attracted a large crowd to the Police Ground in Harare. Neil Edwards was captain of the Barbarians for the third consecutive match and, until the dying moments, an unbeaten tour record was

on the cards. The denouement in Harare was to prove eerily reminiscent of Moscow two years earlier.

Again the Barbarians were winning with the finishing line in sight and again they were to be overhauled at the last gasp. This time it was nothing so splendid as a length-of-the-field try but an opportunist drop goal by fly-half Marthinus Grobler to snatch the game at 23–21. Earlier, a try by Glasgow and two penalty goals and a conversion by Williams had helped the Barbarians to a 13–7 lead at the break. Another penalty by Williams and a try by Bidgood stretched the lead to 21–7, and there seemed no cause for alarm. To Zimbabwe's credit they finished strongly, sparked by a brilliant try by wing Victor Olonga. He had already scored after a fine team attack in the first half but his second effort was exceptional as he took a pass only a few metres from his own line and made such an explosive burst past the remnants of the startled Barbarian defence that it was reported he 'virtually walked to the try-line amid a carnival from the delighted crowd'. Grobler's conversion brought his side to within one point before he applied the finishing touch with his 35-metre drop goal. A final defeat again failed to dampen the Club's spirits, with Geoff Windsor-Lewis reporting:

> We achieved everything we set out for with three matches of good quality and we saw as much of Zimbabwe as was physically possible in the timescale. The tour was a great success and the players responded outstandingly to all the various demands. It was a happy tour, as well, and we had a great deal of fun and brought back many happy memories.

The trips to Russia and Zimbabwe had rekindled the touring habit and in 1996 the Barbarians set out on the longest journey of all when they went to Japan. The Great Hanshin Earthquake of January 1995 had particularly affected the city of Kobe and in its aftermath a charitable fund had been set up to assist with rebuilding and recovery. The invitation to the Club to travel courtesy of Japan Airlines and to play two fund-raising matches in Kyoto and Kobe was further recognition of the power of the Barbarians' unique brand, even in the professional age. As Micky Steele-Bodger explained, 'Charity-related games such as these were probably unique in Japan but the tour was important not only for the financial benefits to the charity, though they were not inconsiderable, but also as a goodwill gesture from the UK and beyond to Japan via rugby concerning this particular tragedy.' The Kansai Rugby Union of west Japan had organised the games and the tour. The first game, in Kyoto, was against a President's XV and the second,

Martin Haag prepares to pass to Rhodri Jones against Zimbabwe with Neil Back on hand to lend support. (© Kevin Stewart)

three days later, against the Kobe Steel club. The latter was a company club that had won seven consecutive national championships and had also pioneered the recruiting of foreign

Fly-half Aled Williams attacks the Zimbabwe defence at Harare. (© Kevin Stewart)

143

players to the country. One of the great characters of the Russian tour, Maru Hayashi, was by then back in his home country and working as forwards coach of the national team. From the moment the tour was announced it had attracted great interest in Japan and both games were scheduled for live television coverage. The quality of the 22 players selected served only to heighten the expectation. Andy Robinson was named as tour captain and with him were international players from all four home countries and the All Black Mike Brewer. A capacity crowd of 20,000 saw the first game at the Nishi Kyogoku Stadium in Kyoto, when 22 tries were scored. The President's XV included only two Japanese players, alongside a dozen New Zealanders and a Canadian, and led throughout a match played in great humidity. In the circumstances the tourists did remarkably well to stay in contention as it was less than 48 hours after they had stepped off their aircraft. The team's 10 tries included a hat-trick by the Cardiff number 8 Howard Stone, celebrating his belated Barbarian debut at the age of 35, while Austin Healey, playing on the wing, and lock Nigel Redman scored two each. Lee Jarvis also scored 19 points with 7 conversions and a try, but the honours went to the hosts, who finished as 76–66 winners.

After the free-running sport of the first game, the time spent in Kobe was a salutary experience. Even 18 months after the disaster the ravages of the earthquake were still evident, with bridges and flyovers still in a precarious state as city life gradually returned to normal. The relevance of the Barbarians' visit was underlined by the British Ambassador to Tokyo, Sir David Wright, in his message to the citizens of Kobe and to the team.

The two games in Japan in 1996 supported the rebuilding fund after the Hanshin Earthquake. (© Barbarian Archive)

He wrote:

> It is a great pleasure for me to welcome the Barbarians rugby team to Kobe . . . not just because they are one of the most famous rugby teams and not just because it is so unusual to see them in Japan. It is also because their visit marks a further stage in the remarkable recovery which Kobe has made from the terrible earthquake it suffered just over a year ago . . . The Barbarians are a welcome sight . . . and their visit is a sign of the deep and increasing links between Japan and the United Kingdom

which extend throughout society, from trade and industry to sport and the arts.

The game against Kobe Steel was played at the Universiade Stadium and was another high-scoring affair. The opposition was this time made up of Japanese players, though one of their number, the 1994 Cambridge Blue David Bickle, held the distinction of being the first Englishman to play international rugby for Japan. The star turn, however, was the right-wing Yamanaka, who scored five tries as his side went on to win 63–43. The Irish lock Gerry Halpin scored two of the Barbarians' seven tries, with Jon Sleightholme, Healey (this time at scrum-half), Jim Hay, Andy Gomersall and Jarvis, who also converted four, claiming the others. The team were obviously disappointed not to have recorded at least one victory on the tour, but there was satisfaction from the knowledge that the charity fund had reached a new figure of nearly £150,000.

In 1997 the Barbarians made their second visit to Italy. The first had been in 1985 to play the national team at the Stadio Flaminio in Rome. That had been a whistle-stop weekend visit and a successful one at that, with a 65-yard penalty goal by full-back Paul Thorburn setting the team off towards a memorable 23–15 win. By half-time the lead had increased to 19–4, as Thorburn converted tries by Keith Robertson and Rory Underwood, and Phil Davies also touched down. The evening heat took its toll after that, with only four more points for the Club when Richard Cardus scored the final try.

Twelve years later the trip involved two matches, one back in Rome and the second in the northern city of Brescia. The opposing teams in both matches were invitation clubs, Lupi and

CONI   FIR

ITALIA - BARBARIANS
Stadio Flaminio - ore 20,30
Roma, 26 maggio 1985

The first trip to Italy in 1985 obviously stimulated a sense of tradition in the hosts. (© Barbarian Archive)

Zebre, with the second expected to be the tougher assignment. The captaincy of the touring team was awarded to the Sale and New Zealand forward John Mitchell, but the game was effectively lost in the first half. By the interval the Barbarians trailed 5–31, their only score being a try by fly-half Simon Mannix. They fared little better in the second period, failing to score at all and losing the match 5–36. The trip to Brescia involved a coach journey of several hours, but the three days that followed were an opportunity to meet not only the officials of the Zebre club but also those of the

145

French Barbarians, who were paying a courtesy visit. Everyone again wanted to meet the Barbarians, with the mayor of Brescia hosting a civic reception on the morning of the match. As anticipated, the Zebre team was particularly strong, with 12 Italian internationals and the French back-rower Xavier Blond. Players such as Massimo Cuttitta, Alessandro Troncon and, especially, Diego Dominguez were to be in the vanguard of Italy's rise to Six Nations status in the 1990s and they provided the sternest test of the Barbarians at the Stadio Comunale in Brescia. Yet the visitors started particularly well, despite conceding the first try from a driving lineout. Jon Callard kicked a penalty goal and converted a captain's try by Mitchell, and when Mannix added the extra points to another try scored by the Blackheath number 8 Mike Harris, the lead had stretched to 17–7. A Dominguez penalty goal did little to dent the Barbarians' confidence and another try, scored by Scott Hastings and converted by Callard, sent them into the half-time break with a comfortable 14-point cushion. The restart signalled a flurry of scoring, with

Callard again converting a try by flanker Marcus White to cancel out seven points by Zebre. But in the final half-hour the only further points were from a try by Graham Dawe converted yet again by Callard, and they were more than cancelled out by four home tries, all converted by Dominguez. An injury-time penalty goal completed an unexpected turnaround and a 48–38 win for Zebre.

The Club's Latin connections were further strengthened when a three-match tour to South America was undertaken in 1998. This was as ambitious and ground-breaking as the earlier trips to Russia and Japan, with fixtures scheduled for Montevideo in Uruguay and Tucuman and Buenos Aires in Argentina. The opponents in each case were the South American Barbarians, whose president was the legendary Argentinian fly-half Hugo Porta. The 25 players in the party included 15 new Barbarians, a further indication that the committee was having to spread its net far and wide to select players not required for the ever-growing frequency of overseas tours by the

Club physiotherapist Steve Cannon is at the back left of this team photo taken during the trip to South America in 1998. (© Barbarian Archive)

home countries. Nevertheless, there was again a good cross-section of international and club players. Mike Brewer, who had been such a good tourist in Japan in 1996, was the player–coach, and he was joined by his fellow New Zealander the Cambridge Blue Steve Cottrell. Also included were three Fijians – Tanielu Qauqau, Kiliraki and Sailesi Nawarui – who had helped the Club win the Middlesex Sevens at Twickenham a few weeks earlier. In the opening game at the British Schools ground in Montevideo the opposition was an unknown quantity – and much the same could be said of the Barbarians' goal-kicking, as their five tries went unconverted before they went on to win the match 25–14. The games in Argentina were, as anticipated, much tougher. A close game in Tucuman was lost 33–44, an occasion of truly mixed emotions for the Northampton lock Jon Phillips. Having won his Club colours in Montevideo he marked this second game with a try but then broke his arm. His disappointment didn't end there, because later on in the same week he was due to be married. Fortunately, although his tour was over, the wedding went ahead. With the bridegroom already on his way home, the last few days of the tour were spent in Buenos Aires and among several pleasant excursions was a visit to the River Plate, where the Second World War battleship the *Graf Spee* had been scuttled. Unfortunately, in the final match, it was the Barbarians who almost sank without trace. The squad had suffered more than its fair share of injuries: a succession of pulled hamstrings as well as Phillips' misfortune, which, allied to the usual wear and tear of the touring experience, left everyone exhausted long before the end of a match played in stifling heat. Their South American counterparts converted all 11 of their tries for a resounding 77–31 victory. It was a far-

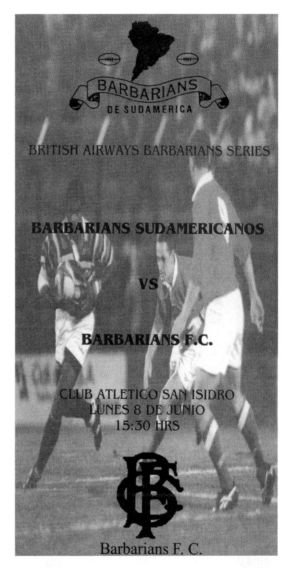

The last of three games against Barbarians Sudamericanos was played in Buenos Aires. (© Barbarian Archive)

from-ideal end to the tour but, again, there were consolations. Crowds of up to 10,000 had turned up at the grounds to watch the matches and there was enthusiasm from all age groups, including the youngsters who adapted the cut-off sleeves of Barbarians jerseys as impromptu

Another touring tradition is for everyone to wear a panama hat with the band of the Club's colours . . . well, Micky Steele-Bodger is an exception here.
(© Steele-Bodger Collection)

and apparently very fashionable headgear. The Club's cause is spread in many mysterious ways.

The Barbarians' connections with France have ensured that there have been several fixtures in recent years. The Racing Club fixture of 1908 was admittedly a distant memory by the time a second match was arranged 74 years later but a French connection has never been far away from the Club's activities. The early game in Paris, played at the Polo Ground in the Bois de Boulogne and watched by a crowd of over 3,000, had been won by 13 points to nil, but a second match scheduled for two years later had been cancelled because of flooding. In 1982 the situation was very different. Racing Club's centenary was celebrated in great style, with two star-studded XVs. The opposition fielded under the banner of 'Equipe Yves de Manoir' and were suitably captained by Jean-Pierre Rives, a leading light of the French Barbarians

who had also given great service to the Club in major games against the All Blacks and Lions and at Easter time in south Wales. The Club's team, in turn, was led by the All Black Graham Mourie, thus establishing a scenario with two great flankers and captains directly opposing each other. Rives' contribution to the game in general was something very close to the hearts of Micky Steele-Bodger and the committee. Asked to select a typical Barbarian, the president had no hesitation in nominating the Frenchman among his short list. He said, 'Jean-Pierre is the archetypal Barbarian. Quite apart from the excellence of his play there is also his piratical image with the flowing blond hair, his face usually covered in blood and indefatigably courageous. Off the field, too, he absolutely threw himself into the Barbarians way of doing things. In the evenings after a match he was marvellous company, playing the piano and drinking beer not wine – he never failed to remind me that "I quite like this beer!"'

Rives was at his best in the celebration game at Parc des Princes, watched by 15,000 fans. Serge Blanco, playing at centre, contributed two tries and the prolific Didier Camberabero another try plus ten points from the boot as the home side won 22–17. Mourie scored two of the Club's three tries, the other coming from scrum-half Ian George, with Gary Pearce converting one and kicking a penalty goal. The game had certainly been a success and perhaps indicated a visit to play in Paris was long overdue. The first French player to be selected for the Barbarians had been the international wing Michel Pomathios, reputed by Micky Steele-Bodger to be such a proficient wine-taster that he would confidently send back corked bottles of celebrated vintages at the very best restaurants and hotels, much to the chagrin of the waiters. Pomathios had been a big hit on the Easter tour of 1951 and, in the late 1960s, Claude Lacaze, Jean Gachassin, Jo Maso and André Campaes had been equally impressive. Pierre Villepreux and several others carried on the new tradition into the next decades as the Gallic approach to the game found a natural home with the Barbarians.

Back in France the French Barbarians were also making a name for themselves, warranting fixtures against the touring teams from the southern hemisphere rather like their forerunners on the English side of the Channel. The 50th anniversary of the liberation of Paris provided the ideal opportunity for a game between 'Barbarians Français' and 'Barbarians Britanniques' on 6 September 1994. The setting was the Stade Charlety in Paris and, as with the Racing Club fixture 12 years earlier, there was no shortage of headline grabbers on view. As well as a full quota of French stars, the host club also included the Wallabies David Campese and Nick Farr-Jones while, not to be outdone, the visitors included another eminent Australian, the lock John Eales, plus the gifted Springbok full-back Andre Joubert and, in the pack, a Canadian, Al Charron, and an American, Chris Lippert. Despite a day of heavy rain the game and the occasion lived up to expectations. Ten minutes before kick-off one of the teams involved in a preliminary match brought a new meaning to the term 'curtain-raiser' by stripping off and dashing en masse to the centre field. The large and enthusiastic crowd was already having its money's worth and the entertainment improved as the night wore on. Patrice Lagisquet, reliving old glories, glided in for a true winger's try in the corner and Campese was having the freedom of the park from full-back. The visitors were still catching their

In 1994 the Stade Charlety in Paris provided the backdrop for the match with the French Barbarians. (© Barbarian Archive)

breath, with four tries already on the board against them in the first half-hour. No sooner had Lagisquet departed the scene with a damaged hamstring than his replacement, Willie Jefferson, another American, had touched down twice and Denis Charvet added the fourth. The Barbarians finally broke their duck with a drop goal by Paul Hull and a try by Joubert. But they were swimming against the Parisian tide, their only other marker being a trademark length-of-the-field attack that Joubert again finished off. The Springbok also kicked a penalty goal and a conversion to complete his side's scoring in an 18–35 defeat. The French finished with a flourish with tries

by another legend, Philippe Sella, and the Paris University replacement wing Arthur Gomez. All-in-all it had been the exercise in *joie de vivre* that both groups of Barbarians had set out to deliver.

In the summer of 1997 a return visit was made to the Stade Charlety to play in the Air France Sevens, a weekend that doubled up as a convention for Barbarian clubs worldwide. Meanwhile, other European fixtures were appearing on the Club's calendar. With teams in France and Italy already established among the opposition, the next stop, in August 2000, was Hanover, for a match against the national team of Germany. This was another 100th birthday celebration and was won 47–19 in front of another new audience of around 5,000 fans. It was further proof that the new millennium would herald a series of new staging posts as the Barbarians travelled the world. The most recent of all was in June 2004, when the Club returned to Lisbon. A previous call had been made there for a sevens tournament in 1990. Now it was for a centenary match but also to acknowledge the burgeoning two-way links between the Barbarians and Portugal. A great figure in Portuguese rugby, Pedro Ribeiro was as delighted as anyone. He wrote:

> To end our season of centenary celebrations the Barbarian FC was invited to come to Lisboa to play Portugal. The match was played in a very good spirit, plenty of attacking rugby in the very long Barbarians tradition and a pleasure to watch. The Portuguese Rugby Union owes thanks to the Barbarian committee for the acceptance of this invitation and is very proud to be one of the growing number

of countries in the world that the Baa-Baas have visited and played.

Luis Pissarra had played for the Club against the Combined Services in November 2003. So too had full-back Goncalo Malheiro and prop Joaquim Ferreira. All had distinguished themselves in good company on a wet and miserable evening. They proved equally effective in opposition for their national team in the heat of high summer in Lisbon. The match was a joyous occasion played at the Estadio Universitario. The final score was 66–34 to the Barbarians – 100 points shared in recognition of a Portuguese centenary. Wherever the Club goes, something memorable, if not unique, is usually served up.

Rob Baxter of Exeter Chiefs captained the Barbarians against Portugal in 2004 and here he celebrates the winning of another trophy with the president. (© Gordon H. Brown)

VIII

THE PERFECT HOSTS

'We have started something which I hope will never finish . . . the Barbarians should be on the fixture list of every future touring side.'

– Arnold Tancred, Australian Manager, 1948

Long before 1948 the Barbarian Football Club had established for itself an enviable position in the world of rugby union. Its very uniqueness, whereby players could only be invited to play in the black-and-white jersey, was itself part of the mystique of the Club. Players who were invited readily admitted that to play for the Barbarians was a step up from their own local clubs, however famous, and only a notch below a full international cap. Indeed, for the players who hadn't yet achieved their international pinnacles, it was regarded as a stepping stone – and the final one – to the big stages at Twickenham, Cardiff Arms Park, Murrayfield or Lansdowne Road. The Club's fixture list, rarely more than half-a-dozen matches in any one season, was a thing of beauty, very much a case of quality rather than quantity. The big English club of Leicester, the tradition of the Mobbs Memorial Match against the East Midlands, and the Welsh foursome at Easter could hardly be bettered for an institution that realised that, like all the great performers in other walks of life, you should leave the audiences and the fans at the end craving for more of the same. The limited appearances every year achieved that and were another reason for the blessed few to always accept the

invitation to play if and when it came. If there was one piece of the jigsaw missing for a player, it was the mystique of playing a match against such gifted teams.

For most of the twentieth century, that criterion certainly applied to the three major rugby-playing countries in the southern hemisphere. Like the Barbarians, the All Blacks, Springboks and Wallabies were rarely seen in Britain and when they were it was a moment for every rugby aficionado to treasure. Each of them in rotation only came to Europe every three or four years and two world wars had disrupted even that strict ration. When they did, the tours were invariably long, of at least four months and thirty matches and encompassed five international fixtures, the clubs of Wales, the counties and universities of England, the districts of Scotland and the provinces of Ireland. The Barbarians were not part of the established structure – but in 1948 that scenario changed.

The tour of the Australian Wallabies that began in Cornwall in September 1947 was typically long. They were the first international touring team to play in Britain since the All Blacks of 1935–36. Ahead of them lay twenty-nine matches in the British Isles and five in France, followed by a long sea journey home the following February. But they were part of an era when players and spectators wanted more rather than less top-class sport. The long years of war had whetted appetites. In the case of the Australians it also nurtured a commendable wish to play even more rugby on their way home via North America. Midway through the tour it was decided that an extra game could be played at Cardiff Arms Park, a venue where a capacity crowd was guaranteed, and that the proceeds would cover any financial shortfall of the main tour and the cost of the subsequent six matches in Canada and California. Representatives of the Four Home Unions Tours Committee and the Australian Rugby Union met on 22 November 1947 on the weekend of the Wallabies international against Scotland and the project received their full backing. The opposing team would be the Barbarians. Fittingly, Micky Steele-Bodger was invited to play in the match and, looking back over half a century, he has no doubt about its significance. He said, 'The Club has had many great days but this was probably the greatest. It stands out because by playing the Wallabies we became a world side. By that I mean that suddenly we were known even more than before outside the confines of British rugby. We, in turn, had a world perspective. If the match had been a flop, the prospect of similar fixtures in the future was finished.'

It was far from being a flop – and the fixture was the first of 23 similar occasions between then and 2004. As if that was not enough, Barbarians v. Wallabies at Cardiff Arms Park on Saturday, 31 January 1948 has gone down in the game's folklore as one of the defining moments in the move towards 15-man, fluent rugby.

For some observers the prospects ahead of the game were not entirely auspicious. There were concerns about its unofficial billing as 'the match of the century'. The Club's committee was equally uncomfortable about such hyperbole. For them it was a club match, not an international, but one that should be worthy of an important development in its history. It later emerged, too, that among the doubters were members of the 1938 British Isles team that had toured South Africa and who were holding a reunion to coincide with the match. 'They were staying at the Royal Hotel with us,' said Steele-Bodger, 'and some of them were of the opinion that we had a scruffy pack and that the whole thing was being blown up out of all proportion.' Interestingly, the Club's honorary secretary, Jack Haigh Smith, had been assistant manager of the 1938 Lions and the scrum-half, Haydn Tanner, was about to captain the Barbarians in the 1948 game. The selection of the team inevitably attracted a lot of interest, though at least one critic wondered whether it was 'a shade too full of players past their best'. That, uncharacteristically, came from O.L. Owen in *The Times* (seven of the selected team were indeed well past their

thirtieth birthdays) but his general feeling was far more positive. On the morning of the match he wrote:

> For some years those who had seen in the Barbarian idea much that was best in British rugby as a whole have hankered after a fixture between them and a touring side from one of the Dominions. It has now come about more by chance than anything else and it is enough to welcome it as the large Cardiff crowd are certain to enjoy and cheer it.

That large crowd numbered 45,000, then the official capacity after the ravages of war had

The team that beat Australia in the first-ever match against one of the Big Three from the southern hemisphere in 1948 – back row: R.F. Trott, K.D. Mullen, I.C. Henderson, M.F. Turner, W.I.D. Elliot, S.V. Perry, W.E. Tamplin, H. Walker, C.B. Holmes; middle row: J. Mycock, H. Tanner (captain), H.A. Haigh Smith (hon. sec.), E. de Lissa (president), H.L. Glyn Hughes (hon. treasurer), T.A. Kemp, B.L. Williams; on ground: W.B. Cleaver, M.R. Steele-Bodger.
(© Barbarian Archive)

left their mark on the old ground, and all the tickets had been sold several days beforehand. The committee had selected the team with impressive astuteness. The five Welshmen were all members of the Cardiff club, then enjoying its most successful season in over 40 years. Tanner was captain of Cardiff, Wales and now the Barbarians, though injury had forced him to miss the international match against Australia a month earlier. Three of his Barbarian teammates – Bleddyn Williams, Billy Cleaver and Bill Tamplin – had already shared in two famous victories for club and country over the tourists at the Arms Park. The fifth Cardiff selection was the full-back Frank Trott. The Barbarians also selected seven Englishmen in their side: Harry Walker at prop; Joe Mycock in the second row; Steele-Bodger and his fellow Cambridge Blue Sam Perry in the back row; while behind the scrum Tommy Kemp partnered Tanner at half-back and the wings were Martin Turner and Cyril Holmes. The two Scots in the pack were prop Ian Henderson and wing-forward Doug Elliot, and Ireland was represented by the future captain of the 1950 Lions, Karl Mullen. Turner was the only uncapped member of the side, Tamplin the only new Barbarian, and Mullen at 21 and Steele-Bodger at 22 its youngest members. It was an interesting combination.

The Wallabies' reputation over the previous months, when they had beaten Scotland, Ireland and England, was built on opportunist attacking and resolute defence. Though they had lost to Wales and France they had not conceded a try in any of the five international matches. They were a true international team that would test the Barbarians to the limit. Tanner's team proved more than equal to the task. On a fine winter's day they had the wind

at their backs in the first half and opened the scoring after 15 minutes. A writer of fiction could not have come up with a better choice of the first Barbarian to score a try in the saga of matches against touring teams: Micky Steele-Bodger. A break by Tanner on the blind side of a scrum set up a link with Holmes, and it was the wing's kick ahead that was pounced on by the wing-forward for an unconverted try. The tone had already been set for an all-action game and it was soon realised that an exceptional match was unfolding. An important factor was the pre-match gentleman's agreement that the wing-forwards would stay down until the ball was out of the scrums, thus giving the half-backs more room to mount attacks. Not that that prevented Steele-Bodger and his fellows from playing a full part in the proceedings. Williams, Turner, Kemp, Elliot and Perry all went close to adding to the Barbarians' try tally and Max Howell (part of the Canadian opposition nine years later), Cyril Burke and John MacBride were equally dangerous for the Wallabies. Yet the only other score before half-time was a penalty goal for the visitors that Arthur Tonkin kicked into the teeth of the wind and with the aid of the crossbar. The Barbarians almost regained the lead when, as *The Observer* reported, 'There was the run of the match, 80 yards by Bleddyn Williams, nearly 50 yards of sidestep and speed. Perry took his pass and crossed the line but knocked into the corner-flag and the cheers died in disappointment.'

The half-time score of 3–all barely reflected the quality and excitement of what had gone before, but the drama was only just beginning. In the opening ten minutes of the second half the Wallabies almost scored on three occasions: from a brilliant break by full-back Brian Piper;

then a hooked attempt at a penalty goal by Tonkin; and finally a foot rush by Nick Shehadie. The Barbarians were far more clinical, with Williams again in the thick of the action. From another scything break, Tamplin, Perry (again) and Mycock were on hand before Henderson provided the final pass to Holmes. Twelve years earlier the Manchester wing had sprinted for Great Britain at the 1936 Olympics in Berlin. At Cardiff Arms Park no Australian could get near him as he raced over for his team's second try.

In a game of many stars Tanner's play was proving exceptional. In defence he thwarted the Wallabies' vice-captain, Colin Windon, as he closed in on the try-line. Moments later, in attack, he started and finished his team's third and decisive try. The ball was spun wide again from a scrum, with Kemp and Cleaver moving the ball to Turner, and it was the captain who appeared outside the far wing for the scoring pass and the touchdown at the corner. The pace of the game was taking its toll, with several walking wounded on both sides. For a while Cleaver was receiving treatment on the touch-line and Turner moved into centre and Steele-Bodger out to the wing. But the Baa-Baas were back to their full complement when their opponents claimed the try they richly deserved. With about six minutes left a scrum in midfield provided the perfect launch pad for a back movement in which MacBride provided the cutting edge and Edmund Broad and the captain Trevor Allan the vital links before Tonkin scored wide out on the right. The game ended with the Wallabies attacking and the Barbarians defending their 9–6 lead. The capacity crowd burst out into spontaneous applause for both sides. In his capacity as rugby correspondent for the *Scottish Sunday Express* Jock Wemyss wrote:

Scrum-half Haydn Tanner (left) was the outstanding figure in what was considered to be a great match in 1948. (© Barbarian Archive)

> It was one of the finest matches ever seen and . . . living up to their high reputation for playing adventurous, carefree rugby the Barbarians won their greatest victory in a thrilling and exciting game before a capacity crowd at the famous Cardiff Arms Park.

Other observers concurred. In the *Western Mail* J.B.G. Thomas concluded:

> It was a classic encounter that will long be remembered. No tour in the past had ended on such a joyous note and Welsh rugby followers feel proud that Cardiff Arms Park, the scene of so many historic encounters, was the honoured ground for such a great occasion. Throughout the full 80 minutes of fast-moving play there was a dominating spirit of true sportsmanship and the quality of the

football could not have been bettered had every move been planned beforehand.

At least three salient points are touched upon in this report. Firstly, the importance of concluding a major tour with a high-profile fixture other than a full-scale international and, as Thomas astutely says, on a 'joyous note'. Secondly, there was the choice of Cardiff Arms Park as the venue. At the time, apart from the obvious advantages of a reliable fan base, it had been selected because the Cardiff club secretary, Arthur Cornish, had been on hand when the powers-that-be met in Edinburgh to make their final decision. If not difficult, it had nevertheless been an inspired choice and would remain automatically so for the next 20 years of matches in the series. Finally, and almost intangibly, there was the element of unpredictability about the play and generosity of spirit by everyone involved. Barbarian rugby was indeed different and would remain the attraction as successive touring teams from the other side of the world returned to share in a new tradition that quickly established itself in the rugby scheme of things.

Other traditions also emerged. The post-match dinners attended by a galaxy of the sport's stars from past and present would always be a natural extension to the rugby earlier in the day and, during them, presentations would be made. In the case of the 1948 match the Australian captain Bill McLean, who had missed most of the tour through injury, was made an honorary member of the Barbarian Football Club – a rare accolade that had previously been given to E. Gwyn Nicholls, the Welshman who led his country to victory over New Zealand in 1905 and then

became a distinguished administrator, and Jack Manchester, the captain of the 1935–36 All Blacks. McLean, who had bravely seen out the tour though able to play in only six of the thirty-four matches, accepted his membership with humility, adding, 'It is an honour that rugby men all over the world try to achieve and I am very proud of it.' Underlining everything was the conclusion of the Wallabies' manager, Arnold Tancred, when he said, 'Through the good offices of the tour committee and the Cardiff club, who arranged this match, we have started something which I hope will never finish. The Barbarians should be on the fixture list of every future touring side. Again we have finished the tour with good luck and enthusiasm and today's match has done a great deal of good for the game.'

Thus, when the next major tour, that by the Springboks in 1951–52, was planned there was never any doubt that a final curtain call against the Barbarians at Cardiff would be an automatic inclusion. Resisting all attempts to select a British representative side, a pressure that increased in the wake of the successful tour by a South African team that ranked with the finest to tour Britain, the committee reiterated that the Barbarians were a club who were privileged to stage another end-of-tour fixture. Not for the last time were there some voices in the opposition camp that doubted the Club's intentions. The South African journalist R.K. Stent was one of them, noting in his tour book *The Fourth Springboks*:

> There was much insistence before the game that the opponents were in no way representative of Britain but merely a club side. Nevertheless, it was quite apparent that, within the framework of

BARBARIANS		AUSTRALIA	
Black and White Hoops, Black Shorts		Light Green, White Shorts	

Full Back	**FRANK TROTT** (16) Cardiff and Wales	(1) **B. J. PIPER** Randwick and N.S.W. **Full Back**	
Left Wing	**C. B. HOLMES** (11) Manchester & England	(4) **A. E. J. TONKIN** Gordon and N.S.W. **Right Wing**	
Left Centre	**W. B. CLEAVER** (12) Cardiff and Wales	(6) **T. ALLAN, Capt.** Gordon & N.S.W. **Outside Centre**	
Right Centre	**BLEDDYN WILLIAMS** (14) Cardiff and Wales	(7) **M. J. HOWELL** Randwick & N.S.W. **Inside Centre**	
Right Wing	**M. F. TURNER** (15) Blackheath	(8) **J. W. T. MacBRIDE** Eastern Sub. & N.S.W. **Left Wing**	
Outside Half	**T. A. KEMP** (10) Richmond & England	(12) **E. G. BROAD** Sydney Un. & N.S.W. **Five-eighth**	
Inside Half	**HAYDN TANNER, Capt** (9) Cardiff and Wales	(13) **C. T. BURKE** Newcastle & N.S.W. **Scrum Half**	
	Forwards—	Forwards—	
	H. WALKER (8) Coventry and England	(20) **C. J. WINDON, Vice-Capt.** Randwick and New South Wales	
	C. MULLEN (7) Old Belvedere and Ireland	(16) **A. J. BUCHAN** Randwick and New South Wales	
	I. C. HENDERSON (6) Edinburgh Acads. and Scotland	(29) **D. H. KELLER** Drummond and New South Wales	
	J. MYCOCK (5) Sale and England	(18) **G. M. COOKE** Brisbane and Queensland	
	W. E. TAMPLIN (4) Cardiff and Wales	(22) **P. A. HARDCASTLE** Eastern Suburbs and N.S.W.	
	W. I. D. ELLIOTT (3) Edinburgh Acads. and Scotland	24 **N. SHEHADIE** Randwick and New South Wales	
	S. V. PERRY (2) Cambridge Univ. and England	(26) **W. L. DAWSON** Manly and New South Wales	
	M. R. STEELE-BODGER (1) Edinburgh Univ. and England	(27) **E. TWEEDALE** Paramatta and New South Wales	

Referee—Mr. A. S. BEAN (Sunderland)

Touch Judges		
BARBARIANS— Mr. H. A. HAIGH-SMITH (Sec., Barbarians R.F.C.)		AUSTRALIA— Mr. J. O. STENMARK

A memento of the after-match camaraderie when both sides and the referee signed this souvenir team-card.
(© Barbarian Archive)

their rules and regulations, the Baa-Baas chose the best available talent from the four Home Unions.

This wasn't strictly true. As Stent conceded, France played Ireland on the same day and that immediately made the likes of Jack Kyle, Karl Mullen, Noel Henderson – all Lions in New Zealand two years before – together with the fearsome back row of Bill McKay, Jim McCarthy and Des O'Brien, unavailable for the Barbarians. There were only two survivors from the 1948 game against the Wallabies – Bleddyn Williams, who would be vice-captain, and Doug Elliot at wing-forward, the only Scotsman in the team. Despite the international in Paris, Ireland was represented by Jimmy Nelson, who was also appointed captain. Micky Steele-Bodger's playing career had by then been cut short by his cruel knee injury, but the wing-forward position was now filled by another great Barbarian committeeman and

officer of the future, Vic Roberts. Thirteen of the side were from England or Wales, including the entire back division. Another Williams, Gerwyn from Llanelli, was at full-back. With Bleddyn Williams at centre was Lewis Cannell of St Mary's Hospital, and Ted Woodward of Wasps and another Olympic sprinter, Newport's Ken Jones, were the two wings. The Cardiff pair of Cliff Morgan and Rex Willis were the half-back combination. In the pack Rees Stephens joined Elliot and Roberts in the back row, another Neath man, Roy John, packed down with Nelson at lock and two

By the time of the match against South Africa in 1952, Micky Steele-Bodger had joined the committee and was also touch judge. Back row: Windsor H. Lewis, H. Waddell, B. Mullan; standing: W.E. Crawford, H.L. Glyn Hughes, W.I.D. Elliot, J. MacG.K. Kendall-Carpenter, J.R.G. Stephens, E.R. John, J.E. Woodward, R.V. Stirling, M.R. Steele-Bodger, H.A. Haigh Smith; sitting: G. Williams, B.L. Williams, J.E. Nelson (captain), D.M. Davies, K.J. Jones; on ground: L.B. Cannell, C.I. Morgan, W.R. Willis, V.G. Roberts.
(© Barbarian Archive)

Englishmen, Bob Stirling and John Kendall-Carpenter, propped the Welsh hooker Dai Davies.

Strictly speaking the Club had played a South African representative side before. On 20 November 1915 a match at Richmond Athletic Ground was variously reported as 'British Services (Barbarians) v. South African Services' or 'Barbarians v. South African Contingent', or, simply, 'Barbarians v. South Africans'. The handwritten record book compiled by Emile de Lissa lists it as the latter, though, confusingly, his published work in 1933, *Barbarian Records*, refers to South African Services. A pedantic point, perhaps, but what is beyond question is that the Barbarians, captained by the England international 'Dreadnought' Harrison, played a team of fifteen South Africans, won the encounter by nine points to three, and the proceeds of the match went towards the war effort, specifically the Comforts for Colonial Troops Fund.

On 26 January 1952 at Cardiff Arms Park the context of the game was more familiar: a very successful Springbok side that had been beaten only once in twenty-six matches on tour, and with another four victories in France to follow after the Barbarians match. Another capacity Arms Park crowd, now set at 55,000, eagerly anticipated a thrilling game and a Barbarians victory. They were to be disappointed on both counts. For half an hour Nelson's men had kept the Springbok tide at bay and had even posted the first score. The nature of it had given hope of more spectacular rugby to follow. Cliff Morgan, who had been well marshalled in two earlier games for Cardiff and Wales against the tourists, made a much more positive start in this game and it was his interpassing with Bleddyn Williams, aided by the centre's defence-splitting sidestep, that opened up the gaps for Doug Elliot to have a clear run in and dive for a try near the posts. Barely 23 minutes were on the clock but it was to be the Club's only score. Without a recognised goal-kicker the duty was shared around three players. Elliot and Stephens had already missed with penalty attempts and Woodward fared no better with the conversion attempt. It was a shortcoming that they would pay for, and the Springboks soon equalised while Nelson was off the field receiving treatment. Taking full advantage of another failed attempt at a penalty goal by Stephens, they ran the ball back out of defence to set up an attacking position on the Barbarians' 25. From there a hoisted kick by the right-wing Buks Marais was collected in full stride on the far touch-line by Chum Ochse, who touched down for the equalising try.

The score remained at 3–all until the interval but after that it became one-way traffic after a tactical switch by the Springboks. Without their Test match fly-half Hannes Brewis they had started the game with Paul Johnstone, a wing, in the pivot position. Throughout the first 40 minutes the South African back line had stuttered and almost stalled. There was little improvement in the opening play of the second half. If the Springboks were to capitalise on their forwards' supremacy, it was time for remedial measures. The acting captain Hennie Muller first switched Johnstone with another wing, Ochse. That proved no more fruitful. With half an hour left to play a second experiment was tried. This time Johnstone went to full-back and Jakkals Keevy moved up. It was to prove an inspired choice. As well as bringing his centres into play with a smoothness that had previously been lacking,

he kicked two medium-range penalty goals for a 9–3 lead. Despite the best efforts of the Barbarians pack, in which Kendall-Carpenter was particularly prominent, the game was drifting away. Throughout the tour many Springbok attacks had been spearheaded by their forwards, who ran and passed with a proficiency rarely seen before. Here it was the giant lock Salty du Rand who did the damage, bursting through the heart of the opposition before linking with Muller, and then the backs carried on the move. Ochse injected pace, centre Ryk van Schoor the deft final short pass, and another tearaway forward, Basie van Wyk, was bursting over for the decisive try. Keevy's conversion and another penalty goal from 40 yards by Johnstone stretched the winning margin out to 17–3.

The defeat was a timely reminder to the Barbarians' many admirers, rather than the committee and players, that such games against major touring teams would never be easy, even more so as the years went by and scratch sides would need all the brilliance of individuals and sometimes external factors to repeat the success of 1948. The Springboks had proved ruthlessly efficient in victory but it remained a game played in the best spirit. As with the Wallabies four years earlier, the South African captain Basil Kenyon was duly made an honorary member of the Club.

Having tasted Australian and South African rugby at its best, the Barbarians now looked forward to the third challenge that would complete a full hand of super-power opposition. In 1953–54 the All Blacks toured Europe and there was an interesting sub-plot when they arrived at Cardiff Arms Park for their final game against the Barbarians. They had already played there twice and lost both times. The Barbarians,

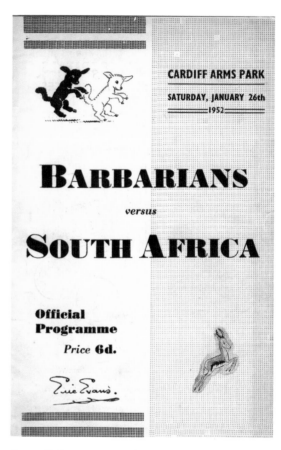

The programmes for the first matches against the Wallabies, Springboks and All Blacks.
By 1954 the glossy magazine-style issue was being produced.
(© Barbarian Archive)

with four of the triumphant Cardiff team in their ranks, plus another three who had helped Wales to victory, hoped to complete an unwanted hat-trick of defeats for the New Zealanders. This time the match did not clash with an international fixture but there was no Scottish player in the selected side and only one Irishman, the prop John Smith. England supplied seven, including four players from Northampton. Three of them were in the pack – Ron Jacobs at prop, the uncapped Dick Hawkes in the second row and Don White at wing-forward. All of them had performed outstandingly for several seasons in the East Midlands teams in the Mobbs Memorial matches. The fourth Northampton Saint was Jeff Butterfield in the centre, where he partnered Phil Davies of the Harlequins. Completing the England contingent were Ian King at full-back and Eric Evans. Cardiff's four representatives included Willis and Morgan, again at half-back, Gareth Griffiths on the wing and Sid Judd, who had scored tries for both club and country against the tourists, at number 8. The other three Welshmen were Ken Jones on the right wing and Rees Stephens and Clem Thomas in the

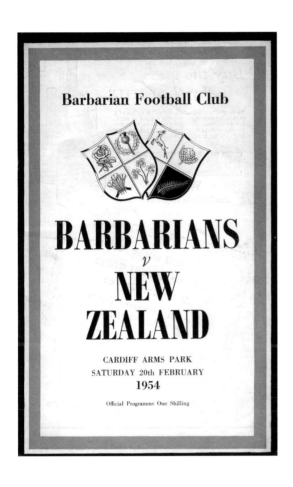

the game would go some way towards rivalling the pioneering match of 1948 in its quality and spectacle. If anything, it raised the reputation of the Club and the fixture even higher. There was no glorious victory but the ebb and flow of the play satisfied everyone. Reflecting on what had been seen, the rugby correspondent of *The Guardian* wrote:

> Every rugby god must have smiled on South Wales at three o'clock on Saturday. A dismal forecast of rain was disproved and the ground, waterlogged the previous day, had recovered splendidly under a brilliant sun. The scene was set for great football, but only the actors could make it so. They did. The first half of a rich, unfolding afternoon produced some of the best football that has ever been seen in Cardiff and that is saying much.

Shades of 1948, indeed. The Barbarians cast list undoubtedly contained its fair share of star performers. They were matched by the All Blacks, from Bob Scott at full-back, through the try-scoring wing Ron Jarden to several world-class forwards including the mighty Kevin Skinner at prop, Tiny White behind him and, in the back row, the outstanding captain Bob Stuart. All the ingredients for a memorable match were in place and so it proved to be. The kick-off was preceded by the ceremonial haka and the final whistle was immediately followed by another Maori tradition, the singing of 'Now is the Hour'. On the pitch 30 players and the referee linked arms and sang; on the terraces and in the stands all of the record 60,000 crowd stayed in place and joined in. The 80 minutes of rugby sandwiched between haka

pack. The choice of Willis as captain was particularly noteworthy. Earlier in the tour, after being part of the history-making Cardiff and Wales teams, he had reportedly told the All Blacks players and press corps, 'I won't see you fellows again because Cardiff will be playing in Dublin when you meet the Baa-Baas.' When it was suggested that, surely, he and Cliff Morgan would be together again for the end-of-tour match, he replied, 'I don't think so, but I hope so. God, I'd love to play for the Baa-Baas.' His wish had been granted.

Other hopes also bore fruition, not least that

The Club's first match against the All Blacks was preceded by a unique joint-team photograph. Seated either side of Barbarian captain Rex Willis (with the ball) are Bob Scott (on the left) and All Blacks captain Bob Stuart. The Barbarians in the picture are: back row: W.P.C. Davies, C.R. Jacobs, R.C. Hawkes, J.H. Smith, S. Judd, E. Evans, M.R. Steele- Bodger (touch judge); seated: R.C.C. Thomas, J.R.G. Stephens, W.R. Willis, I. King, K.J. Jones; in front: D.F. White, J. Butterfield, G.M. Griffiths, C.I. Morgan.
(© Barbarian Archive)

and hymn had earned the appreciation of everyone in attendance.

The Barbarians had again started well, with individual forays by Morgan particularly testing the All Blacks' defence. Then it was the turn of the visitors' superior teamwork to establish prolonged periods of territorial advantage, but the scoreboard remained blank for over half an hour. Scott was at his impish best, readily joining in attacks as few players in his position had rarely ventured in the history of the game. When all else failed, he was always prepared to chance his arm with a snap drop goal. One such effort from halfway fell inches short and, ironically, it was a stumble by him that paved the way for the Barbarians' opening try of the game. It would be wrong to say that Scott was responsible for the opposition's score because when Gareth Griffiths scooped up the loose ball bouncing away from the helpless full-back there

was still no real danger to the All Blacks' line. The Cardiff wing had other ideas. Hemmed in near the left touch-line he sidestepped twice at great pace and left four defenders in his wake on the way to a try converted by King. A five-point lead was all the Baa-Baas could have hoped for given the growing intensity of the All Blacks' play. Shortly before half-time, however, Scott made up for his earlier error. With White ruling the lineouts the Baa-Baas were understandably reluctant to put the ball out of play unless as a last resort. That could be one explanation for a wayward punt into midfield by Rees Stephens when a kick to touch was the more obvious option. Scott gratefully caught the high ball and unhurriedly and unfussily thumped over a drop goal from all of 40 yards. Five points to three ahead at the break the Barbarians could not have foreseen the black tide that would dominate them in the second 40 minutes. Seven minutes into the half the Maori scrum-half Keith Davis capped a brilliant individual performance by scoring a try under the nose of Willis. Jarden converted and the tourists were on their way. Soon, attacks were being mounted from every position. It was 15-man rugby at its best. Scott essayed another outrageous drop-goal attempt from his own half and it rebounded high off an upright. Undeterred, he joined in another back-line attack to create the extra man and, after a dazzling run, sent Jarden over for a try that the wing converted himself. The final 15 minutes must have seemed like an eternity to the Baa-Baas as the All Blacks dominated possession. The other wing, Maurice Dixon, scored an interception try and at the very end the game's outstanding forward, Tiny White, claimed the final touchdown of the match. It was a precursor of what would happen ten years later when Wilson Whineray and his All Blacks next played the Barbarians at the Arms Park. The 1954 match had ended 19–5 in favour of the All Blacks, and Bob Scott, as well as his captain, Bob Stuart, was carried off on the shoulders of the Barbarians.

The Club had far from disgraced themselves but already in only their third game against a top international side there was the evidence of how such fixtures would unfold over the years. Periodically – and gloriously – the Baa-Baas' improvisation and individual genius would unsettle and overcome the finely tuned machines that came from the southern hemisphere. More often than not we should expect the efficiency and teamwork of the visitors to hold the upper hand. There would always be much to admire in the latter, sometimes a brilliance all of its own, but on the days when the 15 individuals prevailed it was a time for everyone to give thanks for the

Rex Willis had wondered whether he would be selected for the game. He needn't have worried because he was captain and gave an impressive performance at scrum-half. Other Barbarians in the picture (left to right) are Rees Stephens, Sid Judd, Ron Jacobs and John Smith. (© Barbarian Archive)

Barbarians way of doing things. Yet, even in 1954, it would have taken a rugby prophet to foresee just how good the whole experience would become.

The cycle of incoming tours to Europe continued in 1957–58 with the return of the Wallabies. The three-to-four-year gaps between the visits served only to increase home appetites for seeing the visitors, even when a particular team might be relatively unsuccessful. That was the case with this particular vintage of Wallabies. Their results were moderate, including defeats in all five international matches, but the pulling power of the Barbarians and the growing reputation of their games against overseas visitors was enough to fill Cardiff Arms Park again on 22 February 1958. The Wallabies had saved their best until the last game of the British

leg of their 36-match tour and contributed fully to a thrilling encounter.

By now no one seriously questioned the committee's reasoning in its team selections. Players such as Ron Jacobs and Cliff Morgan were regarded as automatic choices both for their ability and for their identification with the Club's ethos. Others, such as Tony O'Reilly and Andy Mulligan, were understandably becoming particular favourites with the alickadoos. The new generation also included the likes of Arthur Smith, Ronnie Dawson, David Marques and Adam Robson: all 'natural' Barbarians and all included in the team. What was different in 1958 and was to prove a popular innovation was the selection of a senior player from the Wallabies squad to play against his own men. In this instance there was an obvious candidate: Nick Shehadie, later Sir Nicholas Shehadie, the sole survivor of the 1947–48 Wallabies and a world-class prop highly regarded for his sportsmanship wherever he played. So it was that he packed down in the Barbarians' front row alongside Dawson and Jacobs. Behind them, at lock, Marques was joined by Roddie Evans and in the back row Robson formed a mobile unit with John Faull and Peter Robbins. It was a skilful pack. Morgan and Mulligan were natural soulmates at half-back, both gifted footballers but also young men of the world who realised there was more to life than rugby. When they played it, though, everyone sat up and watched. Morgan, in his third game for the Barbarians against a touring side and his last season of playing, was the automatic choice as captain. O'Reilly and Smith were world-class wings. Inside them at centre was England's Malcolm Phillips, like O'Reilly only 21 years old, and Gordon Wells of Wales. At full-back

was Scotland's Robin Chisholm. It was another good side, but one that could not be regarded, Shehadie apart, as a Lions team in disguise.

Naturally, both sides entered into the spirit of the occasion with a tacit agreement that open rugby was what the players and the spectators – there was another 50,000 crowd – wanted. Unfavourable ground conditions on the day failed to deter them. *The Times* captured the mood perfectly (and rather idiosyncratically):

> Conditions were all against this [open] type of game: a grey, weepy sky, a soapy ball and a surface that put a frightful tax on quick turning. Yet there was nothing lachrymose about the play, for the conditions were overcome on both sides and a generous crowd was impartially uproarious in its approval. Some of the handling, indeed, and especially by the Barbarians, verged on prestidigitation, and to see defence turned instantly into attack in which the direction was switched half-a-dozen times in one movement, with the ball flung in all directions by forwards and backs alike, led almost to dizziness. Certainly there was no tense restricting background to the match, but here was hard, clean, carefree rugby at its best.

Newspaper readers in the 1950s presumably knew at a glance that 'prestidigitation' was (of course) conjuring. Even those with a more limited vocabulary on the terraces saw with their own eyes the full gamut of the tricks of the fly-half's trade again on display from Cliff Morgan. In his final months as a player the Barbarians brought out the best in him, both three months later on tour in South Africa and here on his old stamping ground at the Arms Park. Against the Wallabies, one of his breaks, reported Vivian Jenkins in the *Sunday Times*, 'left a vapour trail'. A good description but trumped again by *The Times* correspondent in full flow:

> It was just the sort of game in which Morgan delights, cutting loose in incalculable sallies and giving full rein to his enterprisingly unorthodox outlook. As ever, he would often start by running backwards, but he is a master of *reculer pour mieux sauter*.

Or, as some of us would say, take one step back and two steps forward. (They really were an educated readership in those days.) Morgan and his brilliant outside backs certainly spent most of the afternoon on the front foot, and no one more so than O'Reilly, who went looking for work when the ball failed to reach him out on the wing. The forwards were also enjoying the fluidity of the play, with wing-forward Peter Robbins particularly outstanding as he snapped up loose balls, pounced with intuitive interceptions and generally caused mayhem among the opposing backs. It was by no means one-way traffic, and the Wallabies had attacking threats of their own from left-wing Ken Donald, who was a handful for Arthur Smith throughout the 80 minutes, and the uncapped fly-half Ron Harvey, who had been drafted in at the eleventh hour and put down his marker for future Test selection.

The game was testimony to the fact that, rather like in 1948, there doesn't have to be a bucketful of points scored for the entertainment value to be high. For the first 20 minutes the play ebbed and flowed, with both sides not quite able to finish off promising attacks. O'Reilly, Smith and Robbins all had their opportunities in the Australians' 25 and 19-year-old Terry Curley, another of the new breed of attacking full-backs, was equally threatening for the Wallabies. It was the tourists who indeed scored first after fine work by Harvey and Donald and then Rod Phelps and Tony Miller before second-rower Dave Emanuel reached Donald's kick-ahead first for the touchdown. The score only served to spark even more unorthodoxy by the Baa-Baas, with passes being thrown high and low, short and long, and attacks mounted from all areas of the field. It was breathless stuff and gained its due reward on the verge of half-time. Robbins again harried the Wallabies' half-backs and the entire pack seemed to be part of a foot rush with Robson, Jacobs and Marques in the vanguard while Roddie Evans claimed the try. With neither side able to convert, the half-time score of 3–all was the ideal platform for more high-quality play in the second half.

The Wallabies might have taken the lead again but Jim Lenehan, a top-class full-back in later years but in this match playing at centre, ignored an overlap outside him and went for an attempted drop goal. Not only was it charged down by Malcolm Phillips in front of his own posts, but the ball was hacked upfield with O'Reilly leading the way, only to stumble as he aimed to gather and complete an audacious break out. There was no reprieve for the Wallabies, however, as Phillips was on hand to claim the unconverted try. The Barbarians' third try again had its roots in a counter-attack out of defence, this time sparked by Morgan with O'Reilly again on hand to put in a high kick ahead and then dispossess Curley as he caught the ball. Showing great anticipation, hooker Ronnie Dawson appeared as if from

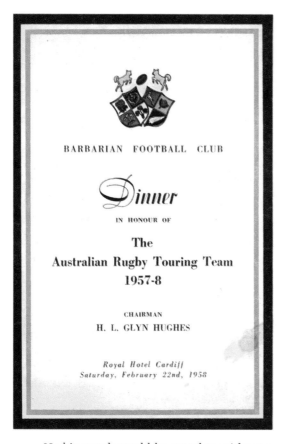

BARBARIAN FOOTBALL CLUB

Dinner

IN HONOUR OF

**The
Australian Rugby Touring Team
1957-8**

CHAIRMAN
H. L. GLYN HUGHES

*Royal Hotel Cardiff
Saturday, February 22nd, 1958*

No big match would be complete without a
formal post-match dinner, and the menu cards,
like the match programmes, have become
collectors' items. (© Barbarian Archive)

nowhere to boot ahead again and drop on the ball for a try under the posts. Faull's simple conversion stretched the lead to 11–3. In the closing moments the Wallabies had the satisfaction of at least scoring the final try of the match and the tour, fittingly by Ken Donald as he showed a range of skills, catching a high kick by Harvey and showing nimble footwork to beat Smith and dive over before the covering defence could reach him. Eleven points to six in favour of the Barbarians was a fair reflection on another pulsating game and the final whistle was followed by now familiar scenes. This time the crowd sang 'Waltzing Matilda' before both the old warrior Nick Shehadie and his opposite number Bob Davidson, the tourists' captain, were carried shoulder high from the field. Afterwards, Davidson was made an honorary Barbarian. It had been another joyous day. A winning double over the Wallabies was also something to savour. It could be tempered by the knowledge that, before the 1980s, Australian rugby, good though it undoubtedly was, was not quite on the same level as their southern hemisphere neighbours. Having fallen well short in the matches of 1952 and 1954, the Barbarians were entitled to wonder whether the scalps of the Springboks and All Blacks would always be just out of their reach. That question was soon answered in the following two decades – and gloriously so.

THE HISTORY MAKERS

'The basic idea of these matches is to end a tour on a happy
note and to send the touring team away in friendship.'
– U.A. Titley, *The Times*, 1964

In February 1961 the Barbarians met the Springboks for the second time in what were in several respects very different circumstances from the normal end-of-tour matches. The ties between the Club and South Africa, whether through the influence of presidents like Hughie Glyn Hughes or Herbert Waddell, or the great success of the tour there in 1958, had always been particularly strong. For a moment in the week leading up to the match in 1961 there was a blip, albeit a minor one, in the normally cordial relationship. The Springboks who toured Europe that season were not an especially popular group of players. The reasons for that had nothing to do with the Barbarians,

more a case of a dour image, a win-at-all-costs reputation and an unfortunate first appearance at the Arms Park early in the tour. The Springboks had beaten Cardiff easily enough at this first visit, by 13 points to nil, but the game had also featured several instances of over-vigorous play by, it has to be said, both sides, though the host team definitely came off worse. They were losers on points in boxing parlance as well as on the scoreboard. As the last week of the tour approached, with a climax at Cardiff Arms Park, the general feeling was one of 'Thank heavens for the Barbarians', as their match, surely, would restore the proper values. It was almost never played.

Five days before the game the Springboks were still in Dublin. Having beaten Ulster in Belfast the previous Saturday their penultimate match before going to France was against Leinster at Lansdowne Road. It was destined to be their 29th fixture and after it they would still remain unbeaten. It wasn't quite the perfect 100 per cent record as they had been held to a draw by the Midland Counties at Leicester in the first month of the tour. But it was still the best-ever performance by a Springboks team in Europe. Only the Barbarians were left with a chance to lower their colours. Then came an unprecedented request from their manager, Ferdie Bergh, to the Club president, Glyn Hughes. All was revealed in a press statement by Bergh:

> The position regarding sick and injured players is becoming increasingly so serious that there is a strong possibility that we will be unable to field a full side against the Barbarians on Saturday. The position, it seems, can only become worse, and accordingly I have telephoned Brigadier Glyn Hughes to inform him of it. I have suggested that, if necessary, we will provide as many fit players as possible and that mixed sides be fielded so that this gala game can take place.

Over 60,000 tickets had been sold, a live television broadcast was scheduled and, at five days' notice, the Springboks wanted an exhibition match. It was hard to escape the conclusion that, given the unfortunate situation where several of their leading players were either injured or ill, the team management were seeking to protect their place in the

history books as the first invincible Springboks. The Brigadier made an impressive response. He said:

> The Barbarians understand that Mr Bergh has issued a statement concerning the difficulties he is suffering from illness and injuries to his players and the possibility that he may not be able to produce his best side for next Saturday's match. The Barbarians committee very much appreciate and sympathise with him in his present predicament, and hope that the position may ease before Saturday. All the South African players are so very good that it is difficult to imagine that any 15 of them would not make a very good showing. The real attraction of this game is 15 South Africans against 15 Barbarians. In any case it would be a good game, and as we have always stressed, the result is of minor importance.

Barbarians are ace diplomats as well as gentlemen. The game went ahead, though the difficult preparations were far from over.

Both the selected teams were subject to several late changes in the final 24 hours before the kick-off. In the case of the Springboks, that came as no surprise to anyone. Three first-choice forwards – Frik du Preez, Piet du Toit and Johan Claassen – were all unfit, though the last two reappeared four days later for the first match in France at Bordeaux. They had quality replacements in Martin Pelser, Piet van Zyl and Mof Myburgh. The real difficulties, some of their own making, were behind the scrum. Several of the star performers were fit and well but the question was in which positions would they play, especially in midfield. The withdrawal of Bennie van Niekerk from one of the centre spots set off a chain reaction of mistaken selections. Dave Stewart, a fine player at fly-half and centre, was left in the pivot position and the world-class wing Jannie Engelbrecht was brought into van Niekerk's vacancy. Everyone in the Springbok camp had expected to see the experienced Keith Oxlee at fly-half, with Stewart partnering John Gainsford outside him. Crucially, a further error was to leave out the goal-kicking Test-match scrum-half and vice-captain Dick Lockyear. Instead, he spent the afternoon as a touch judge. His side were to pay dearly for selection errors.

The Barbarians, too, were not without their personnel problems. True to tradition they had included one uncapped player, the 23-year-old Newport lock Brian Price. Elsewhere in the side were familiar Barbarian favourites and well-tried combinations. Tony O'Reilly and Andy Mulligan were among the backs; there was an Irish front row of Gordon Wood, Ronnie Dawson and Syd Millar; and the Cardiff and Wales centres Cyril Davies and Meirion Roberts. The best-laid plans, however, were to collapse soon after the team assembled at the Esplanade Hotel in Penarth on the Friday. Immediately, a series of mini-crises developed. It started with the Wales captain Terry Davies, selected as the Barbarians' full-back, but at Penarth he was suffering from the flu. The committee's preferred replacement was Ken Scotland, but he couldn't be contacted.

Thus they turned to an old favourite of the Club, the Swansea utility player Haydn Mainwaring. In a long career he had played at full-back, centre and wing-forward for an equally wide range of teams, including the Royal Navy, Swansea, Harlequins, London Welsh and the Barbarians. Having been on four Easter tours, his qualities of reliability, courage and of being, in every sense, a safe pair of hands were well known to the committee. He had also played an outstanding match for the Swansea team against the Springboks three months earlier – but as a centre. No one could have forecast that this third-choice full-back would make such an impression at the end-of-tour showcase that it was to become known as 'Mainwaring's Match'. These days he is a respected Club committeeman, renowned for his self-deprecating wit and friendly disposition. His own recollection of his surprise call-up is typically amusing. He said, 'At the time I was working for Lombard Finance and I had a phone call asking me to report to the Esp at Penarth as soon as possible. On my way home to collect my boots and socks I spotted my wife Eryl at the bus stop. I pulled up in the car and told her, "I'm playing for the Barbarians against the Springboks tomorrow." She went one better when she said, "I've got news for you, too – I'm pregnant!" After that I should have known it was going to be no ordinary weekend.'

Yet the Barbarians could be excused for thinking otherwise. Even as Mainwaring was on his way to join them, further new plans were being made. One of the centres, Cyril Davies, was still suffering from a leg injury picked up in the international against England a fortnight earlier. There was still a hope that he could play the following day but, purely as a precaution, Newport's Brian Jones was asked to be on stand-by. He was another player well known to the Club, having been on the South African tour in 1958. His SOS call, however, seemed to be a false alarm. Having journeyed to Penarth, he was then told that Davies would be

After three late changes this was the team that finally played and beat the Springboks in 1961. Back row: M.F. Turner (referee), J.R.C. Young, H.M. Roberts, S. Millar, B. Price, H.J. Mainwaring, R.A.W. Sharp, W.G.D. Morgan, M.G. Culliton; seated: B.G.M. Wood, W.R. Evans, H. Waddell, A.R. Dawson (captain), H.L. Glyn Hughes, A.J.F. O'Reilly, M.R. Steele-Bodger, H.J. Morgan, V.G. Roberts (touch judge); on ground: B.J. Jones, W.R. Watkins. (© Barbarian Archive)

fit for the game, so he returned home to Cwmcarn. On the Saturday morning, thinking he was still on reserve duty, he caught a bus to the seaside once more and as he walked into the Esp the Brigadier was waiting to tell him he was playing.

The drama and the comings and goings didn't stop there. A third invalid was Andy Mulligan, who had been running a high temperature on the Friday. With time running short the committee had taken a further precaution and sent for another scrum-half in the locality – and another Newport player – Billy Watkins. Once again he too thought he wasn't needed after all so tucked into a hearty Saturday lunch at the Esp. At one o'clock he could be excused if indigestion set in: Mulligan

was still unwell and Watkins would be playing. He had won his single cap for Wales against France in 1959.

Mainwaring's inclusion had brought the quota of uncapped players in the team to two, but both he and Brian Price would soon lose that status. Before the end of the season their heroics for the Barbarians against the Springboks would be a major factor in their playing for Wales. The team was still guided by experienced old heads. Ronnie Dawson, who had led the British Isles in Australia and New Zealand in 1959, was appointed captain. He knew exactly what to say to his team in the changing-room before kick-off, as Brian Jones still clearly remembers: 'He never mentioned that we must win, only the importance of upholding the Baa-Baas' traditions. The intention was to play an open game but the pitch was very heavy and along the touch-lines it was like a quagmire.'

What happened next, in the match itself, was still to be the subject of heated debate among aficionados in the days that followed. The intention might well have been to throw the ball around as in time-honoured fashion but, whether because of the heavy pitch or a change of plan, or simply because of the scent of victory as the game unfolded, the Baa-Baas' tactics took everyone by surprise. This was no free-running, sleight-of-hand extravaganza. For once the Barbarians played what could only be called hard-nosed Test-match-style rugby. As the Springboks sank to defeat, many people close to their camp, if not the players themselves, claimed they had been conned.

The events of the first 20 minutes or so almost certainly set the tone for the final hour of the game. The Barbarians, with the strong wind at their backs, kicked off and Stewart did the sensible thing when he gathered the ball: he kicked to touch. The crowd booed. Already they were willing the Springboks to pass the ball, even on the glue-pot pitch, from every position – and all the signs were that, whatever their own pre-match plans might have been, they would try to do just that. To their credit, when the tourists worked their way into opposition territory they did indeed spin the ball and Mike Antelme almost scored on the right wing. Already, though, their goal-kicking shortcomings were being exposed. Blind-side wing-forward Hugo van Zyl, who had not kicked a goal in his nineteen previous matches on tour, failed to capitalise on two penalty awards, one kick falling narrowly short in the wind and the other horrifically hooked. Later

in the game Stewart was to have no better luck from bang in front of the posts. In the ninth minute the Barbarians took a lead they were never to lose. Watkins was already settling in at scrum-half and keeping the ball in front of his forwards for them to chase and harry the uncertain Springboks. A lineout on the Springboks' 25 seemed to pose no real threat until Watkins' opposite number, Piet Uys, had his clearance kick charged down by number 8 Derek Morgan, the Monmouthshire dentist who played for England. The loose ball was quickly regathered by Morgan, who dived over halfway out to the right of the posts. Though Mainwaring failed to convert, the first blow had been struck. Another Springbok attack, spearheaded by Uys and Stewart, was halted at the last minute only yards from the Barbarians'

Tony O'Reilly (right) shows some fancy footwork against the Springboks in the Cardiff mud. Keeping a watching brief are Barbarian forwards (left to right) Ronnie Dawson, Gordon Wood, Roddie Evans and Brian Price.
(© Barbarian Archive)

posts and van Zyl missed with his second attempted goal.

In the twenty-fourth minute the second try again materialised from a seemingly innocuous situation. A long drop-out by fly-half Richard Sharp was easily caught by Springboks full-back Lionel Wilson but his touch-kick, in turn, was blocked by wing-forward Gerry Culliton. As the ball went loose, Sharp was on hand again, this time to attempt a snap drop goal that missed. The comedy of errors continued. From the next lineout Uys was again in trouble behind his pack. This time a fumble had him scurrying back but he was beaten to the ball by a third member of the Barbarians' back row, Haydn Morgan, who touched down a hundredth of a second before him. It was almost a carbon copy of the first try – and again Mainwaring failed to convert. A six-points lead hardly seemed to ensure victory against the unbeaten Springboks, not with the wind at their backs in the second half, not with their increasingly dangerous attacks stretching the defence to the limit, and not with the presumably superior fitness levels and teamwork of the touring team. But those six points, mixed in with several moments of inspiration, were indeed the platform for a famous win.

In the second half the Springboks, with John Gainsford in outstanding form, attacked and attacked. The Barbarians tackled and tackled. And kicked. And then they tackled again. This was a reversal of roles on a grand scale. The defining moment came midway through the half. Avril Malan was not only a great Springbok lock; he was also a great captain and a figurehead. Where he led, others followed. But not in the 63rd minute of this increasingly tense and epic struggle. Again the action took place on the muddy south touch-line of Cardiff Arms Park, from where the fateful two lineouts of the opening stages had led to the Barbarians' tries. This time the set piece was nearer halfway and the Springboks didn't spill the ball. Far from it. Malan had it safely in his grasp and had obviously decided that the shortest and quickest route to the Barbarians' distant try-line was parallel with the touch-line and with his eyes focused on nothing else. Away he went and every man, woman and child in the capacity crowd must have regarded a captain's try and a Springboks comeback as foregone conclusions. And then there was Mainwaring, on the brink of immortality. He was literally the last line of defence as he moved across to cut Malan off on the touch-line. Though he was no shrinking violet himself he was still a couple of stone lighter than the giant forward and there seemed every prospect of him being swept aside. He had other ideas at the time and, years later, still has a clear recollection of his master-plan: 'He'd gone past Billy Watkins and was racing up the touch-line. I thought he would try and pass to the back-rowers on the inside, so that's why I decided to go in high. A low tackle would have been no good as he would be able to offload the ball. So in I went – and down he went.' Or, as Vivian Jenkins interpreted the scene in the *Sunday Times*, 'there was a thud like a comet burying itself into earth'. The 'galloping Goliath', as Jenkins also memorably described Malan, lay prone and temporarily semi-conscious over the touch-line, both the ball and himself out of play. The Springboks as a team were about to be out of the match as well.

The Barbarians scented victory and now Dawson's astute captaincy took over. Brian Price, a middle-of-the-lineout specialist, was given a new role. He remembers: 'Ronnie said to me that as they were a man down I should go to the front of the next lineout. I did and won the ball with something to spare. For the rest of the game, even with Malan back in the line, he was little more than a passenger. So they started throwing long balls to the back and in those conditions everything became a scramble.'

The Springboks had lost their secure platform of possession. The scrums, with Wood, Dawson and Millar packing exceptionally low and getting under the big Springbok props Kuhn and Myburgh, were going no better despite a majority of tight-heads being stolen – not unusual in those days. Not that the Springboks threw in the towel. There was still their record to protect and soon Mainwaring was in the thick of the action again, stopping Antelme before he could get into full stride and Kuhn as he was charging for the line. All afternoon most of the running thrills had been provided by Gainsford. With a six-point cushion and the winning post in sight surely the Barbarians could afford to try something spectacular themselves. Richard Sharp, a classical English fly-half, thought that perhaps they should. He said to his nearest centre, Brian Jones, 'If we get the ball from the next lineout, do you think we should move it?' BJ's answer was short, sweet and unprintable. Sharp duly kicked the leather off the ball.

The Barbarians had beaten the Springboks at their own game. Afterwards, the springbok head, a trophy presented to the first team to beat the South Africans on tour, was gratefully received by the Brigadier from Ferdie Bergh. Avril Malan was made an honorary Barbarian. He was not there to hear his citation. Still nursing his wounds, he was 30 miles away in his hotel room in Porthcawl. At the final hurdle

Springbok number 8 Doug Hopwood bursts into the Barbarians' half as Gordon Wood (centre) and Brian Price (right) give chase. (© Barbarian Archive)

Billy Watkins, one of the three late replacements, pins the Springboks back with another deft kick, much to the approval of his forwards (left to right) Gerry Culliton, Syd Millar, Derek Morgan, Roddie Evans and Gordon Wood. (© Barbarian Archive)

his team had stumbled on the edge of invincibility. When the dust had settled, there were no hard feelings. Barbarian players and committeemen mingling with the Springboks at the official post-match dinner had the distinct feeling that, with another four matches awaiting the South Africans in France, they were relieved to be free of the burden of invincibility. As it happened, they emerged unscathed from France apart from a scoreless draw in a titanic Test match.

Barbarians and Springboks would rub shoulders many times again – but what of Malan and Mainwaring? Thirty years later, on the day the Welshman retired from his business career at Lombard Finance, a fax message arrived in Newport. It read:

> Haydn,
>
> The news of your retirement has reached my ears down here in South Africa. As you were once so lucky to catch me on the rugby field after I barged through a lineout, I thought I would send you a message, telling you how often I have since beaten you in a replay of the incident.
>
> If you have any confidence that you could still catch me today, what about a challenge, seeing that in the near future you will have time to practise and repractise your moves.
>
> Congratulations Old Man, having reached the ripe age of retirement. I still have eight years to go. May your retirement be a very happy and enjoyable period.
>
> Regards and best wishes,
> Avril Malan

The Springboks, then, were not unbeatable after all. The Wallabies, of course, had already fallen twice to the Barbarians. The All Blacks were the final frontier and not one to venture into unprepared. Their 1954 victory had reminded everyone that the wearers of the silver fern were not ready-made fodder for one-off invitation teams, even those as star-studded and famous as put together in Barbarian colours. Despite the euphoria of the Springboks scalp there was little to discourage the belief in the 1960s that the All Blacks were made of sterner stuff altogether. Or, at least, not at first.

The match in 1964 is remembered fondly not for the Barbarians' part in it, not even for the coruscating exhibition of 15-man rugby by the men in black, but for the finale that featured the tourists' captain at centre-stage. Wilson Whineray was no ordinary captain. He led his country in thirty of the thirty-two internationals in which he played over a period of eight seasons, including series victories over South Africa, Australia and the British Isles. He was a prop-forward but not of the gnarled, take-no-prisoners variety. It is not a cliché to say he was a gentleman of the game. It was no surprise when his services to rugby were recognised by first an OBE and then in his own country by a knighthood. His playing career at the top level had ended in 1965 but had reached its apotheosis a year earlier on a late winter's afternoon at Cardiff Arms Park. The Barbarians' second attempt at lowering the All Blacks' colours had floundered spectacularly, to the tune of thirty-six points to three and eight tries without reply. It was the Club's heaviest defeat in such matches, a source of potential embarrassment, but one from which their reputation would eventually recover. In the immediate aftermath, however, attention was understandably diverted to

The programme for the 1964 match against New Zealand. (© Barbarian Archive)

Whineray and his team and the manner of their overwhelming victory.

No one had really seen it coming. The Barbarians had selected what appeared to be a cleverly constructed team. The heroes of the triumph over the Springboks three years earlier were represented in all three rows of the scrum. Ronnie Dawson, who would again captain the team, was at hooker; Brian Price was now an established international at lock; and Gerry Culliton, currently employed in the Ireland second row, would return to blind-side wing-forward where he had displayed such terrier-like qualities in the subjugation of the

Springboks. Culliton would have good company in the back row with England's Budge Rogers on the open side and Alun Pask, a marvellously skilled ball-handler and runner, at number 8. Two other Welshmen, Len Cunningham and Elwyn Jones, were selected at prop and lock respectively. The selection of uncapped Jones was a recognition of his several valiant displays for Penarth in the Good Friday matches against the Barbarians. Whether he had the weight, height or top-class experience to play opposite the legendary Colin Meads was more debatable. The eighth member of the pack, and again a continuation of a developing club tradition, was a member of the All Blacks touring party. Ian Clarke had come to Britain with the New Zealanders ten years earlier; now

Where's the ball? Opposing wing-forwards Budge Rogers (far left in scrum-cap) and New Zealand's Waka Nathan are nearest the ball in 1964 as Kevin Flynn seems to have overrun it. The Barbarian forwards (from the right) are Brian Price, Len Cunningham and Alun Pask. (© Barbarian Archive)

he was the only survivor of that trip. So it was no surprise that the Club invited him to follow in the footsteps of Australia's Nick Shehadie. It was more of a surprise that, having donned the Barbarians shirt at the Arms Park, he caught the ball from a 25 drop-out by his brother Don and, having called a mark, effortlessly dropped a goal from all of 45 yards. The even greater surprise was that those three points, after barely a quarter-of-an-hour's play, would complete the Barbarians' scoring for the afternoon.

On paper, at least, they had appeared to put together a useful, if not brilliant, back division. Stewart Wilson at full-back and Stuart Watkins on the wing had only recently made their debuts for Scotland and Wales; the other wing, the 21-year-old Sandhurst cadet Colin Simpson, was then uncapped. There was more experience at centre, where a survivor of the 1958 win over the Wallabies, Malcolm Phillips, partnered the brilliant Irishman Kevin Flynn, while scrum-half Simon Clarke had been an automatic choice for England in the last ten internationals. The only disappointment before the game was that the original selection at fly-half, Irishman Michael Gibson, was forced to withdraw and for an unusual reason. Seven days earlier he had made a sensational debut at Twickenham, orchestrating an 18–5 triumph over England. Sensing a possible Triple Crown campaign, his country's selectors wrapped him in cotton wool ahead of their remaining international matches. Ironically, in the weeks that followed, Ireland lost to Scotland, Wales and France. Gibson's unavailability caused no particular alarm among the Club committee. Into his place they drafted a member of the 1961 side, Richard Sharp. Unfortunately for the Barbarians as a team, and Sharp as an

individual, history was not about to repeat itself.

Ian Clarke's unlikely drop goal was not the springboard for another famous victory for the Barbarians. It merely kick-started his countrymen into life. In the final ten minutes of the half the All Blacks opened their try-scoring account. Sharp and Clarke were having an unhappy time of it at half-back, the one struggling for match fitness and the other trying to shake off a staleness caused, paradoxically, by too much rugby. Sharp had not played a competitive game for five weeks, while Clarke had played almost non-stop for the best part of 18 months. The All Blacks showed no mercy. First, their centre Paul Little dispossessed Sharp in a tackle and Meads charged on before Kel Tremain scored. Next, a Clarke clearance kick was charged down by Denis Young and Chris Laidlaw. Waka Nathan and Whineray took the ball on before Meads was on hand for the final pass. It was 6–3 to the All Blacks at half-time and some of the names involved in these first scores reveal the size of the Baa-Baas' task in the second period. Whineray, Young, Meads, Nathan and Tremain were part of the finest pack of forwards in the world at the time. Add Ken Gray as the other prop, Allan Stewart alongside Meads and John Graham in the back row and the cast list was complete. Among the reserves was Brian Lochore, then on the brink of his own illustrious career. Laidlaw, at scrum-half, was the perfect operator to be snapping at the pack's heels and there was plenty of that in the second forty minutes. It was as if Whineray's men suddenly realised that they were in the final moments of their long tour and they should leave an unforgettable calling card.

They did just that. Within five minutes the

score had stretched to 16–3, Graham having pounced on another half-back fumble for one try and Nathan on another loose pass from the base of a scrum for another. Don Clarke easily kicked the first two of his six second-half conversions. From this unassailable position the All Blacks indulged themselves in what could only be called Barbarian rugby. Laidlaw was always capable of 30-yard spin passes but now the forwards were joining in as well. It would be no exaggeration to conclude that the Baa-Baas were run off their feet – and yet up in the stands their alickadoos could only sit back and admire what was unfolding before their eyes.

At the post-match dinner the Brigadier readily admitted that when the crowd called for more, more, more, 'We felt like saying "yeah, yeah, yeah!"' as the All Blacks ran in four more tries. Chronicling the tour in *Willie Away*, Terry McLean wondered whether they might have been 'the Marx Brothers playing "A Day at the Rugby" . . . as the zaniest of moves and movements were attempted and completed'. Two touchdowns by right-wing Malcolm Dick and another for Nathan were mere preambles to the unscripted finale for the captain. As the clock ticked around to the full 80 minutes, Whineray entered centre stage. McLean's eyewitness account is worthy of the epic try itself:

> Suddenly, 20 yards from the posts, there was Whineray, going hell for leather, Meads alongside him and Flynn flashing across from the right to make the tackle. The three neared the posts. The Tower of Babel was a quiet country pub at an off-hour compared with the Arms Park. Amid the fantastic noise, Whineray passed. Or so it seemed. His arms moved

out towards Meads. Coincidentally, he side-stepped the other way. It was the dummy pass to end all dummy passes. Hook, line and sinker, Flynn bought it. Whineray, so it seemed, slackened to a trot as he carried the few more yards to the posts and the final try of the tour of Europe.

As the great captain made his way back over the halfway line and Clarke prepared to take his final goal-kick, the 58,000 crowd broke into a spontaneous singing of 'For He's a Jolly Good Fellow'. Soon the final whistle was blown and Whineray, naturally, was carried from the field shoulder-high. When the euphoria had died down, there was the inescapable feeling that the Barbarians, for once, had been onlookers at the feast and, equally inevitably, questions were asked about the quality of their team selection. In *The Times* U.A. Titley mounted a robust defence:

> This Club has always fostered all that is best in an amateur game, whose players and clubs are free – in spite of the current Irish attack of cold [Gibson] feet – to do what they like without dictation. As with anybody else the Barbarians like winning – but they do not mind losing, which is a far from despicable trait. The basic idea of these particular matches is to end a tour on a happy note and to send the touring team away in friendship.

Within a decade the Barbarians had more than repaired any damage to their reputation. A much closer tussle with the next All Blacks in 1967 took them to the brink of victory and the

Noel Murphy, of Ireland, captained the team against Australia in 1967 when Geoff Windsor-Lewis was the touch judge. Back row: G. Windsor-Lewis, K.W. Kennedy, J.P. Fisher, A.B. Carmichael, W.J. McBride, B. Price, J.W. Telfer, N. Suddon, S.J. Watkins; middle row: S. Wilson, T.G.R. Davies, N.A.A. Murphy (captain), F.P.K. Breshihan, D. Watkins; on ground: P.B. Glover, R.M. Young.
(© Barbarian Archive)

reversal of fortunes was completed on another cataclysmic Cardiff day six years after that when the rugby world saluted both teams, and the match and the Barbarian Football Club were etched into the history of the sport forever.

In the interim, also, two other matches were played against the Wallabies and Springboks. The Australian touring team of 1966–67 was considerably stronger than their predecessors in 1948 and 1958. For a start they had world-class half-backs in Phil Hawthorne and their vice-captain Ken Catchpole, the equally celebrated Greg Davis at wing-forward, and an experienced leader in John Thornett. The Wallabies had lost more than their fair share of matches – 13 out of 29 starts – before the final game with the Barbarians but they had also beaten Wales and England in great style. With no records to worry about, the overall quality of the two previous matches between the Barbarians and the Wallabies had exceeded those with the Springboks and the All Blacks. The game at Cardiff Arms Park on 28 January 1967 added to that reputation for excellence and excitement and, at the same time, enhanced the standing of Australian rugby. Any lingering criticism about team selection after the disappointment of 1964 was soon dispelled when the committee announced a team made up of six Scots, five Irishmen, three from Wales and the newly capped England wing Peter Glover. There were three survivors from the All Blacks trouncing: Stewart Wilson, Stuart Watkins and Brian Price. Price was equalling the record of Cliff Morgan and Ronnie Dawson by playing for a third time for the Club against a major touring team; Wilson would follow suit in the All Blacks match later in the year. The strength of the team was further illustrated by the inclusion of eminent forwards such as Jim Telfer, Noel Murphy (who was also named as captain), Willie John McBride and Ken Kennedy. One unwanted example of history repeating itself was that Michael Gibson was again forced to withdraw from the fly-half position, though this time because of injury. His place went to Newport's mercurial David Watkins, taking the Welsh contingent to four, and with Gerald Davies in the early stages of his own outstanding international career also in the backs there was every expectation of a points feast. There were few disappointments in that respect, with eight tries scored and the lead changing hands five times before the Wallabies won the match 17–11.

Noel Murphy and Australia's John Thornett lead their teams onto a very heavy Arms Park pitch in 1967.
(© Barbarian Archive)

From the kick-off, both teams had mounted attacks through straight hard running and one such move, started by Stuart Watkins in his own half and carried on by the lightning-fast Davies, provided the first thrills. However, it was the tourists who provided the only scores of the first half. Throughout the tour the instinctive linking and direct play of Catchpole and Hawthorne had opened up opposition defences and now it worked again. Both players operated close to the ground – Catchpole was 5 ft 6 in. and Hawthorne

barely two inches taller – and short, slick passes sent them weaving inside and outside bemused tacklers. This time it was Hawthorne who burst onto a popped up offering and covered 15 yards before he used all of his 11½ st. to buffet through the last line of defence for the first try. It was a typically audacious effort. That was after 10 minutes of play, and 15 minutes later the visitors scored again from a more familiar sweeping back-line move that set wing Stewart Boyce sprinting for the corner. The Barbarians had contributed fully to the first-half entertainment without disturbing the scoreboard but they soon cancelled out the six-point arrears after the interval. Within seven minutes of the restart one of their own attacks behind the scrum broke down but the hooker Kennedy was backing up for the try. Five minutes after that Wilson kicked a 25-yard penalty and the scores were level.

A classic lineout leap by Brian Price, watched by Ken Kennedy (left), Sandy Carmichael, Willie John McBride, Jim Telfer and Noel Murphy.
(© Huw Evans Agency)

The Wallabies immediately regained the lead. The 37-year-old prop Tony Miller, who, like Jim Lenehan and Thornett, had played in the corresponding match in 1958, charged over for another unconverted try. Ten minutes from the end Lenehan obstructed Stuart Watkins as he chased a kick ahead by Murphy, and Wilson converted the penalty try. At 11–9 it looked as if the Barbarians were about to complete a hat-trick of wins over the Wallabies, but it was not to be. Hawthorne again worked his magic with a miss pass in midfield and outside-centre John Brass found Lenehan up in the line from full-back and again Boyce dashed the final yards for the try. Lenehan converted from the edge of touch and then, with the last move of another brilliant match, the tourists scored their fifth

try when their other wing, Dick Webb, finished off a blind-side move by the deadly Hawthorne–Catchpole duo.

The Barbarians had seen victory snatched from their grasp in the final five minutes. An even more heart-stopping conclusion was awaiting them later the same year when they undertook another new departure. The Wallabies match had been their seventh game against one of the three southern hemisphere powers; all of them had been staged at Cardiff Arms Park. Future games might well have continued uninterrupted in the Welsh capital but for the hastily arranged fixture with the All Blacks in December 1967.

This tour was unusual on two counts. Firstly, it had been inserted into the calendar after a scheduled New Zealand tour to South Africa had been aborted. The All Blacks, last seen in Britain on that glorious Whineray day in 1964, were not due north of the equator again until the autumn of 1972. The eight- or nine-season gaps between tours by each of the Big Three preserved their mystique and increased the sense of anticipation. However, the political problems in South Africa had upset the touring balance, so the All Blacks came to Europe instead. The second innovation was that the tour would start and end before Christmas and entail only 16 matches. Yes, 'only' 16. By the accepted standards of the 1960s this could be described as a short tour. So short, in fact, that there would be no time or room for the traditional final game against the Barbarians. Sixteen became fourteen when a foot-and-mouth outbreak in the farming communities of Dublin and Belfast prevented the All Blacks from crossing the Irish Sea and forced the cancellation of two games over there. They also happened to be the final two fixtures on the original itinerary. Suddenly, the

Two world-class scrum-halfs in the 1967 game against New Zealand at Twickenham
– Gareth Edwards passes as Chris Laidlaw harries. (© Barbarian Archive)

Barbarian match became feasible again. At barely a month's notice the final game of what was now a 15-match trip was to be not against Ireland in Dublin but the Barbarians at Twickenham. There was always the doubt that the infrastructure for such an important match could be in place within a month but it soon was. On 16 December a crowd in excess of 40,000 turned up and they received more than their money's worth.

The All Blacks were unbeaten on their tour, though they had been held to a 3–all draw against East Wales at the Arms Park. Four Cardiff backs from that new combination – Keri Jones, Gerald Davies, Barry John and Gareth Edwards – also won favour with the Barbarians. A fifth Cardiff man, the prop Howard Norris, was appointed vice-captain. The other Welsh selection was Aberavon's Max Wiltshire in the second row. Scotland's Pringle Fisher was named as captain, but when he withdrew, his place as flanker went to Derrick Grant and the captaincy to Stewart Wilson. The third Scot in the team was Frank Laidlaw at hooker. England's contingent numbered six: Bob Lloyd and Rodney Webb behind the scrum, and in the pack Tony Horton, Peter Larter, Bob Taylor and the Saracens number 8 George Sherriff. Because of the farming curfew, Ireland, for once, was not represented in the Barbarians team. The All Blacks included six of the heroes of the 1964 match: Dick, Laidlaw, Gray, Meads, Nathan and Tremain. Lochore had graduated into the team and had succeeded Whineray as captain. It was another outstanding New Zealand line-up.

Both sides scored from drop goals in the opening ten minutes. Firstly, Wilson collected an All Blacks clearance kick that failed to find

touch and struck a beautiful kick from the edge of the left touch-line. Within six minutes Earl Kirton responded after Sam Strahan had won a lineout on the Barbarians' 25. The tourists' play in the first half was reminiscent of their second period in the match of 1964 – a surfeit of possession and a series of sweeping attacks that stretched the Barbarians' defence. The crucial difference was that, this time, passes were being dropped at vital moments. The result was half an hour of thrills and spills but no further scores. The Barbarians might even have held a lead, but Wilson, otherwise playing a fine game, missed with four attempted penalty goals, two of them rebounding off an upright. The general impression remained that Wilson's men were hanging on by the skin of their teeth.

By the end of the match the All Blacks would have won 45 of the 56 lineouts so there was a desperate need to make full use of any

It's classic opposition ball for the All Blacks as Colin Meads dominates the lineout at Twickenham.
(© Barbarian Archive)

possession that came the Barbarians' way. Two such opportunities presented themselves midway through the second half, both from spilled passes in the Barbarians' half. From the first, Keri Jones, a Commonwealth Games sprinter, scooped the ball up and headed for the distant try-line. He was cut off by full-back Fergie McCormick, who forced the wing to kick, and the chance was lost. Then Gerald Davies was gifted a similar opportunity but again the adroit McCormick blocked Davies' path and his inside pass went astray. But by then the Baa-Baas had sneaked ahead when Barry John chipped a kick behind the defence and into the corner where Bob Lloyd dived on the try and a 6–3 lead. For the next 20 minutes that lead was held and as injury time approached the drubbing of three years before seemed certain to be avenged. Then, with only a minute of normal time left to play, the left-wing Tony Steel came in from the blind side and burst through midfield, and centre Ian MacRae scored the try that levelled the scores.

So near yet so far, but a 6–all draw was a creditable and fair result. In the end, though, it wasn't even that. In the fourth minute of injury time Wilson failed to find touch with what would have been the final kick of the match. Cruelly, at the very spot on the left touch-line where Wilson himself had caught a stray kick and opened the scoring 75 minutes before, the ball now dropped into the arms of Lochore. Captain to captain – but it was the one in black who was to now taste the fruits of victory. Veering infield, he drew the first tacklers before passing left to the looping Kirton. Outside the fly-half, in turn, was Steel and he was away for the winning try. McCormick's conversion gave him exactly 100 points in 12 matches on the tour and his team an 11–6 victory.

Gareth Edwards was appointed captain against the Springboks in 1970. Back row: R.P. Burrell (touch judge), J.J. Jeffery, R.J. Arneil, K.E. Fairbrother, T.M. Davies, A.M. Davis, D.B. Llewelyn, D.J. Duckham, M.G. Molloy (replacement), G.C. Lamb (referee), M. Joseph (touch judge); middle row: I.S. Gallacher, A.T.A. Duggan, C.M.H. Gibson, G.O. Edwards (captain), F.A.L. Laidlaw, J.S. Spencer, J.P.R. Williams; front row: N.C. Starmer-Smith (rep), J.V. Pullin (rep), B. John, C.M. Telfer (rep).
(© Barbarian Archive)

The All Blacks returned home unbeaten; the Barbarians were left to ponder whether last-gasp defeats were becoming a habit. Still, there were several consolations. The Club had retained its role on the touring-team calendar, and had contributed fully to another high-quality match. The agonies of 1964 had been overshadowed by the good performances against the Wallabies and the All Blacks in the two matches since. And the experiment of playing at Twickenham had been proved a success.

Consequently, when the next Springboks team came to Britain in 1969–70, the Rugby Football Union ground was again allocated the Barbarians fixture. It was an end-of-tour occasion unlike any other. At a time when the anti-apartheid movement was at its most active,

the Springboks had journeyed around the British Isles in a manner that no touring team had ever done before. When not playing, personal security dictated that the players were confined to hotel quarters; when playing most of their 25 matches, the pitch became a target for a variety of missiles, including smoke bombs, and invasions. That situation prevailed right up to and including the Twickenham finale. It was not an environment that the Barbarians were familiar with. The Club's policy had always been to keep politics out of their sport and to play matches wherever and whenever they had been invited. In the summer of 1969 the Barbarians had completed a successful six-match tour of South Africa and Rhodesia; on 31 January 1970 they played hosts to the Springboks at Twickenham.

As an occasion the match didn't quite have the special feel of its forerunners at Cardiff Arms Park since 1948 or, indeed, the All Blacks match at Twickenham a little over two years before. Attendances were generally down throughout the tour, partly because of the unrest at several grounds and partly, it has to be acknowledged, because individuals boycotted them as a matter of principle. The crowd at Twickenham numbered around 30,000. The Springboks didn't have the aura of their predecessors and had already lost five and drawn four of their twenty-four matches before facing the Barbarians. The Club's selectors, nevertheless, assembled a particularly strong line-up. Only Barry John, Gareth Edwards and Frank Laidlaw had played in the 1967 game, but the newcomers were an impressive bunch. J.P.R. Williams was at full-back; Michael

Police security at Twickenham is very much in evidence as Rodger Arneil clashes with the Springboks' pack in 1970; Mervyn Davies is on the left. (© Barbarian Archive)

Gibson partnered John Spencer in the centre and there was another Anglo-Irish duo, Alan Duggan and David Duckham, on the wings. In the pack, Barry Llewelyn and Keith Fairbrother were the props, Mike Davis and Stuart Gallacher were at lock, and the back-row unit was John Jeffery, Rodger Arneil and Mervyn Davies. They were expected to do well and they didn't disappoint in the opening ten minutes. Laidlaw stole a Springbok-scrum put-in and Edwards ran to the blind side before putting Arneil over for the try. Then another blind-side snipe by the scrum-half, this time deep in his own half, sent Duckham on his way, spectacularly sidestepping his opposite number Syd Nomis and two other cover-tacklers, for a marvellous second unconverted try. Better goal-kicking would have meant a ten-point lead and the platform for glory. When Edwards almost scored a third try, only for the preceding ruck to be penalised, it still looked as if the Barbarians were in control. The Springboks, however, responded with their best rugby of the tour. Jan Ellis scored a try and Dawie de Villiers kicked the conversion from the right touch-line. The Baa-Baas reaffirmed their lead when Spencer dummied and broke through the midfield and Duggan accepted the scoring pass. Again the conversion was missed, whereas de Villiers, in contrast, was relishing his unfamiliar role as his side's goal-kicker. His penalty goal brought the score back to 9–8 in the Barbarians' favour at the break.

The pattern of the game changed completely in the second half. Spearheaded by Ellis at flanker and Frik du Preez, still one of the great ball-carrying locks at the age of 34, the Springbok pack rampaged all over the pitch. Fly-half Mike Lawless dropped a goal from a scrum-heel against the head and de Villiers converted tries by wing Andrew van der Watt and Ellis. At the very end Fairbrother flopped over from a lineout for a consolation try and a final score of 21–12 in favour of the Springboks. A difficult tour had ended for them on a bright note. Brigadier Glyn Hughes extended more than the usual courtesies to them at the official dinner in the Savoy Hotel. As well as making their outstanding captain Dawie de Villiers an honorary Barbarian, he presented a Barbarian monogram to each of the Springboks, including the players who had departed the tour early because of injuries.

The 1970 match against the Springboks had been the ninth such fixture against a major touring team since 1948; the Barbarians had won three of them and lost six, a respectable record for any club. They had also played, or were about to play, two other international teams in Britain. In 1962 they had drawn 3–all against Canada and later, in 1970, they were beaten 29–9 by Fiji. Both of these games were played at the County Ground in Gosforth and were very different in character.

The Canadian match was a fitting gesture in return for the pioneering tour made by the Club to their country in 1957. The visiting captain was 41-year-old prop Buzz Moore and the Barbarians, never ones to miss an opportunity to honour their own, appointed Ron Jacobs, who had been injured in the first match in 1957, as leader for the day. It was a role he assumed with relish, greeting every member of his team with a glass of sherry as they arrived in the foyer of their base at the Whitley Bay Hotel. Despite failing to win any of the first 10 matches on their 16-match tour, the Canadians were not taken lightly. Six of the Barbarians team – Arthur Smith, Malcolm Phillips, Richard

A great Springbok, Frik du Preez, epitomises the power of the opposition as he peels away from a maul. (© Barbarian Archive)

At the end, Springboks' skipper Dawie de Villiers is carried off the pitch shoulder high by Michael Gibson (left) and Gareth Edwards. (© Barbarian Archive)

Sharp, Brian Price, Peter Robbins and Ron Jacobs – had appeared for the Club in the big end-of-tour games at Cardiff Arms Park, and thirteen of the side were internationals. Unfortunately, the elements conspired against an exciting match. Rain, wind and eventually a blizzard made expansive play impossible and at half-time neither side had scored. Eventually, as conditions deteriorated even further, the Barbarians settled for a penalty goal by Ken Scotland. To the delight of the partisan crowd – for once on the side of the touring team rather than the Baa-Baas – this was cancelled out by a similar effort by Don Burgess and that was the sum total of the scoring.

Eight years later the frozen wasteland had given way to a sunny autumnal afternoon for the visit of the Fijians, and the Gosforth crowd were treated to champagne rugby but not of a nature they might have anticipated. With luminaries such as J.P.R. Williams, Spencer and Duckham, Phil Bennett and Edwards in their back division the scene was set for a master class in back play from the Barbarians. It didn't quite work out that way. At the end of an extraordinary afternoon the names on everyone's lips were Barley and Batibasaga, Tuisese and Tikoisuva, and Naucabalavu and Ravouvou. The Baa-Baas had been taken to the cleaners at their own game, outscored by seven tries to two, and in a breathtaking fashion. There was no indication of the carnage to come when John Spencer scored the opening try of the match in the ninth minute after good work by Derek Quinnell and Gareth Edwards. In fact the Fijians' attempts at passing movements too often floundered on careless handling. It was first-half injury time before one of their centres, Senitiki Nasave, pounced on a loose ball for the equalising try. The fun and games

really started in the second half, with three tries in fourteen minutes. Full-back Josaia Visei started the points spree running onto an audacious long pass by Latilevu and then two front-row forwards, Atonio Racike and Jona Qoro, ran in for further scores. Qoro, in particular, was a remarkable handler and runner and was good enough to be invited back to England five months later, along with fly-half George Barley, to be part of the President's World XV that played England and the regional sides as part of the RFU's centenary celebrations.

The Barbarians did manage to stem the tide for a while in the middle of the half. A Williams penalty goal held the score at 6–18 but there was another rush of tries in the closing stages. The most spectacular was by the flamboyant Batibasaga, who ran around the back of a lineout on the 25, collected the throw-in in full stride and dummied Williams, a feat that few attackers had successfully executed against the impregnable full-back over the years, and swallow-dived under the posts for a try. Immediately from the restart the two locks Naucabalavu and Ravouvou ran the ball back again and Tuisese scored. Batibasaga, who had kicked two conversions at the start of the half, added the extra points to these tries as well. A seventh try by Ravouvou completed the rout before, at the very end, a defiant counter-attack resulted in a try for David Duckham.

A 9–29 defeat was something that few onlookers had anticipated. The players were similarly taken by surprise. Fergus Slattery, the Irish flanker who, with his fellow back-rowers Rodger Arneil and Derek Quinnell, had fought a rearguard action for most of the second half, remains philosophical to this day. He says, 'In many ways it was an unreal atmosphere and we were caught on the hop. Our team performance was very disjointed, with young Quinnell, then only 21, one of the few glorious exceptions. We probably underestimated the opposition but, unlike when we played the All Blacks or Springboks or Wallabies, we really knew very little about them. In those days there was no video footage of their earlier matches readily available. And, of course, they were doing things we'd hardly ever seen before – overhead 30-yard passes, outrageous switching of direction, it was complete chaos. There's no point in analysing it, simply have a smile when thinking back about it. I can assure you that the committee were equally bemused!'

The 1960s had begun with the famous victory over the Springboks at Cardiff, but had rather lost some of its glitter with the subsequent heavy loss to the All Blacks, a close defeat against the Wallabies and a later All Blacks team, and a draw against Canada. With the losses to the Springboks at Twickenham and the Fijians in Gosforth, the 1970s seemed to be continuing in a similar vein. That trend was reversed, however, in the finest manner imaginable when the Barbarians returned to Cardiff Arms Park on 27 January 1973.

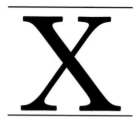

THE EPITOME
OF
PERFECTION

'For 80 minutes we didn't drop a pass and the skill levels were exemplary.'

– John Dawes, 1973

'I can remember the surge of excitement I felt before the start. A match like that needs a catalyst and that first try scored by Gareth Edwards right at the beginning was the catalyst of all the drama that followed.' The recollection of Michael Gibson could be that of any one of the 15 players who wore the Barbarians shirt that afternoon in 1973 – or in the 58,000 crowd or among the millions of television viewers who were surely as entranced as the lucky ones packed into Cardiff Arms Park. It was the day when rugby became the beautiful game, when, for one afternoon, it reached a level of excellence rarely seen before or since. John Dawes was captain of the Club against the All Blacks and he knows why it was so special: 'For

80 minutes we didn't drop a pass and the skill levels were exemplary; it was the epitome of perfection.' Gibson, who partnered him in the centre, agrees: 'The simple things were done efficiently and consistently, even though they were done under the pressure of the highest pace of international rugby. We did nothing elaborate. The ball was used intelligently and it was moved quickly.' The Barbarians beat the All Blacks 23–11, but that was only half the story.

From the very outset the match promised to be unlike any other undertaken by the Club in the 80 years and more of its existence. The alickadoos might still regard the 1948 pioneering fixture against the Wallabies as its greatest day; the clinical defeat of the Springboks in 1961 might have won the approval of the doubting few who hitherto muttered about the Baa-Baas' tendency to indulge in what they would call 'fancy-Dan football'; and the early overseas tours in the '50s and '60s might still be treasured for spreading the gospel to distant shores; but none of them would subsequently rank alongside the daring deeds that began to unfold in the old Welsh theatre of sport shortly before three o'clock on the afternoon of Saturday, 27 January in 1973.

Yet the build-up had featured mini-dramas and major policy decisions all of their own. Once again the spectre of the Barbarians as closet Lions raised its head. This time it had more contextual relevance than ever before. Eighteen months earlier the Lions – the British Isles – had returned from New Zealand after their greatest achievement of all. The two-matches-to-one triumph in the Test series had guaranteed their place in rugby history. But very few of the game's fans in Europe had seen their heroics at first hand, while the television coverage amounted to scratchy black-and-white films. The supporters wanted more of the same and nearer home and as the Lions never played there everyone wanted the Barbarians to fill the void. Now, as luck would have it, the All Blacks, the vanquished New Zealanders of 1971, were bringing down the curtain on their largely successful 28-match tour at Cardiff Arms Park – against the Barbarians. Surely this time the Baa-Baas would oblige an expectant public and pick the Lions again. They almost did.

Geoff Windsor-Lewis, secretary of the Club, freely admits that there were several key personnel involved in the British Isles tour who were pinpointed by the committee. At the top of the list was John Dawes. He had captained the Lions in their conquest of New Zealand and, immediately afterwards, retired from international rugby. 'That made him doubly attractive as a selection option for us,' said Windsor-Lewis. 'We wanted him to lead the side. He was highly regarded as one of the best captains of his generation, irrespective of what he had achieved with the Lions. Now that he no longer played for Wales we could fairly argue that we were not picking a team to represent the best of British rugby. But John still played for London Welsh and continued to be a fine centre in his own right. I have always said that one of the features of Barbarian rugby is the ability to give a pass a yard early rather than a yard late. There was no better exponent of that skill than John.'

It was by no means certain, though, that Dawes would be available for the Barbarians on 27 January. London Welsh were doing particularly well in the RFU's cup competition and in the next round were drawn to play local neighbours and rivals, London Scottish – on 27 January. When Windsor-Lewis met Dawes for lunch at Oxford a week or so before the team was selected, the possible problem was broached. As the prospective captain pointed out, 'I explained to Geoff that, having retired from international rugby, my first consideration had to be for the impending cup match and I would need the permission of the London Welsh committee to play for the Barbarians.' Thankfully, common sense prevailed. The officials at Old Deer Park duly met and approved their captain's involvement in the big game – but only by a majority rather than unanimous vote. Selection of the team was, of course, the prerogative of the Barbarian

John Dawes leaves no one in doubt who is in charge as he prepares the team for the epic match against the All Blacks on the following day. Among those listening (on the far right) is Bob Wilkinson.
(© *Western Mail and Echo*)

committee but Windsor-Lewis sounded out their captain-elect on one or two possibilities. Whatever the intentions to avoid the Lions issue it was an undeniable fact that the majority of the British team that had taken New Zealand by storm were also what Brigadier Glyn Hughes would call 'good Barbarians'. Players like J.P.R. Williams, Gerald Davies, Gareth Edwards and Derek Quinnell from Wales; David Duckham and John Pullin from England; the Scottish prop Sandy Carmichael; and Ireland's Fergus Slattery, Ray McLoughlin and Willie John McBride certainly fitted the Brigadier's bill. They had played in previous end-of-tour matches for the Club at Twickenham and the Arms Park so they would be natural selections for the latest chapter in the series. It would be stretching the point to say that the fact they were also 1971 Lions was incidental; but it could be equally argued that the primary criteria for their selection was that

they were proven Club members who were in good form and would help to constitute the nucleus of a competitive team. No one, after all, wanted a repeat of the one-sided encounter of 1964.

Other well-tried principles also came into play. The team would consist of players who had already represented the Club. There would be no 'new Barbarians'. Of course, in 1973, that still left the committee with a rich vein of talent to choose from. They would be hard pushed to find a top-rank player who had not appeared in the black-and-white shirt at some time in the previous few seasons. Then there was the tradition of including an uncapped player in the team. That, incidentally, was not quite as set in stone as is generally assumed. The Barbarian teams that played against the Springboks in 1952, the Wallabies in 1958 and the All Blacks in 1967 had all contained 15 capped internationals, but it was, most of the time, a preference – and it helped to maintain a club identity. In 1973, however, the committee had in their minds a young lock whom they thought might hold his own in the highest company. Bob Wilkinson had already played against the All Blacks for Cambridge University and Midland Counties (East). In the first he had done particularly well; the second was less memorable. He had also been king of the lineouts in the recent Varsity match. More importantly, perhaps, he had been observed at close quarters. Though still only twenty-one years old he had already played for the Club five times, including the Easter tour of 1972. Contemporary reports wrongly suggested that he was a new Barbarian in 1973. The committee had no qualms about including him as the uncapped player in the side. The young man himself was reasonably sanguine about what lay in store at the Arms Park. 'I really had no inkling that I was in the frame for selection,' he said. 'With the benefit of hindsight I suppose I realise that I fitted the Barbarians profile. I was a Cambridge Blue and was known to Geoff Windsor-Lewis, Micky Steele-Bodger and the committee. As well as the Easter tour the previous year I had also been picked for the match at Leicester at Christmas-time so perhaps they were having another look at me there.'

The selectors must have liked what they had seen and their judgement was more than vindicated. Wilkinson was to be one of the shining lights of the match and he still thinks that was partly due to the way in which he was integrated into the team that weekend. He said, 'I could be forgiven for being awestruck when I arrived at the Royal Hotel in Cardiff. The other players were so good to me and made me feel welcome and part of the whole operation from the first moment. Gareth [Edwards] was particularly good and has continued to be whenever we have met in the years since.' Clearly, the intention was to put together a team that gelled off the field as well as on it. Privately, the committee felt that this was the Club's best chance yet of beating the All Blacks. They would want the players to turn on the style, but a victory would raise the game to a higher plane altogether. With Dawes safely ensconced as captain and Wilkinson pencilled in as the surprise choice, the other 13 names soon fell into place. Apart from Dawes there were nine Test players from the matches in New Zealand in 1971. All of them had strong Barbarian credentials.

J.P.R. Williams at full-back, Gerald Davies and David Duckham on the wings, and Gareth Edwards at scrum-half were automatic selections. Davies had represented the Club against the Wallabies and All Blacks in 1967;

Further preparations for the match with this time Willie John McBride holding centre stage with another attentive audience, including (left to right) Gareth Edwards, Gerald Davies, who was forced to withdraw from the match with an injury, John Pullin and Derek Quinnell.
(© *Western Mail and Echo*)

the other three against the Springboks and Fijians in 1970. Edwards had also played against the 1967 All Blacks. Then there was Michael Gibson. Having been unavailable for three previous end-of-tour matches because of the Irish selectors, injury and a foot-and-mouth outbreak, he had finally played against the Springboks in 1970. Now, at the third attempt, he would be playing against the All Blacks as well. That made six Lions in the back division. The odd man out was at fly-half – Phil Bennett, still establishing himself in his first full season in the Wales side following the retirement of Barry John. In the pack, meanwhile, only three of the selected eight had been regulars in the Test matches Down Under: John Pullin at hooker, Willie John McBride in the second row and Mervyn Davies at number 8. Of the others, prop Ray McLoughlin had been invalided out

of the tour before the Test matches, Fergus Slattery had also not played in the Tests and Derek Quinnell had made one appearance. With the Llanelli prop Barry Llewelyn completing the team at tight-head prop, the committee could fairly claim that this was indeed a Club side.

John Dawes, however, wanted one other person he had worked with before involved. He explained, 'The well-known tradition with the Barbarians was that they were not coached but simply had a bit of a pep talk about open rugby and then went out and tried to put it into practice. I had no problems with that but by 1973 the world was changing. All the international sides had been coached for at least five years and much the same was happening in club rugby. Given the players we had in the team for the All Blacks match it made sense to invite Carwyn James to say a few words to the team beforehand.'

James was a Barbarian in his own right, having played in the celebration match against Ulster in 1957. More pertinently, of course, he had coached Dawes and his men to victory in New Zealand and then Llanelli to a similar triumph over the current All Blacks. When the players and officials gathered in Cardiff 48 hours before the match, it was agreed that James should be invited to speak to the team. The best-laid plans almost backfired. Dawes described what happened: 'I had expected Carwyn to turn up when we were having a run-out on the Friday but there was no show. He eventually appeared on the morning of the match and I arranged with Geoff Windsor-Lewis that we could have a private meeting with him. At eleven o'clock the players assembled in my room at the Royal Hotel, not expecting anything more than a captain's talk

from me. Then the door opened and in walked Carwyn. You could say that the next few minutes had the desired effect. Basically he told us to go out and express ourselves and to take them on early. He particularly stressed this to Phil Bennett, reminding him that he had the beating of these fellows if he was prepared to try something. We all know that Benny took his advice to the letter.'

James' advice was not confined to the prettier aspects of the game in prospect. Fergus Slattery, for one, was given a specific task against the perceived fulcrum of the All Blacks machine: their scrum-half Sid Going. Slattery confessed, 'Carwyn pointed out that Going was carrying a leg injury and that it was my job to try and flatten him when he tried one of his favourite darts around the back of a lineout. I duly obliged and jumped on him.' It was effective advice. Going departed the match injured midway through the second half.

Not everything went to plan, however. In a turn of events reminiscent of the build-up to the match against the Springboks in 1961 the Barbarians were forced to make three changes to their original selection. Perhaps it was a good omen. The first player to pull out early in the week of the match was Barry Llewelyn, who had a knee cartilage injury. His place was taken by Scotland's Sandy Carmichael. Like his fellow prop McLoughlin he had been badly injured in New Zealand a week before the first Test. The other two changes were very much at the eleventh hour. On the morning of the match the two Davies, Gerald and Mervyn, were both declared unfit to play. The wing had pulled a hamstring and the number 8 had a heavy cold. Two other Welshmen, John Bevan and Tommy David, were called into their places. Both necessitated further positional changes in the

BARBARIAN FOOTBALL CLUB v. NEW ZEALAND

At Cardiff, 27th January, 1973.   Barbarians 23 pts   New Zealand 11 pts

The great team of 1973. Back row: E.M. Lewis (touch judge),
G. Windsor-Lewis, J.V. Pullin, W.J. McBride, R.M. Wilkinson,
D.L. Quinnell, A.B. Carmichael, D.J. Duckham, G. Domercq (referee),
D.O. Spyer (touch judge); middle row: G.O. Edwards, C.M.H. Gibson,
H.L. Glyn Hughes, S.J. Dawes (captain), H. Waddell, J.C. Bevan,
R.J. McLoughlin; front row: J.F. Slattery, T. David, P. Bennett,
J.P.R. Williams. (© Barbarian Archive)

line-up. Bevan was a natural left-winger, so David Duckham was switched to the right. Afterwards, Duckham felt it was a blessing in disguise because from the right touch-line he had more opportunities to mount counter-attacks from wayward All Black kicks. He said, 'I waited for the right moments, and when they came I was not anxious to release the ball immediately, although I managed to persuade a number of New Zealand defenders that I had done so more than once.' The dummies, sidesteps and swerves served up by the dashing Englishman remain among the most indelible images of the match. Tommy David's inclusion necessitated Derek Quinnell, originally selected at flanker, moving to the

number 8 position. Despite Mervyn Davies' standing as a world-class player, his absence in no way weakened the team's performance on the day. David, like Quinnell, had already played for the Llanelli team that had beaten the All Blacks, but he had never played for Wales. Bevan and David were new Barbarians and David became the second uncapped player in the side.

As kick-off time approached, there was no escaping the feeling that, despite all the protestations to the contrary, the match that was about to be played was the unofficial fifth international of the All Blacks tour. They had already beaten Wales, England and Scotland and drawn with Ireland. Of the team selected against

the Barbarians, only the hooker, Ron Urlich, and the flanker, Alistair Scown, had not been in the Test XV against Ireland the previous week. The team had not been a particularly popular one, handicapped by a self-imposed darkness and rigidity of purpose that was personified by the fondness of several senior players for wearing black berets and gaucho hats that earned them the sobriquet of 'The Mafia'. This didn't seem to unsettle them at all; rather, some of them rejoiced in it. The net result was to make them unpopular, not least in Wales. Yet, on several occasions on tour, including the opening match against Western Counties and, three days before the Barbarians match, against a combined Neath and Aberavon side, they had displayed the finest 15-man attacking rugby imaginable. Even so, one of their own countrymen, Terry McLean, who had penned such a vivid account of Whineray's team in 1964, entitled his book on the 1972–73 All Blacks *They Missed the Bus*. At Cardiff Arms Park against the Barbarians, however, they went a long way towards putting everything back on track.

They started the proceedings in the best possible manner. For the first time on tour the All Blacks performed the haka. The war dance then was not the fearsome, in-the-opposition's-face fandango that it later became. Then it was a much-loved tradition that was performed as a ceremonial pre-kick-off piece of theatre, done in fact facing not the opposing team but the spectators in the main grandstand. For reasons best known to themselves the All Blacks had voted not to perform it at any one of the previous twenty-seven matches. Now they wisely relented. At their final stop at Cardiff Arms Park it had become a public relations exercise. It was a healthy sign of the positive mood everyone was in.

The Barbarians were doing pretty well themselves. Their high spots in the next 80 minutes were destined to become among the most well-known – and well-loved – snippets of sporting action of modern times. It was the first great rugby spectacle of the video age and to choose the greatest moment of all would be nigh impossible. The majority vote would go to Edwards' try, *that* try, in the third minute. It would be hard to argue against it. John Dawes believed it was the greatest try he had ever seen so early in a game. Michael Gibson identified its true worth with his reference to it being a catalyst. He said: 'It summed up all we believed in about the importance of correct decision-making, the transfer of the ball and the need for total support of the player in possession. The effect of the try was incredible. The noise from the crowd came over the pitch in waves. The score had set a standard and now we had a duty to maintain that standard for the rest of the match.'

It is remembered so well. Fergus Slattery saw the action unfold closer than most: 'When Bennett started that run from his own lines like everyone else, I was just concentrating on getting back behind the ball to cover. Then, suddenly, all the traffic was going the other way. There were a lot of us in a congested group in midfield trying to work out what was going to happen next. Typically, Gareth Edwards was tracking events from the very middle of the pitch. We always reckoned he patrolled that area rather than the edges, but then he popped up for that final pass and the glory of the try. I enjoyed watching it.'

The entire passage of play, from Phil Bennett's impersonation of a startled hare under the shadow of his own posts, through the contributions of J.P.R. Williams, John Pullin,

Tommy David rose from relative obscurity to star billing by being a
vital link in Gareth Edwards' legendary first try. (© *Western Mail and Echo*)

Dawes, Tommy David and Derek Quinnell, culminating in the triumphant try-scoring dive of Gareth Edwards at the other end of the field, is certainly the most celebrated and recalled piece of action the sport has seen. It seemed only appropriate that up in the roof of the South Stand the television commentator describing the unfolding drama was Cliff Morgan. The great Barbarian of yesteryear might also have sown the seeds of one myth when he described Dawes' part in it and, with a marvellous economy of words, commended the captain's 'great dummy!' Years of watching and re-watching the video clip have failed to convince many fans that the All Blacks were mesmerised by any such skill. Dawes has the perfect answer whenever he's asked: 'If Cliff Morgan says it was a dummy, then that's what it was . . . Actually, if you look at it closely you'll see that my intention was to pass the ball to John Bevan. My body angle

shows that I was shaping to do so. Then I didn't. That's a dummy!'

If this was a normal game, everything that followed the opening gambit would have been an anticlimax. But, of course, it wasn't. The play continued at a pace and with an ambition that was unique. For the next half-hour the game went to and fro, the All Blacks forever attempting to set up attacking platforms, the Baa-Baas counter-attacking from deep. In the final ten minutes of the half the Baa-Baas, as Terry McLean said, 'went completely bonkers'. Bennett kicked a penalty goal after Edwards had caught Going in possession and Alex Wyllie had fallen offside. Almost immediately, Slattery pounced on the loose ball after Edwards had again rattled the struggling Going at the base of a defensive scrum and Bennett's conversion stretched the lead to 13 points. The half ended as it had begun, with a spectacular Barbarians try

For sheer power, nothing could equal wing John Bevan as he scored the third try of the coruscating first half.
(© *Western Mail and Echo*)

in the south-west corner. Slattery was again in the action when he caught fly-half Bob Burgess as he struggled to secure another poor pass from Going. Quinnell was at his elbow to charge on and link with Bennett and Dawes as the move swept infield and to the left. The running onto the ball stretched the defence to the limit but Bevan still had a lot to do when he took his captain's pass. The winger's game was built on power as much as pace and his opposite number, the equally sturdy Bryan Williams, was held off as he literally crashed over for the third try of the half.

The Barbarians led 17–nil at the interval. Surely the game was won and lost. The All Blacks thought otherwise. Their captain, Ian Kirkpatrick, dropped the ball in the process of scoring their opening try but Joe Karam kicked a penalty goal. By midway through the half they had reduced the deficit to six points with a brace of tries by Grant Batty. There was

no shortage of action to grab the attention. Before Batty's second try Going had accepted the inevitable with his leg injury and walked off to be replaced by Lin Colling. The little winger was himself involved in an altercation with the towering Tommy David on the touchline after he took exception to what he thought was a late tackle. What might have developed into a nasty incident quite out of tune with the rest of the proceedings ended with the flanker ruffling Batty's hair in admonishment. But he was no naughty schoolboy and moments later his second try as he chipped over J.P.R. Williams' head and regathered confirmed him as an international wing of the highest quality.

It was not always about fancy-Dan attacking, as J.P.R. Williams demonstrates in his tackle of danger-man Grant Batty.
(© *Western Mail and Echo*)

At 17–11 John Dawes concedes that his team might have gone on to lose the game if the All Blacks had scored again. Happily, this was a side that stuck true to its principles of ball-in-hand rugby and attacking the opposition rather than, in the modern parlance, sitting on a lead. Their reward summed up the match. A sustained attack seemed to have ended when Colling picked up a loose ball on his line and kicked to touch. Not quite. Duckham kept the ball in play and, for the umpteenth time in the afternoon, weaved his way infield past several would-be tacklers. By the time he was held, a generous blind side was available back to the right touch-line. Quinnell was on hand for the recycling and Dawes, Williams, Gibson, with a feint and dummy, and Slattery mesmerised the defence before J.P.R. touched down in the corner. With the minimum of fuss Bennett stroked over the conversion from the edge of the right touch-line.

Several more minutes of end-to-end attacking followed but there were no further scores. The Barbarians had won by 23 points to 11. At the dinner in the Royal Hotel Brigadier Glyn Hughes gave his assessment: 'It is the best match ever in the series against touring teams. I believe the victory and the manner of it will provide a big boost to morale in British rugby.' The New Zealand manager, Ernie Todd, agreed and added, 'The Barbarians played a type of rugby we have not met on tour before . . . we

The picture tells its own story as John Dawes is chaired off in triumph. (© *Western Mail and Echo*)

salute them for their champagne rugby. I am sure our players learned a lot today. We will always remember this match.'

No one would disagree with that conclusion. If there was one downside it was that the match set such a high standard of performance and established such a sense of expectation among the public that every match played by the Club against successive touring teams since then has paled in comparison. But so would any game of rugby union. Barbarians v. All Blacks in 1973 was, after all, the epitome of perfection.

XI

ONWARD
AND
UPWARD

'The Barbarians' very name creates a flavour and a passion which is denied all others, recognised, imitated, even envied the world over.'

– Gerald Davies, 1988

So how do you follow a match such as the 1973 classic at Cardiff Arms Park? There was a ready-made answer. In the autumn of the next year the pride of New Zealand rugby was returning to Britain, for the first time not on an epic four-month odyssey but on one of the shorter tours that were to become the norm within the next two decades. The trend towards these whistle-stop visits would eventually pose a particular problem for the Barbarians and the survival of their traditional end-of-tour fixture. But not in 1974. The driving force for the tour was the centenary of the Irish Rugby Football Union, and six matches were scheduled against the provinces

and an international at Lansdowne Road. The Welsh Rugby Union and the Rugby Football Union requested fixtures in an extra week of the tour. The IRFU, the official hosts, agreed, on the understanding that the match against Ireland was the only international on the itinerary. A compromise agreement was reached: in Cardiff the All Blacks would play a midweek match against a Welsh XV and on the following Saturday at Twickenham the opposition would be the Barbarians. Immediately, the expectation of another extravaganza on the lines of 1973 was born. Depending on your point of view, it was either a fortuitous coincidence or an unwanted burden that, in the summer of 1974, another British Isles team had gone to the southern hemisphere and, this time, overwhelmed South Africa. The subtext to the impending Barbarians v. All Blacks match was inescapable. History was repeating itself with a vengeance.

The Club's selectors went only part of the way towards distancing itself from the concept of another Lions-in-disguise formation. The entire British Isles Test pack from the summer was selected to represent the Barbarians at Twickenham, with Gareth Edwards at scrum-half and Andy Irvine at full-back. In fairness the committee was merely doing the sensible thing. These All Blacks were a strong side. They had won every match in Ireland and then defeated what was in effect if not name the full Wales team in Cardiff. Anything less than a strong Barbarians pack would be overpowered and probably overrun. As events transpired, even this strong combination proved incapable of beating them. Five of the backs came from outside the Lions squad: Gerald Davies and David Duckham were still the best wings around but had made themselves unavailable for the trip to South Africa; the Englishmen Peter Warfield and Peter Preece were at centre; and the uncapped player at fly-half was John Bevan, not the powerhouse wing of that name but an Aberavon clubman. In addition, Andy Irvine had played on the wing rather than at full-back for the British Isles. Only four of the heroic team of eighteen months earlier – Duckham, Edwards, Willie John McBride, now the captain, and Fergus Slattery – were at Twickenham for the return match. Gerald and Mervyn Davies, the two eleventh hour withdrawals at the Arms Park, would now get their chance, while Sandy Carmichael and Derek Quinnell were named among the replacements. The All Blacks had ten

of the 1973 side in their ranks, including Ian Kirkpatrick, though he had surprisingly lost the captaincy, and, ominously, a fully fit Sid Going. Their new captain was another back-rower, Andy Leslie. Any attempts to shake off the glorious shadow of the earlier match were obviously doomed from the start: the two games even had the same referee, Georges Domercq of France. The scene was set, then, for The Greatest Match, Part Two. But as Fergus Slattery said, 'You can't manufacture these situations.'

The 1974 match was a perfectly acceptable encounter in its own right. Indeed, Peter West reported in *The Times* that it was 'throbbing and thunderous'. It was not short of impressive individual performances. Kirkpatrick again displayed the qualities that made him a world-class flanker. Going relished the chance to, as it were, put the record straight after he had hobbled off in Cardiff. Grant Batty was still a jack-in-the-box wing, alert for any opportunity that came his way. The Barbarians' pack had all the nuggety efficiency that had made them unbeatable in another guise in South Africa. As a contest it could not be faulted, but it lacked the *joie de vivre* of its forerunner. The two great wings, Gerald Davies and Duckham, received the not-so-grand total of four passes in the eighty minutes. From one of them, Davies linked with Irvine for the full-back to hoist the kick that led to the match-saving try. That was with less than ten minutes left to play. The only Barbarians points in the first hour and more of the game had come from three penalty goals from Irvine, two of them mighty efforts from a 50-yard range. The All Blacks had looked the likeliest to score tries throughout the match, though when they did they were scrappy affairs. Leslie scored the first after Gerald Davies was trapped as, perhaps sensing the

Mervyn Davies had been forced to pull out of the 1973 match against New Zealand, but at Twickenham the following year he was in the thick of the action and scored the Barbarians' try as two All Blacks tried in vain to stop him. (© Colorsport)

need to light a spark on the match, he tried to sidestep out of his own 25. Joe Karam had already kicked a penalty goal that secured a 7–3 lead at the interval.

Two second-half penalty goals by Irvine gave the Barbarians a flattering 9–7 advantage before the All Blacks claimed their second try. It was a tribute to opportunism and at least a little vision, if not brilliance, as Batty, at the base of a ruck, kicked to the open side of the pitch where Bryan Williams collected the ball for what appeared to be the decisive score. Karam's conversion stretched the lead to 13–9. Then Gerald Davies, Peter Preece and Irvine at last played a part in a late attack and Mervyn Davies stormed up to claim Irvine's kick and stretched out for the touchdown. The match ended as a 13–all draw.

It would be harsh to describe the game as an anticlimax, more a reminder that, however competitive matches after 1973 would be, there would always be a propensity to draw unfavourable comparisons with what had gone before. The 1974 sequel was an occasion worthy of a packed Twickenham, where an unbeaten All Blacks team and the majority of an all-conquering Lions squad could be saluted, and the aura of the Barbarians was retained.

The latter was very important to the Club and its many well-wishers and, over the next 20 years, even as the touring itineraries were shortened and the domestic calendar became more congested, the fixtures against overseas teams continued. The Springboks did not tour Europe again until 1992. However, between 1976 and 1993 seven games were played against the All Blacks and Wallabies. Of the four against the Australian side, the first provided the Barbarians with another victory.

At Cardiff Arms Park on 24 January 1976 the Barbarians team was built around a nucleus of players who had served the Club well for several seasons. Under the captaincy of Mervyn Davies there was a gifted back division that included Michael Gibson, Gerald Davies, Gareth Edwards and Phil Bennett, while Andy Irvine had replaced the original selection, J.P.R. Williams. In the pack there were Sandy Carmichael, Gordon Brown and Fergus Slattery. There was certainly a sense of continuity, of 'good Barbarians' again answering the call of duty. With them were others who had emerged more recently and would appear again in the future. Ray Gravell, J.J. Williams, Peter Wheeler and the uncapped Cardiff prop Mike Knill toured North America with the Club later in 1976. The unsung hero of 1973, Bob Wilkinson, had also not been forgotten and was included among the replacements. He was still playing for the Barbarians on the Easter tour of 1984, twelve years after his debut, when Geoff Windsor-Lewis reputedly told him, 'I don't think we can go on picking you much longer!' The touring-team game was, again, a case of a reunion for current players as well as alickadoos and that was another important factor in its enduring success. The occasional victories also helped and, though the 19–7 defeat of the 1976 Wallabies was by no means a glorious one, it was nevertheless another important feather in the Club's cap. Curiously, the star-studded back division, even with a good supply of possession, stuttered rather than shone throughout the match. The Wallabies had a similar tour record to many of their predecessors: eighteen victories in twenty-four outings before the Barbarians fixture and beating only Ireland in the four internationals. They were well led by scrum-half John Hipwell and had other fine players such as Paddy Batch on the wing, Paul McLean at fly-half or full-back and, in the pack, Mark Loane and Greg Cornelson. Unfortunately, only Loane was fit to play in the final match. That made the Baa-Baas even more the pre-match favourites and they just about justified the tag. Once again Georges Domercq was the referee.

On a cold winter's day the inevitable capacity crowd again turned up at Cardiff Arms Park. By half-time they were already sensing that the match was destined to splutter along on three cylinders. A penalty goal by full-back Jim Hindmarsh had given the Wallabies a fourth-minute lead and it wasn't until over half an hour had been played that the Baa-Baas overtook it. From a ruck on the visitors' 25, Edwards, Bennett, Irvine and J.J. Williams combined before the fly-half reappeared in the

A typical Barbarian attack against the Wallabies in 1976, spearheaded by Gareth Edwards with Andy Irvine backing up. (© Colorsport)

In defence the Barbarians were equally formidable, as Mervyn Davies shows when stopping a Wallaby attack. (© Huw Evans Agency)

201

Hooker Peter Wheeler finishes off a Barbarians attack with a try at the posts against the Wallabies. At the back is Fergus Slattery and to the right is Allan Martin.
(© Huw Evans Agency)

move to take the wing's inside pass and dash over for an unconverted try. The Wallabies regained the lead when wing Jim Ryan crashed

over in the corner early in the second half. Sensing an unexpected defeat, the Baa-Baas roused themselves. Hooker Peter Wheeler scored under the posts. Bennett converted and kicked a penalty goal to put his side in control at 13–7. There had been very little spectacular back play but, as the final whistle approached, the crowd at least had the satisfaction of seeing the former sprinter J.J. Williams pick up a loose pass, admittedly with the suspicion of a knock-on, and go on an arcing run to the posts for the final try, converted again by Bennett.

Given the insatiable demands from near and far for the Barbarians to recognise their alleged duty to pick Lions-strength teams whenever the Wallabies, All Blacks or Springboks loomed on the horizon, it was ironic that in September 1977 the Club was invited to play the Lions in aid of the Appeal Fund for the Silver Jubilee of Queen Elizabeth II. It was also a great honour and the committee made sure that they picked a side fit for the occasion. The Lions had returned from New Zealand with a record not quite on a par with their predecessors of 1971

Win or lose, the Barbarians and their overseas opponents, in this case the Wallabies of 1976, finished their matches still the best of friends. (© Colorsport)

THE HOME RUGBY UNIONS

LIONS

v

BARBARIANS

TWICKENHAM Saturday, 10th September, 1977

Official Programme: Twenty Five Pence

Another memorable day for the Club as, for the first time, the Barbarians play the Lions at Twickenham in front of a 70,000 crowd and in aid of the Silver Jubilee of Queen Elizabeth II. (© Barbarian Archive)

and 1974. The Test series had been lost 3–1, cruelly so courtesy of a last-minute try in the fourth Test. A month later, 13 of the British Isles XV in Auckland faced the Barbarians at Twickenham. The Club's line-up benefited from the fact that three leading backs, J.P.R. Williams, Gerald Davies and Gareth Edwards, had not been available to tour with the Lions. As good Barbarians they were obvious selections. Also in the side was Bob Wilkinson at lock and an all-French back row of Jean-

Pierre Rives, Jean-Pierre Bastiat and Jean-Claude Skrela. A feast of rugby was in the offing and a capacity crowd was in attendance. The Barbarians were outgunned by the powerful Lions' Test pack and handicapped by the lack of a goal-kicker, but they matched their opponents try for try. They were also not disconcerted when they fell behind 15–nil. Andy Irvine kicked three penalty goals and Phil Bennett converted a try by Steve Fenwick. In a second-half comeback Gerald Davies converted a try by Williams and, although they conceded two more Lions tries to Gareth Evans and Irvine, they were far from beaten. In a strong final quarter Rives inspired tries for Ray Gravell and Dave McKay. The final score was 23–14; more importantly, the Barbarians and

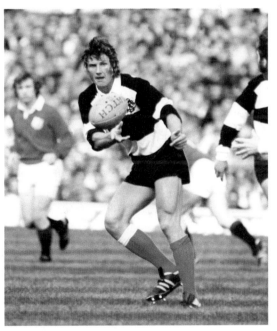

Jean Claude Skrela, of Toulouse and France, in action against the Lions.

(© Colorsport)

the moment the teams were announced. Neither fly-halfs were current internationals and on this occasion that was good news. The Barbarians opted for Phil Bennett, who, like John Dawes in 1973, had retired from Test rugby; that, too, was a good omen. The All Blacks, to their credit, overlooked the utilitarian Doug Bruce, who had guided them to a Grand Slam against the four home countries and selected the mercurial Maori Eddie Dunn. Elsewhere, equally exciting names were announced. In the back row the Barbarians had the French duo Jean-Pierre Rives and Jean-Claude Skrela alongside Derek Quinnell. The Llanelli number 8, in recognition of his fine service to the Club for many years, was a popular choice as captain. Under his charge were three uncapped players, the Richmond prop Will Dickinson, Aberavon's Neil Hutchings in the centre and the Neath wing Elgan Rees, who had toured New Zealand with the Lions in 1977. Quinnell's opposite number as All Blacks captain was Graham Mourie, an intelligent flanker who was later to captain the Barbarians. From these good beginnings a fine afternoon's rugby developed.

Not many points were scored in the first half but that was no indictment of the quality of what was served up. On a fine, clear day the pace of the game was noticeable from the off. Most of it was set by the All Blacks, whose support play could only be achieved by a team that had been together for several weeks. This was their 18th match together and, so far, only Munster, at their fortress of Thomond Park in Limerick, had lowered their colours. As several chances were wasted, the hope was that the Barbarians would follow suit. It was a close-run thing. A try to each side – Brad Johnstone for the tourists in the 24th minute and Mike

Another great French flanker, Jean-Pierre Rives, who also played against the Lions, was nominated by Micky Steele-Bodger as an ideal Barbarian.
(© Colorsport)

the Lions had helped to raise £100,000, the largest single donation, for the Silver Jubilee Fund.

In 1978, again in Cardiff, the Barbarians played the All Blacks for the third time in five and a half years. They had beaten them sensationally, drawn with them fortuitously, and now they were to lose to them at the last gasp. It was a match in the finest traditions of the series. All the signs were favourable from

Slemen for the Club 14 minutes later – had left the score locked at 4–all. Then penalty goals by Brian McKechnie, his only success in nine attempts, and Bennett carried the stalemate forward to 7–all. The points flowed more freely as the second half advanced. Tries by Leicester Rutledge and Bryan Williams seemed to have settled the game in favour of the All Blacks but the Barbarians turned the match on its head. A quickly taken tap by scrum-half Brynmor Williams set up Slemen for his second try. A brilliant touch-line conversion by Bennett and a less difficult penalty goal with only seven minutes left put the Baa-Baas ahead at 16–15. The curse of the last-minute score was about to strike yet again. Dunn, the playmaker selected to oil the wheels of the back division, stood behind a five-metre scrum in the seventy-ninth minute. With a deadly efficiency the ball was spun back to him and over went the drop goal. The All Blacks had won 18–16.

By the 1980s the fixtures had lost their three-to four-year cyclical pattern. The postponement of the match against the Wallabies in 1982 because of a blizzard meant that after the match against the All Blacks there was a six-year gap, the longest in the series, before the Barbarians next played a touring team. The Wallabies were met twice in Cardiff in 1984 and 1988 and, in 1989, the Club returned to Twickenham to host the All Blacks. Not surprisingly, victories were even harder to come by. The long interval had also allowed a new generation of star players to come on the scene and that was especially the case with the Wallabies. Their 1984 team had achieved history by winning an international Grand Slam in the British Isles, powered by marvellous teamwork and supreme backs such as Mark Ella, Michael Lynagh, Nick Farr-Jones and David Campese. Farr-Jones did not play

against the Barbarians but the others did; so too did redoubtable forwards like Steve Cutler, Simon Poidevin and Tommy Lawton.

The Barbarians knew that their excellent three-wins-in-four-matches record against the Wallabies was under threat and that their own side needed a clever balance of ball-winners and ball-users. They again selected two Frenchmen, Serge Blanco and Jerome Gallion, had pace on the wings with Rory Underwood and the uncapped Simon Smith, and ball-winning lineout forwards in Robert Norster and Donal Lenihan. Gareth Davies, no longer in the Wales side, was captain and fly-half. In what turned out to be a helter-skelter of a match the team fell just short of victory. Along with all the other traditions of the fixture it had become expected that a Frenchman would officiate. Georges Domercq had refereed three times in the 1970s. Rene Hourquet was his successor but he was to be too lenient in the matter of knock-ons, forward passes and obstruction and the Wallabies, in particular, took full advantage.

It was undeniably edge-of-the-seat entertainment. A try by prop Iain Milne and two penalty goals by Davies against a Lynagh penalty gave the Baa-Baas an early 10–3 lead. By the interval they were behind 10–15, a sweeping length-of-the-field run setting up a try for lock Steve Williams and a break by Lynagh providing another for Poidevin; Lynagh, playing at centre, converted both. Soon it was 27–10 after Lynagh added two more conversions to tries by Roger Gould and Michael Hawker. For a moment, at least, there were forebodings of a repeat of the heavy 1964 defeat against the All Blacks but these Baa-Baas were made of sterner stuff. The two wings, Underwood and Smith, scored tries and, at the

very end, Gallion dashed over from a lineout and then Davies' pinpoint pass put Blanco over in the corner. But by then the captain Andrew Slack and Poidevin had added further tries for the Wallabies and Lynagh had converted one of them. Still, the Baa-Baas were far from disgraced at 30–37 – and their five tries were more than any other team had scored against the Grand Slam Wallabies.

The majority of the Wallabies stayed together for the rest of the '80s and were generally acknowledged to be the great entertainers of world rugby. A failure to win the first Rugby World Cup when it was played in both Australia and New Zealand didn't put a dampener on the team's aspirations. When they next played the Barbarians in November 1988, the match ended with what might have been a choreographed climax, a moment of individual brilliance fit to rank alongside Whineray's magical finale 24 years before. The star turn was David Campese. The wing who had first displayed his brilliance in 1984 produced something truly unforgettable. As the match entered injury time, with his side already in a winning position at 33–22, he collected the ball in his own half and with the whole Barbarians defence in front of him. With the ball clutched in one hand he sidestepped off his left foot, sold dummies and swerved in and out, turning his would-be tacklers so that they were dizzy, before touching down under the posts. It was a moment of genius. The Cardiff crowd applauded him all the way back to the halfway line and beyond, where he found his teammates also saluting him.

Earlier in the day Gerald Davies had reminded *The Times*' readership of the essence of the Club:

> The Barbarians' very name creates a flavour and a passion which is denied all others, recognised, imitated, even envied the world over . . . The Barbarian flamboyance even makes us critics wonder about the rhymes and rhythms of a game which quite often can fail to amuse and become jaded with too much reasoning and analysis.

Even before Campese's glorious show-stopper the Barbarians and the Wallabies had manufactured another memorable advertisement for the game. Captained this time by the Irish flanker Philip Matthews, the Baa-Baas were starved of possession for long periods but the pack around him never gave up. In the loose, forwards such as David Sole, Robert Norster, Andy Robinson and Matthews chased and harassed their more organised opponents. With Jonathan Davies and Robert Jones at half-back there was always the chance of break-outs and opportunist scores and, to their credit, four tries were scored. An interception by Mark Ring and a run-in by Matt Duncan accounted for the first, but with Gavin Hastings' conversion it was their only score of the first half. Tries by Jeff Miller, Acura Niuqila and Nick Farr-Jones, all converted by Michael Lynagh, had already given the Wallabies an 18–6 lead by then. Campese scored his first try immediately after the restart – another virtuoso effort as he burst through onto a pass from Lynagh and literally strolled to the posts for another converted try. Later in the half Steve Tuynman plopped over from a lineout for the fifth try and Lynagh kicked a penalty goal. Without ever threatening to win the match, the Barbarians never gave up. Hastings scored a try, which he converted himself, and, late in the game, added the extra points to a try by Robinson. When Jonathan

Mercurial fly-half Jonathan Davies was another
great favourite with the Barbarians and he
revelled in the open rugby on show in the 1988
match against the Wallabies. Alongside him is
Andy Robinson. (© Huw Evans Agency)

Robert Jones partnered Jonathan Davies in 22 games for
Wales so it was only natural that they should be paired
together at half-back against the Wallabies. As the lineout
breaks up, Robert Norster looks on.
(© Huw Evans Agency)

Davies collected the kick-off after Robinson's try
and ran straight back at the Wallabies, and Rory
Underwood was on hand to send the uncapped
centre Colin Laity over for another try, it looked
at least as if the Baa-Baas had scored the best try
of the afternoon. Then Campese took centre-
stage. Once again a Barbarians match at the
Arms Park had left everyone with a warm glow
of satisfaction.

David Campese hadn't quite finished with the
Barbarians. A month later he was invited to
make his Club debut in the Christmas match at
Leicester. He scored a try in the 36–19 victory.
He played in the same fixture 12 months later

and in 1990 returned for the centenary
celebrations and turned out against England and
Wales. And then, in 1992, he completed a hat-
trick of appearances for the Wallabies against the
Club. The scene had moved to Twickenham and
another tour was to end on a high note. This
time it was of 13 matches and, although the
Wallabies had lost twice in Wales to Swansea
and Llanelli, and again in Munster, they had
completed the main business of the trip. They
had won the two international matches against
Wales and Ireland; to beat the Barbarians would
be a bonus. Campese and his teammates were
returning to the ground where they had been
crowned world champions a year earlier but
they were keeping everything in perspective.
One of their travelling pressmen, Greg Growden,
revealed their true feelings in the match
programme at Twickenham:

Thank goodness a Barbarians fixture has been organised to put everything back into perspective, remind everyone that touring can be fun, and bring the hardest of Wallaby seasons to an end. The Wallabies have been looking forward to today's fixture as it is the ultimate release, a rare chance to play for the sheer enjoyment, where they can at last perform without fear or favour, and show their proper attacking attributes, without worrying about what will happen if all goes wrong.

Nothing, of course, went wrong. A try to each side in the first half, and better goal-kicking by the Wallabies, established a 13–8 lead at the break. Along with Campese they now had two world-class centres in Jason Little and Tim Horan. It was Little's break after a ruck that set up Horan's try. That was in the 13th minute. Seven minutes later the Baa-Baas responded with the try of the match. Micky Skinner started the move in his own half, Stuart Barnes took the

direct line through the middle and Ian Smith, Will Carling and Scott Gibbs all lent a hand before full-back Mike Rayer, with an exquisitely timed pass, put Ian Hunter over in the corner. The other points of the half came from two Marty Roebuck penalty goals and a conversion for the Wallabies and a Barnes penalty for the Baa-Baas. The Club had a cosmopolitan second row in the pack, with New Zealand's Ian Jones alongside the 19-stone Canadian Norm Hadley. With Jeff Probyn in front of them at tight-head prop and still burrowing away at the age of 36, the forwards were doing particularly well in the scrums. It was only appropriate then that a 5-metre scrum drive enabled Jones to touch down and level the scores in the 55th minute. The match was now in the melting pot but ten points for the Wallabies inside five minutes widened the gap again. Roebuck kicked a penalty and converted a try by prop Dan Crowley. Not to be outdone, Probyn, who had given Crowley a particularly uncomfortable afternoon in the set pieces, matched that effort with a try under the posts that Barnes

Will Carling captained the Club's team against the Wallabies at Twickenham in 1992. Standing: Dr Ben Gilfeather (physio), H. Roberts (rep), I. Hunter, B.B. Clarke, D.F. Cronin (replacement), N. Hadley, I.D. Jones, M.G. Skinner, N.J. Popplewell, J.A. Probyn, N.N. Meek, H. Williams-Jones (rep), C.M. Chalmers (rep), Kevin Murphy; seated: M.A. Rayer, S. Barnes, R.N. Jones, I.S. Gibbs, W.D.C. Carling (captain), I.R. Smith, T. Underwood, J-B Lafond (rep), R.H St B. Moon (rep).
(© Barbarian Archive)

converted. That left the Barbarians 20–23 down with three minutes left but the last word went to the Wallabies when hooker and skipper Phil Kearns burrowed over from a maul and Roebuck converted.

On this occasion there had been no final flourish for Campese but both sides had served up another treat. The great man was glad to be a part of it. He said, 'The Barbarians do rugby a good service. And there is definitely room for a fixture like this one at the end of the tour.' The match may have lacked the intensity of an international but the Wallabies were more than happy with their 30–20 victory. Meanwhile, the traditional principles of the Barbarians were still surviving. In *The Times* David Hands commended them for that:

> If the Barbarians were to shear their eccentricities, the uncapped players for instance . . . and give it the trappings of a third international fixture, they would

stand in danger of losing a fine tradition. They would deprive players, opponents and their own of an outstanding rugby occasion.

The Club had no intention of doing that. Either side of the 1992 match against the Wallabies they played the All Blacks at Twickenham in 1989 and in Cardiff in 1993. The New Zealand side of that era were a special breed. Between 16 November 1986 and 25 November 1989 when they stepped out onto the Twickenham turf to play the Barbarians they were unbeaten in 46 matches, including the first Rugby World Cup in 1987, which they had won with something to spare. Their fourteen-match tour that was ending at Twickenham was no different, with sixty-eight tries scored and only seven conceded. The challenge facing the Barbarians was again considerable. The selectors chose the props and locks that had packed down for the British Isles in Australia

The team that played the All Blacks in 1989 included two sets of brothers – the Hastings and Underwoods. Standing: C.J. Stephens (replacement), L.F.P. Aherne (rep), G. Jones (rep), J.C. Guscott, G.W. Rees, P.M. Matthews, P.J. Ackford, W.A. Dooley, P.T. Davies, S.J. Smith (rep), D.C. Fitzgerald (rep), B.J. Mullin (rep); seated: A.G. Hastings, D. Young, B.C. Moore, D.M.B. Sole (captain), N.C. Farr-Jones, R. Underwood, S. Hastings, T. Underwood, A. Clement. (© Barbarian Archive)

earlier in the year: David Sole plus Brian Moore, David Young, Wade Dooley and Paul Ackford. They would at least provide the platform for a true contest. Philip Matthews, who had captained the Club against the 1988 Wallabies, was in the back row with Phil Davies and Gary Rees. In the backs there were two sets of brothers – Gavin and Scott Hastings and Rory and Tony Underwood. Tony was uncapped. A late change at fly-half saw Anthony Clement drafted in for the injured Craig Chalmers. Completing the line-up were Australia's Nick Farr-Jones, already a big name in the sport, and Jerry Guscott, who would soon rank alongside him as a sporting celebrity. The All Blacks were led by Wayne Shelford, though he was forced to retire at half-time and be replaced by Zinzan Brooke. Other names such as Grant Fox, Steve McDowell, Sean Fitzpatrick, Gary Whetton and Mike Brewer confirmed this as a New Zealand team on a par with the greatest sides in their country's history. It was a measure of the Barbarians' own quality that they led them at half-time and continued to do so throughout the third quarter until the tourists' greater teamwork finally broke them down.

The Barbarians might even have won. The general consensus afterwards was that they had by far the better of the front-five confrontation, were a little off the pace at getting to the rucks and mauls, shaded the lineouts, and were a potent attacking force on the wings. Unfortunately, other parts of their machine functioned fitfully. Farr-Jones and Clement had never played as a half-back combination before – and it showed. Too many moves broke down in midfield and the Underwoods became ever-distant wings. And yet they held the half-time lead at 10–6. In the third minute Matthews supported a snipe by Farr-Jones for a try. It was cancelled out by a try by Craig Innes and converted by Fox midway through the half. Two penalty goals by Gavin Hastings in the final five minutes of the half regained the lead, but that was the end of the Baa-Baas' scoring. In a one-way second half Brooke and Richard Loe scored tries and Fox, who rarely missed anything, converted both and slotted a penalty goal to make the final score 21–10.

The selection of the Underwood and Hastings brothers in 1989 had provided another example of how the Barbarians invariably hit the right notes in so many ways. The next All Blacks encounter, in 1993, offered another family connection, this time of father and son. Twenty years after Derek Quinnell had supplied the scoring pass for Gareth Edwards' match-defining try, a Quinnell was again playing for the Barbarians against the All Blacks. His son Scott was 21 years old and had only recently had his international baptism for Wales against Canada. Wales had lost and the rugby community there had sunk into one of its periodic troughs of despair. The return of the Barbarians provided the perfect antidote but, even as the great deeds of 1973 were rehashed yet again, Quinnell Senior had the right advice for his son. He said, 'Scott doesn't want to hear about history. He's off to play for the Barbarians and I hope he enjoys it. It's a different game.'

It was different for the All Blacks too, because, against all predictions, they had actually lost a Test match on the tour – and to England, at that, a week earlier. When they arrived in Cardiff to prepare for the Barbarians, that setback was preying on their minds more than their record seven-tries and fifty-points annihilation of Scotland earlier in the tour was comforting them. Not that they need have worried. They shot into a 17-point lead, rather like their opponents had done 20 years earlier, and in the end were convincing 25 points to 12 victors. The match confirmed again what many had known for a long time: scratch teams, even those under the prestigious banner of the Barbarians, were less and less likely to beat the touring team as the years went by.

The Barbarians' 1993 team and replacements were drawn from seven countries, including the French lock Olivier Roumat, the Australian Ewen McKenzie, and the uncapped South African centre Christiaan Scholtz. Scott Hastings was captain but even with Scott Gibbs alongside him and Gary Armstrong and Eric Elwood directing operations at half-back the moments of inspiration were few and far between. Nevertheless, there were flashes of inspiration to savour, with Anthony Clement, the fly-half in 1988, far more effective as a counter-attacking full-back. The All Black tide, though, was typically remorseless. A loose lineout tap let in Craig Dowd for the first try; the power and pace of wing Inga Tuigamala accounted for the second. The goal-kicking wing Jeff Wilson converted both and added a penalty goal. Otherwise it was a frustrating afternoon for Wilson. Against Scotland he had scored a hat-trick of tries on his Test debut. Against the Barbarians he was away on the outside of his marker, the Cardiff wing Nigel Walker, three times. Each time he was caught. It was a fine contest within a contest: Wilson had played cricket for New Zealand; Walker had hurdled for Great Britain in the Olympic Games.

For the first time since 1964 the Barbarians failed to score a try. Their only points came from four penalty goals in the first half by Elwood but another goal by Wilson kept the All Blacks ahead at 20–12. The second half was largely even, with the Baa-Baas' defence holding out the persistent All Blacks attacks. Five minutes before the final whistle one more surge at last found a way through. Several All Blacks handled before the lock Ian Jones galloped over for the last try of the tour and a 25–12 win. The try wasn't quite in the class of Campese's magic five years earlier but it was memorable in its own way. Ian Jones had played for the Barbarians against the Wallabies and would do so again in 1996. Before then he was destined to don the black-and-white jersey again against the Springboks – and to share in another famous victory.

HISTORY
REPEATS
ITSELF

'It was amazing that, in two days, players from several different countries came together and gelled so well . . . and it culminated in as good a win as I've ever been part of.'
– Robert Jones, 1994

The Barbarians played the Springboks for the fourth time on 3 December 1994. The match was staged at Lansdowne Road in Dublin, where their only previous appearance had been in 1970 in a match to celebrate the centenary of the Wanderers club. It was also the first time for a traditional end-of-tour fixture to be staged in Ireland. Included in the Baa-Baas team was the Irish hooker Keith Wood. Thirty-three years earlier his late father, Gordon, had also been selected for the Club against the Springboks at Cardiff. On that day the Barbarians had recorded a famous victory. History was about to repeat itself.

Irish players had featured prominently for the Club in the 18 previous matches against the overseas teams. Karl Mullen was in the team that beat the Wallabies in 1948; Jimmy Nelson had been captain in the 1952 match against the Springboks and Ronnie Dawson triumphantly so in 1961; Noel Murphy, Willie John McBride and Philip Matthews had also led teams in the past; and names such as O'Reilly, Slattery, Gibson and Culliton were synonymous with the greatest deeds in the series. So a game between the Barbarians and the Springboks at Lansdowne Road was always likely to be a success.

The reality exceeded all expectations. As the match approached, the Irish rugby community put their full weight of support behind the project. All 50,000 tickets were sold and Edmund Van Esbeck's comments in the *Irish Times* summed up the general feeling of expectation. On the morning of the match he wrote:

> It is remarkable, bearing in mind Ireland's place at the top table of rugby affairs dating back to the 1870s, that this will only be the second occasion for the Barbarian jersey to appear at Lansdowne Road . . . They also played in an Old Wesley centenary match three years ago, but that was in Donnybrook. And however important such centenary occasions are, a match against a touring side is the pinnacle. Selection for it is second only to international honours.

In the same article Van Esbeck added, 'The venue is what one might term an overdue compliment to Ireland and will represent a unique occasion for a capacity crowd to savour and hopefully a match to decorate so notable an event.'

The match was the 13th and final game of the Springboks tour, a feature of which had been some erratic results. The two internationals against Scotland and Wales had been won easily enough, the champion Welsh club Swansea had been overwhelmed 78–7, but a midweek match against Scotland A had been narrowly lost. The word from their camp was that the main business of the tour, to win the two internationals, had been completed satisfactorily and the Barbarians match was a chance to 'let their hair down'. If that was true then the wheel really had come full circle. After all, it was while their 1961 predecessors were in Dublin that the suggestion was made that the imminent match against the Baa-Baas in Cardiff should be called off because of injuries and illness and an exhibition game played in its place. That offer had been politely declined and an epic match had followed. Now, in 1994, promises of gala rugby were being aired again by the tourists.

The Barbarians, meanwhile, prepared their own team selection. Once again no one could accuse them of following a 'best of British' agenda. For a start there was a Frenchman, the wing Philippe Saint-Andre, the Canadian flanker Al Charron and the All Black lock Ian Jones. Among the replacements were the Australian centre Pat Howard and an uncapped South African with the Newport club, Guy Manson-Bishop. Two of the three Englishmen in the starting line-up, Jonathan Callard at full-

In 1961 an all-Irish front row had helped the Barbarians defeat the Springboks. Thirty-three years later in Dublin, Peter Clohessy, Keith Wood and Nick Popplewell prepare to prove that history is about to repeat itself.
(© Barbarian Archive)

back and Neil Back at flanker, were not in the current England team, while Bristol's 6 ft 9 in. lock Simon Shaw was the uncapped player in the side. Elsewhere in the pack Rob Wainwright completed the back row and, with another echo of 1961, there was an all-Irish front row: for Millar, Dawson and Wood Senior in the earlier game, now read Nick Popplewell, Wood Junior and Peter Clohessy. In the back division was a fourth Irishman, Simon Geoghegan, on the right wing with Scott Hastings of Scotland and Mike Hall of Wales at centre and another Scottish–Welsh combination at half-back. Craig Chalmers, who had been forced to withdraw from the Club's match against the All Blacks in 1989, was at fly-half, with Robert Jones at scrum-half. The selection of Jones was particularly well-received. A Barbarian of nine-years' standing, he had already played against the Wallabies twice and against Argentina in the centenary season. He was also one of the

finest scrum-halfs of his generation, good enough to go on two tours with the British Isles and win forty-nine caps for Wales. Unaccountably, in 1994 he was no longer an automatic choice for his country: an oversight that baffled many observers. The Barbarians had no hesitation in inviting him and made him captain as well. He rose to the appointment magnificently. Before the team had even arrived in Dublin, Jones had made a point of telephoning every one of them to offer his congratulations on their selection and to remind them of the honour of playing in such a match. He was also frank enough to admit, 'I certainly want to get back in the Welsh team and I hope this match will help me to do that. I am looking forward to the game. There will be tremendous atmosphere; there always is in Dublin.' The match and its aftermath turned out to be everything he had hoped for.

It was obvious after the first five minutes that the match was not going to be an airy-fairy affair but something with real bite. Though the Springboks had made five changes to the team that had beaten Wales a week earlier, they still had a nucleus of proven performers, including Andre Joubert at full-back, Pieter Muller in the centre, Joost van der Westhuizen at scrum-half, Os du Randt, Mark Andrews and Ruben Kruger in the pack and all under the inspiring leadership of François Pienaar.

Their avowed intention of playing an open game was evident within 70 seconds of the kick-off when Pienaar drove forward, a ruck was won and Kruger received a scoring pass from Gavin Johnson. A five-points start and a real challenge to the Barbarians. Very soon, though, a game plan emerged. Robert Jones was putting together a rich mix of his bullet-like passes, sniping runs and deadly box-kicks.

French wing Philippe Saint-Andre scored the first try of the match against the Springboks in 1994. The Barbarians nearest to him are Craig Chalmers and Jon Callard.

(© Inpho)

And when the ball went to the ground, Neil Back was invariably the first man there to regather it. When penalty goal opportunities arrived, they were at least attempted. Unfortunately, Callard missed three in the first 25 minutes. He eventually found his touch after Saint-Andre dribbled the ball from halfway to score a try that the full-back converted from the touch-line. He added a penalty goal for a 10–5 lead at the interval. Fifteen minutes after the restart the scoreboard hadn't changed. Then the Springboks clicked into gear. Johnson again provided the final pass for a try by Muller and when, two minutes later, Johnson finished off a move himself for the third try his side was ahead 15–10.

The points were now coming with a flourish and soon from the opposite direction. In the 60th minute a Springbok passing move broke down and Pat Howard collected an interception for a long run into opposition territory. Just as he was about to be overhauled he floated a pass to Geoghegan, who ran in for the most popular of Irish Barbarian tries. Another excellent conversion by Callard regained the lead. Four minutes later he kicked another penalty goal and when Chalmers succeeded with the scruffiest of drop goals that went over via the crossbar the Springboks knew it was not their day.

The 23–15 victory was fit to rank with the Club's finest achievements. Geoff Windsor-Lewis freely admitted afterwards, 'I think from my point of view it was as emotional as the win over New Zealand in 1973. We've been close several times in the intervening years but for commitment and huge tackling, teamwork and spirit, this was special. From Thursday night it built up and the boys who really wanted to play well did so and were inspired.' His captain

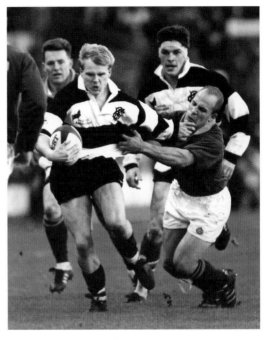

The last and most popular try of all, which sealed a famous win against the Springboks, was scored by Ireland's very own Simon Geoghegan. (© Fotosport)

agreed, saying, 'It was amazing that, in two days, players from several different countries came together and gelled so well. There was a lot of individual pride out there and it culminated in as good a win as I've ever been part of.'

Two days beforehand one rugby writer in a national newspaper in London had summarily dismissed the match in prospect in Dublin. He lamented:

> If only South Africa were playing England instead of the Barbarians on Saturday. Then we would have a clearer idea of how good they really are . . . It is left to the Baa-Baas to provide the final, searching examination. Some hope.

They have assembled a decent collection of players, but the days of a galaxy of star names frightening a successful touring team are long gone. Talent without teamwork counts for nothing. There will be a bucketful of points, smiles all round, and South Africa will head for home after another thumping victory without playing the one side in the UK who could give them a decent run for their money.

He had got everything badly wrong. In Ireland, and admittedly with the benefit of hindsight, the *Sunday Independent*'s Mick Doyle saw things differently: 'Thank you, Barbarians, for bringing real rugby back to us.'

And, a month later, Robert Jones was recalled to the Wales team to win his 50th cap.

The visit to Dublin had been a triumph and the Barbarians' victory reminded everyone that they still had a role to play in the modern game.

The advent of professional rugby in 1995 presented new challenges, with even shorter tours from overseas, now rarely longer than two or three international matches, and a congested domestic calendar that made player availability even more of a problem. Even so, four more matches were played against the Big Three in the course of the next ten years. The Club committee soon realised they would have to spread their net wider when selecting players for these games. At Twickenham in December 1996, however, the team was still predominantly home based. Two exceptions were Norm Hewitt, the All Black at hooker, and Ian Jones, back again in the second row. Another old face was in the opposition, where David Campese was making his fourth appearance for the Wallabies against the Barbarians. This time it was definitely expected to be his last game in the gold jersey. If so, his timing was, as always, immaculate, as the Wallabies were set to complete an unbeaten 12-match tour.

Celebrations all round in the Lansdowne Road dressing-room after the Springboks had been vanquished 23–15. (© Fotosport)

The outcome was as expected in both respects. Campese, of course, scored a try – one of five by his team as they ran away to a 39–nil lead with over a quarter of the game still left to play. The capacity crowd at Twickenham had expected to see a bigger challenge from the Barbarians. There was some consolation in the final stages as Allan Bateman ran onto a flat pass from Gregor Townsend for a try and then Scott Quinnell, who had his younger brother Craig with him in the pack, charged through three Australian tacklers for another touchdown that his captain, Rob Andrew, converted. All of them had been upstaged by full-back Matthew Burke, who had scored twenty-five of his side's points, including two tries. Inevitably, after such a comprehensive 39–12 defeat, questions were again asked about the viability of future matches with the Barbarians. The context, though, was worth remembering: an invincible Australian team had ruthlessly demolished a scratch Barbarians combination. Campese, who had distinguished himself in both jerseys in an illustrious 15-year career at the top, pointed out afterwards: 'I love Barbarian rugby because you can go out there and express yourself . . . and the Barbarians can bring on talent.'

In 2000 and 2001 the Barbarians found a new home for their matches against the Springboks and, again, the Wallabies. The Millennium Stadium in Cardiff had been built for the Rugby World Cup of 1999 and was the natural replacement for the National Stadium at Cardiff Arms Park. Its increased capacity meant that a crowd of 70,000 was present on Sunday, 10 December 2000. That was a record for a Barbarians match, and it had two other 'firsts': it was played under a closed roof and the Barbarians included thirteen southern hemisphere players in the starting line-up. The latter was unavoidable. There was a full programme of league rugby throughout the four home countries and in France, and the clubs were reluctant to release their players. There were two notable exceptions. The captain of the Barbarians was Lawrence Dallaglio and in the back division was the rising new star of British and Irish rugby, Brian O'Driscoll. And if you are going to trawl the world for players then at least get the best. Hence, at full-back, the Club had Christian Cullen. Another All Black at fly-half was Carlos Spencer, with Neil Jenkins waiting to take his turn from the replacements bench. Matthew Burke, the twenty-five-point Wallaby of four years before, was one of the wings. Agustin Pichot of Argentina, a self-confessed Barbarian to the core, was at scrum-half. The likes of Naka Drotske, Jim Williams and Ron Cribb were ideal foils for Dallaglio in the pack. For a long time it looked as if the Club's astute recruitment would pay off. Shortly before half-time Dallaglio's men led 31–12. O'Driscoll, Pichot, Cullen and the Australian wing Chris Latham had scored tries; Burke had converted all four and also kicked a penalty goal. Another score then and the match might have been won. Unfortunately, the next score went the other way. Chester Williams, the wing who had scored the first try of the match in the second minute, claimed another in stoppage time. The other Springbok wing, Breyton Paulse, had also opened his try-scoring account midway through the half and, at 31–17 at the break, the game was far from over.

The breathtaking pace of the game affected the Barbarians more than their opponents in the second half. The Springboks had passed and run to such an extent that they did not

The Barbarians' first game at the newly opened Millennium Stadium in Cardiff was in December 2000 against the Springboks. The Australian full-back Matt Burke, playing on the wing, was among a host of big names in the black-and-white jersey.
(© Getty Images)

kick the ball out of hand until the 59th minute. Three tries followed in a ten-minute spell, one to Ollie le Roux and two more to Paulse for his hat-trick. Percy Montgomery, who had added the points to Williams' early try, converted all three. After that the score stayed at 38–31 for 23 minutes. With only one goal's difference the Baa-Baas harboured hopes of salvaging a draw. But with 82 minutes' playing time on the stadium's clock the Springboks were awarded a penalty inside the Barbarians' 22. Ever the pragmatist, their captain Andre Vos called up replacement Braam van Straaten to kick the goal. He duly did so and the Springboks had won by 41–31.

Eleven months later the Barbarians returned to the Millennium Stadium to play the Wallabies on a Wednesday evening. There was

a bigger representation of European players in the team: the Frenchmen Stephane Glas, Olivier Magne and Raphael Ibanez and three Welsh internationals, the props Darren Morris and David Young and the skipper and scrum-half Robert Howley. Percy Montgomery, Breyton Paulse and Braam van Straaten were now in the black-and-white jersey as, again, were All Black lock Ian Jones and Wallaby centre Pat Howard.

The match followed a similar pattern. An early 14-point lead for the Baa-Baas was established by tries from Paulse and Glas, both converted by van Straaten, but in the second quarter the superior teamwork of the Wallabies was crucial. Five tries were scored in a twenty-minute spell. Scott Staniforth scored two of them and completed a hat-trick in the second half. Toutai Kefu, Chris Latham, Elton Flatley and, in the second period, Ben Tune were the other try-scorers; five were converted by Flatley and two by Manny Edmonds. Pat Lam replied for the Barbarians and Braam van

The All Black Christian Cullen was another world-class player on duty against the Springboks. (© Getty Images)

Straaten finished with five conversions in five attempts. His fellow South African upstaged him. Breyton Paulse, having scored a hat-trick of tries against the Barbarians a year earlier, now finished with a hat-trick for them. This time, though, he was on the losing side as the Wallabies won 49–35.

Despite the two defeats at the Millennium Stadium the Barbarian committee could still feel pleased that their matches against the overseas teams were proving successful. The near-capacity Sunday-afternoon crowd against the Springboks had been followed by a healthy turn-out of 40,000 on a Wednesday evening against the Wallabies. More importantly, a greater number of home-based players of top international pedigree had played for them in the second of the two matches. However, a watershed was reached when the Barbarians played the All Blacks at Twickenham on 4 December 2004. Another crowd of nearly 60,000 were attracted to the match. The significant difference was that, for the first time ever, the Club fielded a team exclusively of overseas players. The XV that started was made up of nine Australians, three South Africans, two New Zealanders and a Fijian. It was an unavoidable development. On the same weekend there was a full schedule of European Cup rugby clashing with the fixture. That immediately removed from the selection equation all the club-contracted professional players. One of them was the French centre Thomas Castaignede and he readily admitted that he was immensely disappointed. He wrote in his weekly column in *The Guardian*, 'I had agreed with [my club] Saracens that I would be able to play but then politics got in the way of it, because the Premiership clubs [in England] agreed they would not send any of their

Brian O'Driscoll in Barbarian colours up against Percy Montgomery, himself a fine Baa-Baa when not playing for the Springboks. (© Getty Images)

players.' The international stars from overseas had no such barriers and, under the captaincy of the 77-times-capped All Black scrum-half Justin Marshall and the coaching of Bob Dwyer and his assistant Rob Howley, they assembled in London for a full week's preparation.

In the first half, at least, they more or less held their own against an All Blacks side that contained several players endeavouring to establish a place in future New Zealand international teams. Xavier Rush, the Auckland number 8, scored a try against his own countrymen, and the Australian fly-half Matt Giteau converted. Though the All Blacks were to finish with seven tries, the Baa-Baas kept in touch at 12–26, after a try by replacement prop Andrea le Cicero. A 70-minute effort by lock Albert van den Berg, with Matt Rogers'

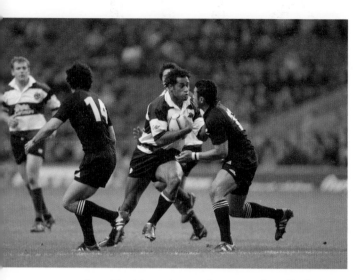

Lote Tuqiri on the attack against the All Blacks at
Twickenham in December 2004.
(© Getty Images)

conversion, pulled the score back to 19–40.
One try had been scored against them after a
blatant late tackle but the final result was
hardly affected. In the end the All Blacks
pulled away for a 47–19 win.

No one was pretending afterwards that the
match was one of the greatest of the 23 that had
been played since the inaugural fixture against
the Wallabies in 1948. The initial disappointment
would soon die down. Thomas Castaignede
touched the nub of the situation when he wrote:

> This won't be the last time that questions
> are asked about the Barbarians' status in
> the modern game: there are so many
> divergent interests that old institutions
> will always run the risk of being
> squeezed. But they are an institution
> that we need to retain because they are
> magic and always will be.

TOURING BARBARIANS-STYLE

'I've found it fascinating because of the cross-pollination between the likes of the South Africans, the French and the Irish.'

– Anton Oliver, June 2004

Anyone doubting the ongoing magic of the Barbarians in the modern professional age should have been at the playing fields of Madras College in St Andrews on the early summer morning of 21 May in 2004. As players from eight countries in the thirty-man squad had their final run-out before the opening game of the Staffware Challenge Tour against Scotland the following day, there was no shortage of excited onlookers on the sidelines. The World Cup-winning Aussie coach Bob Dwyer was with the likes of Christian Cullen and Brian O'Driscoll among the backs and Bobby Skinstad and Anton Oliver in the forwards as they went through their training

routine. Boys and girls from seven local schools were there, waiting for a training session of their own with the world stars; so, too, were television cameras, press photographers, a couple of hundred fans of all ages – and, watching unobtrusively from the back of the crowd, a royal presence: Prince William. When the Baa-Baas are in town, there is no limit to the possibilities of who might turn up.

Once again the Barbarians had assembled a squad of all the talents from the four corners of the rugby world and over the next ten days their itinerary would centre on matches against teams representing Scotland, Wales and England. By 2004 the summer tour had quickly

established itself as one of the highlights of the Barbarians' season. Several factors had contributed to its development over the previous five years. Its roots lay in an apparently unconnected spring-time match at Twickenham in 1996 that was an early attempt to maximise the sponsorship opportunities of the new professional rugby age. That had been the Sanyo World Challenge, a fixture between the champion club of England and a World XV. The sponsorship meant that players could literally be invited from all around the world and that they could be coached by Bob Dwyer. Leicester were that season's club champions and, with their large fan base, the success of the venture was guaranteed. A crowd of 35,000 turned up, but, in the next two years, when Wasps and Newcastle were champions, the attendances were less impressive. After three years the matches were beginning to lose their appeal. Into the breach stepped Sponsorship Bureau International Ltd, Scottish Amicable's consultants, who approached the match organiser, Steven Berrick of International Sports Investments. It was immediately obvious to all parties that a Barbarian fixture held many attractions, not least that their participation would give future fixtures a more prestigious identity. At the same time the Leicester v. Barbarians match at Twickenham on 23 May 1999 was to be another important staging post in the Club's development in the modern professional climate.

The Barbarians won the match 55–33. The success of the venture provided further food for thought. If players were being flown over from all parts of the world to play in what had become the Scottish Amicable Trophy then why not broaden the concept into a two- or three-match tour? It quickly became a common

objective for the Club, ISI and the sponsor to develop the short-tour concept. In May 2000 a slight window was identified in the fixture calendar and, with Ireland for the IRFU's 125th anniversary and Scotland for the Scottish Amicable Challenge added as fixtures, the summer tour became a reality.

Player recruitment proved to be far less of a problem than some doubters had anticipated. The very physical and mental intensity of the modern game was increasingly resulting in many top players retiring early from the international stage to prolong their careers at club level. Others may have lost their places in national teams through the whims of selectors and coaches. More than anything, though, was the affinity that so many felt for the Barbarians as a team and institution. Put simply, they enjoyed playing for the Club. From 2000 onwards it has been commonplace for squads drawn from seven or eight nations to be assembled, enjoying a Barbarian-style tour both on and off the field.

Those who assembled for the first tour in 2000 were indeed a team of all the talents and there was a nucleus of loyal Barbarians of many years' standing. Thomas Castaignede, Ian Jones, Lawrence Dallaglio and Neil Jenkins needed no introduction to the ways of the Barbarians and one of the delights of the gathering that year was that it also marked the beginning of several other long-term connections with the Club. In succeeding summers, Adrian Garvey, Waisale Serevi, Mark Andrews and several others returned to readily wear the black-and-white shirt.

Apart from the playing element, the actual style of the Barbarians was an attraction in itself. The new millennium had seen Cotton Traders appointed as the official kit supplier, thereby renewing the Club's association with the former England rugby captains and Barbarians Fran Cotton and Steve Smith. Their company provided world-class playing and leisure kit for all those invited to play for the Club. Given the relative scarcity of Barbarian kit it has always proved very popular with players and supporters alike, drawing much comment and attention when the squad is travelling from match to match.

If anything, the squad of 2000 was too strong for club opposition. Two narrow wins over Ireland (31–30) and Scotland (45–42) were followed by a remarkable performance at Twickenham. In front of a crowd of 52,263 the Baa-Baas overwhelmed Leicester, again the club champions, by 85–10. In the process, they scored 13 tries and caused another rethink about the viability of club fixtures as a worthwhile contest. Beforehand, Bob Dwyer, again the coach, had said that his selection for the game was the strongest invitation XV the world had seen in the 30 years since the RFU president's team had toured England. The result supported his claim. In the *Daily Telegraph*'s match report Brendan Gallagher concluded, 'There isn't a club side in the world who could contain this Barbarian team.' The next logical step was to replace the club opposition at Twickenham with a full England team. In 2001 that duly happened.

The three matches in 2001 against Wales, Scotland and England were watched by crowds totalling over 120,000 and again they were all won. Given the glittering array of talent on show, neither fact was surprising. Among the former Barbarians returning to play were Jonah Lomu, Jeremy Guscott and Robin Brooke; the new Club members included Percy Montgomery, Joost van der Westhuizen

Two world-class players, François Pienaar and Zinzan Brooke, hold the Scottish Amicable Trophy aloft after the 55–33 victory over Leicester in 1999. (© Getty Images)

The World Cup-winning Wallaby centre Tim Horan was only one of a galaxy of stars recruited for the summer tours that started in May 2000. Here he is in action against Wales in 2001. (© Getty Images)

223

The Springbok scrum-half Joost van der Westhuizen
made his Barbarian debut on the 2001 tour against Wales.
(© Getty Images)

the three countries had good reason to seek a long overdue win over the Barbarians.

That in itself would not be sufficient to guarantee future summer tours. All of the committee were aware that the annual three-match adventure around the international stadiums of the British Isles since 2000 had breathed new life into what was threatening to become an ailing patient. Equally, the tours themselves would never have seen the light of day without considerable sponsorship. In 2004 new sponsors had come on board. Gartmore, a company specialising in investment management, were the Club's sponsors. Its chief executive, Glyn Jones, said, 'Our two brands are very similar because they both place an emphasis on heritage, trust and loyalty.' In return for its sponsorship, Gartmore received advertising rights at stadiums, in match programmes and, the highest profile of all, on the playing kit. For the tour itself, Staffware, a global leader in business-management software, had negotiated title sponsorship. So the renamed Staffware Challenge Tour succeeded the earlier tours that had been supported in turn by Scottish Amicable in 2000 and 2001, and then Prudential and Lloyds TSB in successive years. This time, the games against Scotland, Wales and England would each be for the Staffware Challenge Trophy. Also supporting the tour were five associate sponsors, the airlines BMI and bmibaby.com, the sports-drink firm Powerade, Walker Morris Solicitors and the BMS group. These were the Barbarians of the modern age: playing strong opponents and supported by high-tech and professional companies.

and Gary Teichmann. Between them the 30-man squad had totalled nearly 1,300 international caps. Wales were beaten 40–38, thanks to an injury-time try by Friedrich Lombard that was converted from the right touch-line by Braam van Straaten. Scotland succumbed 74–31, with Lomu claiming four of twelve tries. England fared no better, going down 43–29 with Lomu again among the try-scorers. In 2002, England gained their only victory in the series, winning 53–29 before the Barbarians, coached this time by another eminent Australian, Rod Macqueen, headed off to Scotland and Wales for two big wins. By then the three matches had been re-branded as the Prudential Tour. With Alan Solomons as coach there was another Grand Slam in the Lloyds TSB Tour of 2003, so, by the time the fifth tour was being planned in 2004, each of

Two months before the 2004 tour kicked off, everyone connected with the Club was saddened by the death of the vice-president,

Vic Roberts. His passing on Sunday, 14 March shook everyone who knew the placid, cheerful and proud Cornishman, none more so than Micky Steele-Bodger. The sporting lives of the two men had run uncannily parallel on and off the field for nearly 60 years and now there was much to reflect on. If there was one difference it was that Roberts' playing career had been much longer than his unfortunate contemporary's. Whereas the seemingly indestructible president had been forced to hang up his boots in his early 20s after his serious knee injury, Vic had played on well past his 30th birthday and was still knocking on the international door 10 years after his debut on the big stage in 1946–47.

Victor George Roberts had been born in Penryn in 1924 and he was to be never far from the sea for most of his life. During the Second World War he was first a naval cadet and then an officer involved in the training exercises for the D-Day landings. After the war he joined the water-guard branch of Customs and Excise. Happily, this meant that he could continue to play rugby in his native county. He was still a member of the Penryn club when he won his first England cap against France at Twickenham in 1947. His fellow flanker was M.R. Steele-Bodger. A few weeks later he made his Barbarians debut against Penarth. Micky, also in the Easter tour party, was watching from the stand. Later that weekend they packed down together again against Newport. Vic went on to play thirteen times for the Barbarians, including five tours to South Wales, missing his first one in 1950 when he was selected for the British and Irish Lions team that went to Australasia. He also captained England twice in his sixteen internationals and when his career postings

The Barbarians came back from nil–25 down to beat Wales 40–25 in 2002 with an injury-time try by team captain Pat Lam (centre) completing a remarkable comeback. (© Getty Images)

Leicester and Ireland utility back Geordan Murphy displays all his running skills against Scotland in 2001. (© Getty Images)

The Club's only defeat in four tour matches against England was in 2002, but even then there were five glorious tries, including two from Scottish back-rower Simon Taylor. (© Getty Images)

The vice-president Vic Roberts (left) on tour in Zimbabwe in 1994 with fellow committeeman and honorary treasurer Gordon Ferguson. (© Kevin Stewart)

took him away from Cornwall he played a season for Swansea (while having the unlikely responsibility of monitoring possible smuggling on the Carmarthenshire coast) and then combined his work as senior Customs officer at Heathrow Airport with eight years at the Harlequins. He often joked that his seniority at the airport made him a popular figure with rugby tourists of later generations whenever they returned overloaded with gifts and luggage from all points of the globe and headed for the 'nothing to declare' channel.

On the Lions tour to New Zealand the local critics had noted Vic Roberts to be 'a bustling, determined player' and, indeed, he played in 12 of the games, but on his return to England he was to concentrate on club and county rugby before returning to the international scene in 1956 after a five-year gap. His final game for the Barbarians was at Newport the following year and he immediately began his 47-year service as a committeeman and, eventually, combined the vice-presidency with his meticulous work as the Club's registrar. Micky Steele-Bodger has no doubts about his great friend's qualities and contribution: 'In 1947 I competed with Vic for a place in the England back row. We never again competed. He became Barbarian registrar and my vice-president and his integrity and friendship were vital. His handshake was a reflection of all that was meaningful and to be trusted.'

In the weeks that followed Vic Roberts' death there would be memorial services in Cornwall and Sussex and hundreds of friends and former colleagues would pay their respects to a great Barbarian and gentleman. Meanwhile there was no escaping the preparations that went ahead for the Staffware Tour.

Once again it was to be the jewel in the

crown of the Barbarians' season. The majority of the players flew into Heathrow Airport on Tuesday, 18 May, four days before the opening game against Scotland. The new Barbarians among them would immediately be impressed by the level of organisation and real sense of style in everything that was laid on. The tour started that day at the Pennyhill Park Hotel, the five-star venue in the Surrey stockbroker belt that had long since been the second home of Sir Clive Woodward's England teams. The Baa-Baas had been using it as a muster base for several years themselves and as each overseas star arrived this time, as always, almost the first person they met was Micky Steele-Bodger. Generous amounts of playing, training and leisure kit were allocated, a team meeting was held, and soon the first social gathering of what would be an exhausting 13-day programme of social and sporting commitments was under way.

The cast list was again impressive. Among the backs there were the Irishmen Brian O'Driscoll, David Humphreys and Shane Horgan, plus quality All Blacks in Christian Cullen, Bruce Reihana and the outstanding scrum-half from the 2003 tour, Mark Robinson. The other scrum-half was the Springbok World Cup player Neil de Kock, and also from South Africa came two exciting wings, Breyton Paulse and Stefan Terblanche. The international contingent didn't stop there because also on board were a great Wallaby, the 76-times-capped Matthew Burke, and another Waratah, Nathan Grey, who was to prove to be the outstanding centre on the tour. France's midfield maestro Thomas Castaignede would be joined later in the week by a member of the current French team, Damien Traille. Completing the attacking options were two

dynamic wingers, Vilimoni Delasau, a strapping Fijian based in New Zealand, and Paul Sackey, an England A representative from London Irish. Both of them would have their tour cut short for very different reasons: Delasau after being injured at Murrayfield, and Sackey, before he had even played, was called into the England camp and would actually turn out against the Barbarians at Twickenham.

There were even more distinguished names among the forwards. Anton Oliver and Taine Randell had both captained New Zealand and had other capped All Blacks alongside them in the prop Greg Feek and the versatile lock or back-rower Brad Mika. Another Test captain, South Africa's Corne Krige, had been forced to withdraw because of a suspension but the green and gold were still well represented by Mark Andrews, Bobby Skinstad and three giant props, Richard Bands, Cobus Visagie and Ollie le Roux. Joining Andrews in an intriguing set of lock-forward options were Mark Connors of Australia and Ireland's Malcolm O'Kelly. The back-row complement was arguably even stronger, with, as well as Skinstad, Randell and Mika, the New Zealand-born Italian international Aaron Persico and the Irish Lion Eric Miller. It didn't stop there, because, in the second week, they would all be strengthened even further by the arrival of three more quality players in the French flanker Olivier Magne, another Springbok Test skipper, Andre Vos, and, straight from the Super 12 final in Canberra, the ACT Brumbies' enforcer Owen Finegan. In such company the only uncapped forward, the Ulster hooker Matt Sexton, might be expected to take a back seat, but one of the triumphs of the next couple of weeks was the way everyone was integrated into the team. One other name needed to be mentioned. Another late arrival, scheduled for the second half of the tour, was the world-record cap-holder Jason Leonard. He was bound to be a leading figure when he enlisted. Having retired from the international scene only a few weeks before, with 114 caps under his belt, a Barbarians tour that would climax in front of 72,000 fans at Twickenham promised to be the perfect curtain call on an exceptional career. As events transpired, Leonard disappointed nobody.

The final piece of the jigsaw in the Barbarians party was probably the most important. Every summer tour since 2000 had benefited from the direction of a proven international coach and now the Australian World Cup-winner Bob Dwyer was back again. He was a great favourite with the Barbarians and he was certainly an inspired choice. Players of the pedigree assembled in 2004 needed careful handling based on a fine balance between leadership and inspiration. A heavy-handed disciplinarian was the last thing that players who had travelled the length of the world needed. From the outset it was obvious that Dwyer was more of a patrician and a confidant who coaxed and encouraged rather than cracked whips and issued orders. Ironically, as he was to reflect himself early on in the proceedings, one of the things he disappointed some players in, at least initially, was his refusal to provide the rigid structures and game plans that seemed to be everywhere in the modern game. With a wry smile on his face after the Scotland game, he said, 'A few of the guys have asked me about the structure we are trying to play. I told them that we're not into structures. My priority – and theirs – is *shape* and the freedom to express themselves.' Throughout the tour, and especially when he addressed a fascinated audience in Cardiff at a Friends of the Barbarians lunch, his message was, 'When you receive the ball, you have three choices – you can run, you can pass or you can kick. That's the game plan we have – it's as simple as that.' Understandably, he wasn't at all amused when one wag suggested a fourth possibility, that of dropping the ball. Dwyer, like all the best coaches, placed a heavy premium on individual skills.

Dwyer's affinity with the Barbarians had grown since he had first coached them in 1999, though his admiration for the club went back to his days as the Wallabies' coach. His first direct contact had been in 1988, in the days when an end-of-tour fixture against the Barbarians at Twickenham or Cardiff Arms Park was set in stone in the rugby calendar. Then and later the prospect of preparing an Australian side to play them was something that he relished: 'I will admit that my selection policy when we were playing the Barbarians tended to be different from the full-blown Test matches. There would be a variety of considerations. One or two guys might have missed out on a few big games during the tour, so it was an opportunity to give them a run in a high-profile match. There might also be players at the end of their careers and a match such as this would be a fitting finale for them, the proper stage on which to bow out.'

To his credit, Dwyer was also wary of the Barbarians game being wrongly regarded as some sort of festival match and it was something that he did everything to ensure would not happen: 'Beating a star-studded Barbarians team is always a worthwhile scalp. Sometimes, as in 1988 when we had lost to England, it was an early opportunity for the players to redeem themselves. And over the years I have always approached the game as an important one to win. In 1992, thirteen of the Test side played against the Barbarians at Twickenham. I also impressed on everyone that there is always the trap of trying to play basketball rather than rugby and that had to be avoided at all costs.'

Dwyer's strictures obviously worked because, in 1988 at Cardiff Arms Park, the Wallabies beat the Barbarians by 40 points to 22 with the highlight being the second of David Campese's two tries as he swerved, sprinted and bemused all the defence in a magical run from halfway. Four years later the Wallabies completed a double for their coach with a 30–20 win at Twickenham. For Dwyer there was never any difficulty in generating motivation with the players, for, as he pointed out, 'The players want to be part of a Barbarians match because they say they enjoy it and of course the mystique of the Barbarians and all they stand for is a significant part of the attraction. For my own part the great tradition of the club, alone, defines its reputation.'

No surprises, then, when Bob Dwyer jumped at the offer to move from one dug-out to another, as it were, to coach the Barbarians. That came in 1999 with the first of the Scottish Amicable Trophy matches, against, ironically, one of his former clubs, Leicester. Return invitations to take charge for the games against the Springboks and the Wallabies at the Millennium Stadium and the first two summer tours in 2000 and 2001 were made almost a matter of course. By the time the 2004 tour was about to start Dwyer made no secret of the fact that he was proud of a track record of seven Barbarian victories in nine starts.

Not the least of Dwyer's contributions to the success of each tour that he was involved in was the manner in which he nurtured a sense of teamwork among hitherto often unforgiving rivals on the field, supported by an off-the-field atmosphere that was decidedly relaxed and supportive. He remains impressively modest about that ability, preferring to pinpoint the quality of the players and their personalities. His assessment is that, 'The Baa-Baas are something special and they have allowed me over the years to be involved with men such as Zinzan Brooke, Thomas Castaignede, Lawrence Dallaglio, Brian O'Driscoll, Joost van der Westhuizen and many, many more. The quality of the players and the respect they have for each other has a big bearing on the way these games are played and why the tours are such a success.' To which can only be added the obvious conclusion that Bob Dwyer himself must take some of the credit for a happy state of affairs.

The first full day of the 2004 tour encompassed nearly everything that the Barbarians stood for: a two-hour training run at the Madras Playing Fields with an autograph-signing session for local school children; an afternoon competing in the sponsors' golf day at the Duke's Course on the outskirts of St Andrews; and a dinner and prize-giving in the Road Hole Grill at the team's base, the Old Course Hotel. As if to underline the sense of all-for-one, one-for-all spirit that had been quickly established, no one quibbled when two of the main prizes, including the ever-contentious measurement of the par-three tee-shot nearest the hole, were snapped up by the medical and physiotherapy back-up unit of the team doctor, Donal O'Shaughnessy, the physiotherapist, Steve Cannon, and the masseur, Dave Tottle. These three had been with the Barbarians for several years and were inseparable at all hours of the day and often night. The Doc, as Donal was invariably and inevitably known, was still a full-time GP in Belfast and had a rugby track record that included eight years with the Ireland squad in the 1990s. Steve and Dave were much closer to home. Steve, once a livewire scrum-half, had played for the Cardiff team that beat the Wallabies in 1984 and was now running a very successful clinic in the Welsh capital. One of his employees was Dave, who, on tour, doubled as his straight man in any number of hilarious stunts and leg-pulling exchanges, and who hailed from Taffs Well, a few miles outside Cardiff, where, as the Doc and Cannon never tired of reminding him, half the local rugby club drank at the bar wearing the latest Baa-Baas training kit. Tottle's impression of moral indignation and suppressed outrage at any suggestion of impropriety was one of the great images of every tour.

The golf dinner in the evening was merely

A French genius and a true Barbarian in every sense, Thomas Castaignede, on the attack against Scotland in 2004.
(© Getty Images)

an aperitif, for the players at least, to a sortie into the delights of the ancient town of St Andrews. Among the local guests that later returned with them for a nightcap in the splendour of the hotel's Road Hole Bar was Prince William. The French wizard Castaignede took the Prince under his wing and soon invited him to join the team post-match at Murrayfield two days later. Royalty being what it is, the future heir to the throne, while accepting the offer to go into the Baa-Baas' changing-room, added the rider that there should not be any nudity. 'Don't worry, sir,' reassured Thomas, 'we prefer women . . .'

Thursday moved into Friday, with more training, more locals and royalty in attendance, and a free afternoon when some players had come up trumps in the daily ballot for a tee-off time on the Old Course itself. Fittingly, Matt Burke, the Aussie full-back and a Barbarian to the core, who never failed to greet 'Micky' with a mixture of wonder and amused admiration every time he approached the president, carded a par four at the notorious seventeenth hole – and duly celebrated in the hours that followed. He had no shortage of helpers. The show was well and truly on the road.

Match day itself was equally successful. The Scotland side had been going through a torrid time, suffering a Six Nations whitewash that included defeat against Italy after a dire performance in Rome. The local media and supporters expected – and demanded – better against the Barbarians. The only pity was that the fans didn't turn out in force on a sunny afternoon at Murrayfield. The official attendance was announced as just under 25,000, which could be described as respectable rather than totally satisfactory for both the Scottish Rugby Union and the

Barbarian committee. It was hinted that the latter, at least, were maintaining an open mind about the financial feasibility of the annual game north of the border. All their inclinations were positive and there was certainly a will to continue a fixture that epitomised the strong Scottish connections within the club. That was further underlined at the pre-match function when great figures of both Scottish and Barbarian history, such as Adam Robson and Frank Coutts, were among the first to greet Micky Steele-Bodger on their arrival. A splendid display of Barbarian memorabilia suggested that the powers-that-be in Edinburgh also appreciated the role of the match in their wider calendar.

As for the match itself, Dwyer was taking no chances with his team selection. Christian Cullen was only available for the first part of the tour as he had to fly back to New Zealand, so he was an automatic selection at full-back. Likewise, the Irishmen Shane Horgan and Brian O'Driscoll in the backs and Malcolm O'Kelly at lock, who would miss the Welsh match the following midweek because of pressing international squad matters back in Dublin, would play now and then return in time for the England game. Ironically, amidst the fun and games of the Barbarians tour, the Irish Rugby Football Union was locked in what appeared to be a power struggle with its players over levels of payment for their imminent tour to South Africa. Elsewhere in Dwyer's starting line-up, Thomas Castaignede formed an exciting midfield partnership with O'Driscoll, while David Humphreys and Mark Robinson, who had orchestrated a stylish win over England in 2003, were reunited at half-back. The spine of the pack contained all the big guns: Anton Oliver at hooker, Mark Andrews with O'Kelly in the

engine room, and Bobby Skinstad alongside Taine Randell in the back row. In all, there were seven new Barbarians, including the props Greg Feek and Cobus Visagie, Aaron Persico at flanker, and Vilimoni Delasau on the wing, plus another couple among the replacements.

An interesting sub-plot to the game was that Scotland were now coached by Matt Williams, a fellow Australian who readily admitted he had cut his coaching teeth using Dwyer as his role model. Grinding his teeth looked more like the order of the day as his old mentor showed no mercy in the opening stages of the match. The Baa-Baas attacked straight from the kick-off and, after a couple of near misses, posted their first points in the eighth minute. Robinson slipped through the front of a lineout on halfway with alarming ease and improvised a brilliant inside pass for Delasau to race 40 metres to the line. Humphreys converted with pinpoint accuracy, in marked contrast to his opposite number, Dan Parks, who fluffed a couple of penalty-goal attempts from close range in the next five minutes. When Robinson struck again in the 25th minute, finishing off a devastating incursion by Horgan for Humphreys to again convert, it looked like being a long afternoon for the Scots.

Fortunately, perhaps, the expected points spree never materialised. As Dwyer quipped afterwards, 'We were doing so well at one stage that we came up with a new tactic after we'd gone through a few phases . . . why not hand the ball back to our opponents to see what they could do with it?' Too often as the game wore on, that amounted to aimless kicking away of possession, not at all what Dwyer had in mind when he talked about shape in a game. In the 27th minute, though, the Baa-Baas' gift-wrapped another ploy when a tapped penalty on their own 22 ended abruptly with Parks intercepting a careless pass from Castaignede, intended for O'Driscoll, and racing over at the posts. The fly-half's simple conversion gave an unexpected score of 7–14 and, not for the last time, the Scots sensed that a significant victory was within their grasp. The mood changed again in the final five minutes of the half when Horgan took centre stage. He had a willing lieutenant in Robinson, who first seized on turnover ball in his own half to link with Cullen and Skinstad for the Irishman to touch down and, two minutes later, the scrum-half was at it again with another clean break carried on by Skinstad for Horgan to claim the fourth converted try of the half.

At 28–7 at the interval, the game seemed won and lost. No one, however, and particularly an annoyed Dwyer, had legislated for the Baa-Baas' sloppiness after the restart. In the space of twenty-five minutes, Scotland scored three tries, two of them from turnovers. The Baa-Baas' only response was an admittedly good try of their own by Cullen after another telling burst by the increasingly outstanding Skinstad. But Humphreys had surprisingly missed the conversion and, with less than ten minutes left to play, the lead had been cut to 33–26. Breathing space was regained when the back row drove off a scrum ten metres from the Scottish line and the captain for the day, Randell, scored a try converted by Humphreys. Even then, Barbarian generosity was not exhausted. Straight from the restart the ball was kicked away again and the number 8, Allister Hogg, ran straight through the middle for his second try of the half. Parks' conversion reduced the points gap to seven once more and, in all truth, the Baa-Baas were relieved to play out time without conceding further points.

The post-match rituals these days are much abbreviated, certainly in the formal sense. No big dinner, no over-dressing and no set-piece speeches. Scotland's authorities, to their credit, still staged a buffet for players, guests and sponsors, highlighted by a brief question-and-answer session with the two coaches – affording Bob Dwyer another opportunity to conclude, 'When we had the ball, we went well; then we tried having no ball at all and that didn't go quite as well.' As always, the final word went to Micky Steele-Bodger as he presented ties to the match officials and to Matt Williams and the Scottish captain, Scott Murray, laced with a few trademark put-downs. He finished with 'You still haven't beaten us but keep trying because we will be back next year', and, as the Baa-Baas headed back to continue their celebrations at St Andrews, everyone involved sincerely hoped that, indeed, they would be among those invited there again in 2005.

Next up was the game against Wales but not this time in Cardiff. The Millennium Stadium was unavailable because of the end-of-season football play-offs – a bizarre arrangement whereby a venue primarily built for the Welsh Rugby Union was now contracted to the English Football League. When it became apparent some months earlier that the WRU and the Barbarian committee had at least two options – to call the game off altogether or to play it elsewhere – there was a feeling that the ball was literally being left in the Club's court. Wisely, the committee opted not only to proceed with the fixture but also to stage it as the host rather than the visiting side. So Wales v. Barbarians had become Barbarians v. Wales, with the only issue being where exactly the match should be played. With the club ground at Cardiff Arms Park also unavailable (again because of a commitment with the football authorities, but this time because of a hospitality marquee for the FA Cup final) and the soccer stadium at Ninian Park in Cardiff deemed unsuitable, attention turned to North Wales and the Racecourse ground in Wrexham, another soccer venue but one that had staged Wales internationals in recent years. Hindsight is a wonderful thing but as the second week of the tour proceeded there developed a tacit acceptance among at least some of the committee that the wrong decision had been made. Believing that the official ground capacity of 15,500 at the Racecourse couldn't cater for the expected demand, the game was instead taken to Ashton Gate, home of Bristol City Football Club, essentially on the basis of its greater capacity of 21,500. In the event, that factor proved irrelevant. The Welsh fans stayed firmly on their side of the Severn Bridge, watching the game from the comfort of their armchairs while the expected demand from the rugby heartlands of the West Country barely materialised. When the game kicked off on the Wednesday evening, a large proportion of the eventual attendance of 11,381 were still making their way to their seats. The game might have been played in the Principality after all.

At least the Barbarians had based themselves in Cardiff for three days and nights before the match, and again they had used their time there productively in PR terms. A Monday-morning run-out at Taffs Well Rugby Club again attracted a sizeable gathering of local schoolchildren, this time from Gwaelod-y-Garth, Tongwynlais and Ffynnon Taf, all within a drop-kick of the village that produced, among others, the legendary Cardiff, Wales, Lions and Barbarians centre Bleddyn Williams. The sense of pride in Dave Tottle's whole being was tangible as he rightly proclaimed that the essence of the Barbarians was always to take the game back to its roots and to meet the people. He loved every minute of seeing the world stars sharing time with his neighbours in what was effectively their backyard.

The two Frenchmen, Olivier Magne and Damien Traille, had joined up with the squad the previous evening and so had Jason Leonard, Andre Vos and Owen Finegan, so there was every suggestion that Bob Dwyer had an even stronger hand from which to select the team to take on Wales. That impression proved deceptive. For a start, Finegan was jet-lagged after a 24-hour trip from Australia over the weekend while Leonard, Vos and Magne had all been involved in a gruelling Parker Pen Cup final on the Saturday. And as some new faces arrived, so there were others leaving the squad. Christian Cullen's exit had been prearranged, but following him on another plane to New Zealand went Vilimoni Delasau with a shoulder injury. Paul Sackey had been called into the England squad and a third wing, Stefan Terblanche, stayed on but was ruled out of selection by a hamstring injury. Meanwhile, the three Irishmen, O'Driscoll, Horgan and O'Kelly, had temporarily left for their tour meeting in Dublin. In the circumstances, Dwyer had no option but to request another outside-back to fill the gaps. Luckily, the experienced Wales and Lions wing Dafydd James was available and answered the call. Having been omitted from recent national teams, he jumped at the chance to showcase his talents in front of the new Wales coach Mike Ruddock and, as such, would be a valuable addition to the squad.

Dwyer stuck to his pre-tour plan of making 15 changes in the starting line-up from the Scotland match, handing the captaincy to Matt Burke but in the relatively unfamiliar position of fly-half. That was regarded in some circles as a suprising choice, but the world-class full-back and international centre had also played on the wing for the Club. Another possible area of concern was the second row of the pack, where two natural back-rowers, Brad Mika and Mark Connors, were teamed up as locks. Ruddock's new Wales team were widely expected to concentrate on establishing a platform up front and would test the Baa-Baas' resolve in the front five. So it proved to be the case, but before then the squad had another enjoyable PR occasion at the Friends of the Barbarians lunch at the Hilton Hotel. Once again Dwyer captured everyone's attention in a keynote address that not only outlined his theory of shape rather than structure in a game plan but also recounted his boyhood love of all sports and rugby in particular: 'When me and my mates were kids in Sydney, I dare say it was no different to those of you in Cardiff or the Welsh valleys or anywhere else in the world. A gang of us would go down the local park, or wherever there was an open space we could play on. The dustbins would be our goalposts, a rolled-up old shirt probably served as a ball and the pathway would be the natural boundary. Then we'd run and pass and, of course, we'd all have the parts of famous players in our favourite clubs. That's how we got to know each other, got to know the game and its skills, and, most importantly, nurtured our enthusiasm that was later honed in more celebrated surroundings.

'I think of those days when I meet up with the Barbarians. Here we are, a bunch of people often from very different backgrounds but all committed to getting on with one another and playing the game we love to the best of our ability and having a lot of fun along the way. As I've said many times before, the Barbarians and all they represent are even more important in this professional age than when the sport was completely amateur.'

The sentiments were marvellous and received a warm reception from the lunch-time gathering. Not even the disappointments against Wales the following evening could devalue them, but there is no denying that after that match there was cause to regroup and refocus the rest of this particular tour's priorities. It was another one of those occasions when the critics and fans went deep into the record books, but this time for the wrong reasons, at least for the Barbarians. The scoreline was certainly unacceptable for all involved in the Club: Barbarians 0, Wales 42. It was over a quarter of a century and 195 games since the Club had failed to register a point in 80 minutes of rugby. There were precious few saving graces: one or two early attacks that broke down at the last moment; a length-of-the-field team effort inspired by the ever-dangerous Breyton Paulse that fell on the sword of wrong options; and in the second half a clever incursion by Dafydd James from the blind-side wing that again floundered, with the final pass going astray. By then, though, a scrappy game was long since lost. Fly-half Ceri Sweeney had claimed all thirteen of Wales' first-half points, with two penalty goals and a conversion of his own try after the Baa-Baas' defence had given a passable impression of 'after you, sir' as they waved him on to the line. One controversial incident came when the Scottish referee Rob Dickson, an official curiously ill-suited to a match of this nature, sin-binned the otherwise excellent Nathan Grey in the 30th minute for allegedly killing the ball in a ruck. Dickson went on to award 32 free-kicks and penalties, more or less evenly spread between the teams, as he effectively killed the free-flowing intentions of the players. The Barbarians' patience was already stretched to the limit when he then ignored a blatant tackle off the ball on Paulse as a long-overdue try seemed imminent.

But the longer the game wore on, the more disjointed the Baa-Baas' defence became, culminating in the final three of the Welsh tally of six tries in the match. The appearance off the bench of Jason Leonard in the final quarter raised at least a few cheers from the largely English contingent in the crowd, but it was an evening that ended with a few Barbarian reputations tarnished, if only for the time being. As the squad headed east next morning along the motorway towards London for the final leg of the tour, there was much to reflect on. Anton Oliver, who had joined the proceedings as a replacement midway through the second half, said, 'I am only associated with the Barbarians for one-and-a-half weeks but I felt sorry for the way we let down Barbarians stalwarts like Micky Steele-Bodger. The Welsh were very clinical and accurate and we were beaten by a better team but the fact we scored nil was like rubbing a whole truckload of salt into the wound.'

A day or so later Bob Dwyer was still mulling over the highs and lows of the matches so far. One thing he pondered was why the group had broken with the tradition of showing the squad the in-house video of the Club's history, covering everything from its origins and Easter tours to the legendary moments such as Haydn Mainwaring's earth-shattering tackle on Avril Malan in 1961, David Duckham's blistering sidestepping against a later Springboks team at Twickenham, and Gareth Edwards' legendary try against the All Blacks. 'That short film encapsulates everything that's good about the Club's traditions,' reflected Dwyer, 'and it's always gone down well on previous tours and got everyone in the right frame of mind.' His attention was also drawn to the Wales match report in *The Times* when David Hands, a correspondent widely respected for his balanced observations and vast experience, had noted that, 'Rarely have the Barbarians been such a shambles . . . [they] looked as if they had been enjoying themselves not wisely but too well the night before.' That report struck a chord and Dwyer resolved to put it to positive use ahead of the England match the following Sunday. Much later he also admitted that the abject performance against Wales had provided a 'kick up the backside' for everyone involved, so perhaps there was also an element of self-motivation among the superstars as they prepared for the final hurdle.

Everything about the impending match at Twickenham was different to what had gone before on the tour. The prospect of playing in front of a record 70,000-plus crowd was incentive enough, but events at Bristol had added to the general sense of urgency. A nice personal touch was certain to be the final appearance of Jason Leonard in a competitive match and it was quickly agreed that he would take the field well ahead of the rest of the team to receive the appreciation of the packed stands. But there the sentiment stopped. Dwyer handed the captaincy to Anton Oliver, a hooker who had led the All Blacks on ten occasions in

Bob Dwyer, a World Cup-winning coach who has become a great favourite with the Barbarians.
(© Getty Images)

2001 and who had made a big impression over the course of the previous week. The positive feelings of Micky Steele-Bodger and the committee towards him were reciprocated when he said, 'I've found the tour fascinating because of the cross-pollination between the likes of the South Africans, French and Irish, not just in terms of rugby but also in terms of socialising. It gives you an insight into not just the differences in rugby but of the histories and cultures of different countries.' Whatever his reputation as an abrasive hooker on the field, it surprised no one that, off it, Oliver already had two degrees in physical education and in finance and that he was seriously contemplating enrolling for another in the arts or humanities at one of the Oxbridge colleges.

Established stars like Matthew Burke,

Olivier Magne, Bobby Skinstad and Damien Traille had to be content with seats on the replacements bench as the starting line-up featured Nathan Grey and Brian O'Driscoll in the centre and a big back row of Owen Finegan, Taine Randell and Andre Vos. On paper the team looked by some distance to be the strongest selected and everyone wasted no time in getting down to the preparations. A squad run-out at Richmond Athletic Ground on the Friday morning was followed by another 24 hours later at Hyde Park. The youngsters in attendance for the latter were themselves a special group coming from a voluntary organisation known as the Trevor Leota School of Hard Knocks. Essentially they were children from tough environments who had been given a sense of purpose in a project that the formidable Samoan forward had readily agreed to identify with and play a hands-on role in. In Hyde Park that morning the Barbarians were unstinting in the time they gave to the kids when the formal part of their own run-out was complete. As for Leota, a committed Barbarian in his own right, he would be teaming up with the club again for the trip to Portugal a fortnight later.

The England team selected for the match had an unfamiliar look. With simultaneous tours to Australasia and Canada about to start, coach Sir Clive Woodward had opted for several new faces and nine uncapped players in his starting line-up under the captaincy of the Newcastle Falcons' number 8, Hugh Vyvyan. In such circumstances the capacity crowd was even more remarkable, if partly explained by the staging of four hours of mini and junior rugby festivals throughout the morning and early afternoon. There was an inescapable feeling that the marketing people at the Rugby

Football Union deserved a medal of their own; at the very least they might be subcontracted out to their counterparts in Scotland and Wales, who seemed desperately to need all the help they could get to come up with new and fruitful ideas to attract audiences.

Woodward and the English fans must have been hoping that their rookie team would be spurred on by the possibility of future involvement in the success culture that was the modern Team England. It was not to be, as everyone was upstaged by the individual who had just taken his leave of the national squad. The prolonged applause that greeted Jason Leonard's arrival on the pitch had barely died down when the old warrior, now a couple of months short of his 36th birthday, was smuggled the ball at a short-range lineout and drove over the line for the opening try. Less than three minutes had been played on the clock. Afterwards, he said, 'I was as surprised as anyone to score but I was lucky enough to get my hands on the ball and fall over the line. But to get that kind of reception, well, I'm not an emotional guy but it brought a lump to my throat.'

It was a fitting beginning that gave everyone the chance to continue the mood of celebration but it was hardly the trigger for a festival game. For the next 75 minutes or so England's only route to points-scoring lay with kicking penalty goals; the Barbarians, at least, never lost sight of their try-scoring habit.

Four minutes after Leonard's bravura beginning, O'Driscoll looped outside his wing and put in what was little more than a speculative grubber-kick along the west touchline. There seemed little danger until a mix-up in the England defence allowed the ever-alert Shane Horgan to flop on the loose ball for the

New Zealander Bruce Reihana made a big impression on successive summer tours in 2003 and 2004, scoring tries on both occasions against England. (© Getty Images)

try. David Humphreys, having converted the first try from near the posts, now missed this kick from the edge of touch. Without reaching any great heights, the Baa-Baas were already 12 points ahead. A couple of straight penalty goals by Dave Walder gave England some hope, only for the Baa-Baas to strike again as Humphreys slipped an inside pass for Bruce Reihana to race over unchallenged. After that the game stuttered and started throughout the final ten minutes of the half, interrupted only by another couple of goals by Walder and another for Humphreys in the second minute of injury time. For the Barbarians the game was far from won at 20–12 but a couple of significant interval changes saw Burke replace Castaignede and Skinstad come in for Randell. The Springbok number 8 was soon in the limelight for the wrong reasons.

In the sixth minute of the half the curse of the yellow card that had struck Nathan Grey

The star of the show in the final match of the 2004 tour was Jason Leonard and he takes his bow for the last time at Twickenham. (© Getty Images)

against Wales now appeared again, with Skinstad, in every sense, the unfortunate recipient. The referee this time was Nigel Whitehouse, a traffic policeman in South Wales. Though an experienced international official and respected in many quarters, he had never been quite able to shake off his rather undeserved reputation for blurring the boundaries between his day job and what was presumably his recreational activity. So he whistled away to the extent of nearly 30 penalties, heavily in the home side's favour, and added the sting in the tail of 10 minutes in the sin bin for Skinstad when he interfered with a quick tap penalty. Yet the Springbok got the last laugh moments after he returned to the action and intercepted a wayward pass for a 40-metre jog to the England posts with a huge smile on his face. Humphreys' conversion stretched the lead to 27–12 before the match ended as it had started, with a lineout catch and drive, finished off this time by Malcolm O'Kelly. With Oliver having been replaced five minutes earlier, the captaincy had now passed to Mark Andrews. The giant lock was another about to leave the big stage for the last time so, to everyone's delight, he invoked the skipper's right to attempt the conversion from the right touch-line. He missed the target by a considerable distance but no one begrudged him his moment of fantasy. Afterwards, he contributed a fitting tribute: 'It means a lot to play for – and in – a Barbarian jersey and especially to preserve the reputation of the legends who have played in the past.'

The Staffware Tour of 2004 had ended on a high note and, with even the disappointed England coach Sir Clive Woodward conceding that 'The Barbarians is a wonderful fixture if we can play it with our full-strength team,' there was every reason to believe that there were many more tours to be undertaken in the future. Woodward's England, for one, would want to redress the deficit balance of three defeats in the four most recent matches. And, of course, not many touring teams can claim that they rubbed shoulders with a prince at the beginning and were commended by a knight at the end of their expedition. In the summer of 2004, both on and off the field, the Barbarians remained unique.

BARBARIANS ANCIENT AND MODERN

'For it's a way we have in the Baa-Baas,
And a jolly good way too.'
– Barbarian Football Club song

On 9 November 2004 the Barbarians played the Combined Services at the Army Rugby Stadium in Aldershot. It was the Club's 726th official fixture since its formation in 1890 and a relatively new one on its calendar. It had first been played seven years before, but, given the principles underpinning it and the sense of ceremony attached to it, it was the sort of match and occasion that might have been staged at any time during the previous 114 years. The team selected to wear the black-and-white jersey had been drawn from the four countries of the British Isles, together with three players from Portugal. During the day of the game the Club's president, Micky Steele-Bodger, the secretary Geoffrey Windsor-Lewis,

the treasurer Gordon H. Brown and two other committee members, Haydn Mainwaring and Jeff Probyn, had met and dined with the president of the Combined Services Rugby Union, Major General James Shaw, and several senior officers. Immediately before the kick-off a military band sounded the 'Last Post' and there was a minute's silence. It was the week of Remembrance Day and there was also a poppy collection in support of the Royal British Legion. Then a match was played in the best of spirits and won by an opportunist try deep in injury time by the Services team. As an earlier president of Combined Services, General Sir Roger Wheeler, had forecast at the time of the first match in 1997, 'The attitude and ethos of

both sides in playing the game for the game's sake, but of course to win, encapsulates the Corinthian spirit that we share.'

If the Combined Services match is a modern fixture, the preliminaries attached to it are reminiscent of those that are far longer established for the Mobbs Memorial Match every March. That fixture against East Midlands stretches back to 1921, while not far away in another part of the Midlands the game against Leicester has its origins in 1909. The three games together form the staple domestic diet of every Barbarians season in the new millennium. The summer tours against the international teams of Britain have been a popular addition, while the periodic visits to Portugal, Germany, Russia and elsewhere underline the Club's commitment to developing the game in other countries.

Supporting worthy causes has never been far from the agenda of the Barbarians. In the world wars of the last century, matches were arranged to help recruitment, local hospitals, the Red Cross and a wide range of military charities. In more recent times the good work has continued. Playing the British and Irish Lions at Twickenham in 1977 was both a great honour for the Club and a major sporting occasion; it also raised an unprecedented £100,000 for the Silver Jubilee Fund of Queen Elizabeth II. In the space of three months in 1996 the Barbarians played the Peace International against Ireland, toured Japan to support the charitable fund set up after the Great Hanshin Earthquake, and returned to Britain to play Scotland in aid of the Dunblane Disaster Fund. All of these ventures raised valuable revenue for projects and in areas where it was desperately needed. Sometimes the Club agrees to play matches within a very

tight timescale. On successive evenings in March 2003 they played in London and Leicester. The first match was against London Irish at the Stoop Ground in Twickenham in support of the SALSA Foundation and Jarrod Cunningham, a fine player who had been diagnosed with a form of motor neurone disease. Twenty-four hours later the game against Leicester at Welford Road was to support not only Neil Back's testimonial year but also the families of two officers of the Leicestershire Police Force who had been tragically killed in a traffic accident. Funds are also raised at special dinners. When the players from the 1973 team that beat the All Blacks gathered for their 30th anniversary reunion, the Club staged a gala dinner in London for several hundred guests and sponsors. From the proceeds of the evening, £23,000 was donated to the Wooden Spoon Society, the charity that supports disadvantaged children.

Given the extent of its activities in these fields, in February 2004 the Club took the next logical step and set up the Barbarians Rugby Charitable Trust. Its object is to aid socially and economically disadvantaged individuals and organisations in any part of the world needing support to develop rugby. At the same time the committee of the Club declared a policy of donating any surplus funds to charity, after retaining a reserve adequate to meet future commitments. The trustees appointed were Micky Steele-Bodger, Geoffrey Windsor-Lewis and John Spencer, with Gordon H. Brown fulfilling the role of honorary administrator. This was an important development in the Club's history and already by the early months of 2005 kit and equipment had been despatched or taken to Brazil, Chile, Romania, Portugal and the townships of South Africa.

Another aim of the Trust is to enable the Club to continue undertaking regular missionary tours to the developing rugby nations.

Nearer home the Club has also endeavoured to foster an ongoing dialogue and communication with its supporters and well-wishers. In 1996 an official supporters club was projected and out of that came the Friends of the Barbarians. It was a forum where players and supporters could meet at a variety of social events around the country and be involved in the Barbarian ethos. Its first two presidents were Bill Beaumont and Gerald Davies, two great players who were also marvellous ambassadors for the game and the Club. As well as regular newsletters, golf days and lunches were organised all over the British Isles and were invariably well supported.

The *raison d'être* of the Barbarians will always be the business of playing rugby and, wisely, the committee will always endeavour to play six to seven fixtures every season. The games in Leicester, the East Midlands and now against the Combined Services, together with the occasional anniversary and special fund matches, keeps them in touch with their constituency – the grass-roots players and rugby folk of the British Isles. The big matches against the international teams of Europe and the southern hemisphere are, in some respects, the icing on the cake, and there remains an insatiable public demand for them. It is these fixtures over the decades that have set the imagination racing and have furthered the aura and the legend. The signs are that they will continue to do so.

These are the modern Barbarians, much of whose good work proceeds unobtrusively but to a commendable purpose. The president in 2005, Micky Steele-Bodger, and the committee realise that they have responsibilities to respect everything that has gone before them and to ensure that all that is still to come does so within the accepted principles of the Club. They work together to foster both it and the rugby union game now in a very different environment to when Percy Carpmael and his fellows put down the roots of the Barbarian Football Club on 9 April 1890. That, however, is unlikely to be an insurmountable barrier for an institution that has attracted so much goodwill towards itself and has done so with such a sense of style.

STATISTICAL
APPENDICES

I

MATCHES AGAINST MAJOR TOURING TEAMS

(* – denotes uncapped player at the time of the match)

MATCH 1: 31 JANUARY 1948 AT CARDIFF ARMS PARK

Barbarians 9 Australia 6

Barbarians: R.F. Trott; M.F. Turner*, W.B. Cleaver, B.L. Williams, C.B. Holmes; T.A. Kemp, H. Tanner (capt.); H. Walker, K.D. Mullen, I.C. Henderson, J. Mycock, W.E. Tamplin, W.I.D. Elliot, S.V. Perry, M.R. Steele-Bodger

Scorers – Tries: Steele-Bodger, Holmes, Tanner

Australia: B.J. Piper; A.E.J. Tonkin, T. Allan (capt.), M.J. Howell, J.W.T. MacBride; E.G. Broad, C.T. Burke; E. Tweedale, W.L. Dawson, N. Shehadie, P.A. Hardcastle, G.M. Cooke, D.H. Keller, A.J. Buchan, C.J. Windon

Scorer – Try: Tonkin; Penalty goal: Tonkin

Referee: A.S. Bean (Sunderland)

Attendance: 45,000

MATCH 2: 16 JANUARY 1952 AT CARDIFF ARMS PARK

Barbarians 3 South Africa 17

Barbarians: G. Williams; J.E. Woodward, L.B. Cannell, B.L. Williams, K.J. Jones; C.I. Morgan, W.R. Willis; R.V. Stirling, D.M. Davies, J. MacG.K. Kendall-Carpenter, E.R. John, J.E. Nelson (capt.), V.G. Roberts, J.R.G. Stephens, W.I.D. Elliot

Scorer – Try: Elliot

South Africa: A.C. Keevy; F.P. Marais, R.A.M. van Schoor, M.T. Lategan, J.K. Ochse; P.G. Johnstone, P.A. du Toit; F.E. van der Ryst, W. Delport, H.J. Bekker, E.E. Dinkelmann, J.M. du Rand, S.P. Fry, H.S.V. Muller (capt.), C.J. van Wyk

Scorers – Tries: Ochse, van Wyk; Conversion: Keevy; Penalty goals: Keevy (2), Johnstone

Referee: Captain M.J. Dowling (Ireland)

Attendance: 55,000

MATCH 3: 20 FEBRUARY 1954 AT CARDIFF ARMS PARK

Barbarians 5 New Zealand 19

Barbarians: I. King; K.J. Jones, J. Butterfield, W.P.C. Davies, G.M. Griffiths; C.I. Morgan, W.R. Willis (capt.); C.R. Jacobs*, E. Evans, J.H. Smith, R.C. Hawkes*, J.R.G. Stephens, R.C.C. Thomas, S. Judd, D.F. White

Scorers – Try: Griffiths; Conversion: King

New Zealand: R.W.H. Scott; M.J. Dixon, J.T. Fitzgerald, R.A. Jarden; B.B.J. Fitzpatrick,

R.G. Bowers; K. Davis; K.L. Skinner, R.C. Hemi,
H.L. White, R.A. White, G.N. Dalzell,
R.C. Stuart (capt.), W.A. McCaw, D.O. Oliver
Scorers – Tries: Jarden, Dixon, Davis, R.A. White;
   Conversions: Jarden (2); Drop goal: Scott
Referee: I. David (Neath)
Attendance: 60,000

MATCH 4: 22 FEBRUARY 1958 AT CARDIFF
ARMS PARK

Barbarians 11 Australia 6
Barbarians: R.W.T. Chisholm; A.R. Smith,
   G.T. Wells, M.S. Phillips, A.J.F. O'Reilly;
   C.I. Morgan (capt.), A.A. Mulligan; C.R. Jacobs,
   A.R. Dawson, N. Shehadie, R.W.D. Marques,
   W.R. Evans, P.G.D. Robbins, J. Faull, A. Robson
Scorers – Tries: Evans, Phillips, Dawson;
   Conversion: Faull
Australia: T.G.P. Curley; A.R. Morton,
   J.K. Lenehan, R. Phelps, K.J. Donald;
   R.M. Harvey, D.M. Connor; R.A.L. Davidson
   (capt.), R.W. Meadows, G.N. Vaughan,
   A.R. Miller, D.M. Emanuel, J.E. Thornett,
   N.M. Hughes, W.J. Gunther
Scorers – Tries: Emanuel, Donald
Referee: G.A. Walker (RAF)
Attendance: 50,000

MATCH 5: 4 FEBRUARY 1961 AT CARDIFF
ARMS PARK

Barbarians 6 South Africa 0
Barbarians: H.J. Mainwaring*; J.R.C. Young,
   B.J. Jones, H.M. Roberts, A.J.F. O'Reilly;
   R.A.W. Sharp, W.R. Watkins; B.G.M. Wood,
   A.R. Dawson (capt.), S. Millar, W.R. Evans,
   B. Price*, M.G. Culliton, W.G.D. Morgan,
   H.J. Morgan
Scorers – Tries: W.G.D. Morgan, H.J. Morgan
South Africa: L.G. Wilson; M.J.G. Antelme,
   J.L. Gainsford, J.P. Engelbrecht, B-P van Zyl;
   D.A. Stewart, P. de W. Uys; S.P. Kuhn,
   G.F. Malan, J.L. Myburgh, A.S. Malan (capt.),
   P.J. van Zyl, G.H. van Zyl, D.J. Hopwood,
   H.J.M. Pelser
Referee: M.F. Turner (London Society)
Attendance: 60,000

MATCH 6: 15 FEBRUARY 1964 AT CARDIFF
ARMS PARK

Barbarians 3 New Zealand 36
Barbarians: S. Wilson; S.J. Watkins, M.S. Phillips,
   M.K. Flynn, C.P. Simpson*; R.A.W. Sharp,
   S.J.S. Clarke; L.J. Cunningham, A.R. Dawson
   (capt.), I.J. Clarke, E. Jones*, B. Price,
   M.G. Culliton, A.E.I. Pask, D.P. Rogers
Scorer – Drop goal: I.J. Clarke
New Zealand: D.B. Clarke; M.J. Dick, P.F. Little,
   R.W. Caulton; D.A. Arnold, B.A. Watt;
   C.R. Laidlaw, W.J. Whineray (capt.), D. Young,
   K.F. Gray, C.E. Meads, A.J. Stewart,
   D.J. Graham, K.R. Tremain, W.J. Nathan
Scorers – Tries: Nathan (2), Tremain, C.E. Meads,
   Graham, Dick, Caulton, Whineray; Conversions:
   D.B. Clarke (6)
Referee: D.G. Walters (Gowerton)
Attendance: 58,000

MATCH 7: 28 JANUARY 1967 AT CARDIFF
ARMS PARK

Barbarians 11 Australia 17
Barbarians: S. Wilson; S.J. Watkins, T.G.R. Davies,
   F.P.K. Bresnihan, P.B. Glover; D. Watkins,
   R.M. Young; N. Suddon, K.W. Kennedy,
   A.B. Carmichael, B. Price, W.J. McBride,
   N.A.A. Murphy (capt.), J.W. Telfer, J.P. Fisher
Scorers – Try: Kennedy; Penalty try; Conversion:
   Wilson; Penalty goal: Wilson
Australia: J.K. Lenehan; E.S. Boyce, R.J.P. Marks,
   J.E. Brass, R. Webb; P.F. Hawthorne,
   K.W. Catchpole; J.E. Thornett (capt.),
   P.G. Johnson, A.R. Miller, M.P. Purcell,
   R.G. Teitzel, J. Guerassimoff, J.F. O'Gorman,
   G.V. Davis
Scorers – Tries: Boyce (2), Hawthorne, O'Gorman,
   Webb; Conversion: Lenehan
Referee: R.W. Gilliland (Ireland)
Attendance: 40,000

MATCH 8: 16 DECEMBER 1967 AT
TWICKENHAM

Barbarians 6 New Zealand 11
Barbarians: S. Wilson (capt.); W.K. Jones,
   R.H. Lloyd, T.G.R. Davies, R.E. Webb; B. John,
   G.O. Edwards; C.H. Norris, F.A.L. Laidlaw,
   A.L. Horton, M.L. Wiltshire, P.J. Larter,

R.B. Taylor, G.A. Sherriff, D. Grant

Scorers – Try: Lloyd; Drop goal: Wilson

New Zealand: W.F. McCormick; M.J. Dick,
W.L. Davis, A.G. Steel; I.R. MacRae,
E.W. Kirton; C.R. Laidlaw; B.L. Muller,
B.E. McLeod, K.F. Gray, C.E. Meads,
S.C. Strahan, K.R. Tremain, B.J. Lochore (capt.),
W.J. Nathan

Scorers – Tries: MacRae, Steel; Conversion:
McCormick; Drop goal: Kirton

Referee: M. Joseph (Wales)

Attendance: 40,000

MATCH 9: 31 JANUARY 1970 AT TWICKENHAM

Barbarians 12 South Africa 21

Barbarians: J.P.R. Williams; A.T.A. Duggan,
J.S. Spencer, C.M.H. Gibson, D.J. Duckham;
B. John, G.O. Edwards (capt.); K.E. Fairbrother,
F.A.L. Laidlaw, D.B. Llewelyn, A.M. Davis,
I.S. Gallacher*, J.J. Jeffery, T.M. Davies,
R.J. Arneil

Scorers – Tries: Arneil, Duckham, Duggan,
Fairbrother

South Africa: H.O. de Villiers; S.H. Nomis,
O.A. Roux, J.P. van der Merwe, A.E. van der
Watt; M.J. Lawless, D.J. de Villiers (capt.);
J.F.K. Marais, C.H. Cockrell, J.L. Myburgh,
F.C.H. du Preez, I.J. de Klerk, P.J.F. Greyling,
M.W. Jennings, J.H. Ellis

Scorers – Tries: Ellis (2), van der Watt; Conversions:
de Villiers (3); Penalty goal: de Villiers; Drop
goal: Lawless

Referee: Air Commodore G.C. Lamb (England)

Attendance: 30,000

MATCH 10: 27 JANUARY 1973 AT NATIONAL STADIUM, CARDIFF ARMS PARK

Barbarians 23 New Zealand 11

Barbarians: J.P.R. Williams; D.J. Duckham,
S.J. Dawes (capt.), C.M.H. Gibson, J.C. Bevan;
P. Bennett, G.O. Edwards; R.J. McLoughlin,
J.V. Pullin, A.B. Carmichael, W.J. McBride,
R.M. Wilkinson*, T. David*, D.L. Quinnell,
J.F. Slattery

Scorers – Tries: Edwards, Slattery, Bevan,
Willliams; Conversions: Bennett (2); Penalty
goal: Bennett

New Zealand: J.F. Karam; B.G. Williams,
B.J. Robertson, I.A. Hurst, G.B. Batty; R.E.
Burgess, S.M. Going (G.L. Colling); G.J. Whiting,
R.A. Urlich, K.K. Lambert, H.H. Macdonald,
P.J. Whiting, A.I. Scown, A.J. Wyllie, I.A.
Kirkpatrick (capt.)

Scorers – Tries: Batty (2); Penalty goal: Karam

Referee: G. Domercq (France)

Attendance: 51,000

MATCH 11: 30 NOVEMBER 1974 AT TWICKENHAM

Barbarians 13 New Zealand 13

Barbarians: A.R. Irvine; T.G.R. Davies,
P.J. Warfield, P.S. Preece, D.J. Duckham;
J.D. Bevan*, G.O. Edwards; J. McLauchlan,
R.W. Windsor, F.E. Cotton, W.J. McBride (capt.),
G.L. Brown, R.M. Uttley, T.M. Davies, J.F.
Slattery

Scorers – Try: T.M. Davies; Penalty goals: Irvine (3)

New Zealand: J.F. Karam; B.G. Williams,
B.J. Robertson, I.A. Hurst, G.B. Batty;
D.J. Robertson, S.M. Going; K.K. Lambert,
R.W. Norton, K.J. Tanner, P.J. Whiting,
H.H. Macdonald, I.A. Kirkpatrick, A.R. Leslie
(capt.), K.W. Stewart

Scorers – Tries: Leslie, Williams; Conversion:
Karam; Penalty goal: Karam

Referee: G. Domercq (France)

Attendance: 68,000

MATCH 12: 24 JANUARY 1976 AT NATIONAL STADIUM, CARDIFF ARMS PARK

Barbarians 19 Australia 7

Barbarians: A.R. Irvine; T.G.R. Davies,
R.W.R. Gravell, C.M.H. Gibson, J.J. Williams;
P. Bennett, G.O. Edwards; F.M.D. Knill*,
P.J. Wheeler, A.B. Carmichael, A.J. Martin,
G.L. Brown, T.P. Evans, T.M. Davies (capt.),
J.F. Slattery

Scorers – Tries: Bennett, Wheeler, Williams;
Conversions: Bennett (2); Penalty goal: Bennett

Australia: J.C. Hindmarsh; J.R. Ryan,
R.D. L'Estrange, G.A. Shaw, L.E. Monaghan
(W.A. McKid); L.J. Weatherstone, R.G. Hauser;
J.E.C. Meadows, C.M. Carberry, R. Graham,
G. Fay, R.A. Smith, G.K. Pearse, M.E. Loane
(D.W. Hillhouse), A.A. Shaw

Scorers – Try: Ryan; Penalty goal: Hindmarsh
Referee: G. Domercq (France)
Attendance: 50,000

MATCH 13: 16 DECEMBER 1978 AT NATIONAL STADIUM, CARDIFF ARMS PARK

Barbarians 16 New Zealand 18

Barbarians: A.R. Irvine; H.E. Rees,
R.N. Hutchings*, J.M. Renwick, M.A.C. Slemen;
P. Bennett, D.B. Williams; P.A. Orr (B.G. Nelmes),
P.J. Wheeler, W. Dickinson*, W.B. Beaumont,
A.J. Martin, J-P. Rives, D.L. Quinnell (capt.),
J-C. Skrela

Scorers – Tries: Slemen (2); Conversion: Bennett;
Penalty goals: Bennett (2)

New Zealand: B.J. McKechnie; S.S. Wilson,
B.J. Robertson, W.M. Osborne, B.G. Williams;
E. Dunn, D.S. Loveridge; B.R. Johnstone
(J.C. Ashworth), A.G. Dalton, G.A. Knight,
A.M. Haden, F.J. Oliver, L.M. Rutledge,
J.K. Fleming, G.N.K. Mourie (capt.)

Scorers – Tries: Johnstone, Rutledge, Williams;
Penalty goal: McKechnie; Drop goal: Dunn
Referee: N.R. Sanson (Scotland)
Attendance: 47,500

CANCELLED MATCH: 9 JANUARY 1982 AT NATIONAL STADIUM, CARDIFF ARMS PARK

Barbarians v. Australia – cancelled because of
heavy snow

The selected XV was: A.R. Irvine; T.M. Ringland,
C.R. Woodward, P.W. Dodge, G.R.T. Baird;
W.G. Davies, T.D. Holmes; P.A. Orr, P.J. Wheeler,
R. Paparemborde, W.B. Beaumont (capt.),
M.J. Colclough, J. Squire, W.P. Duggan,
J-P. Rives

Referee: J-P. Bonnet (France)

MATCH 14: 15 DECEMBER 1984 AT NATIONAL STADIUM, CARDIFF ARMS PARK

Barbarians 30 Australia 37

Barbarians: S. Blanco; S.T. Smith*, R.A. Ackerman,
B.J. Mullin, R. Underwood; W.G. Davies (capt.),
J. Gallion; P.A. Orr, M.J. Watkins, I.G. Milne,
D.G. Lenihan, R.L. Norster, S.K. McGaughey,
W.A. Anderson, G.W. Rees

Scorers – Tries: Milne, Smith, Underwood, Gallion,

Blanco; Conversions: Davies (2); Penalty goals:
Davies (2)

Australia: R.G. Gould; M.J. Hawker, A.G. Slack
(capt.), M.P. Lynagh, D.I. Campese; M.G. Ella,
P.A. Cox; S. Pilecki, T.A. Lawton, A.J. McIntyre,
S.A. Williams, S.A.G. Cutler, S.P. Poidevin,
R.J. Reynolds, C. Roche

Scorers – Tries: Poidevin (2), Hawker, Gould, Slack,
Williams; Conversions: Lynagh (5); Penalty goal:
Lynagh
Referee: R. Hourquet (France)
Attendance: 45,000

MATCH 15: 26 NOVEMBER 1988 AT NATIONAL STADIUM, CARDIFF ARMS PARK

Barbarians 22 Australia 40

Barbarians: A.G. Hastings; M.D.F. Duncan,
C. Laity*, M.G. Ring, R. Underwood; J. Davies,
R.N. Jones; D.M.B. Sole, S.J. Smith, D. Young,
W.A. Dooley, R.L. Norster, P.M. Matthews
(capt.), I.A.M. Paxton, R.A. Robinson

Scorers – Tries: Duncan, Hastings, Robinson, Laity;
Conversions: Hastings (3)

Australia: A.J. Leeds; A.S. Niuqila, M.T. Cook,
L.F. Walker, D.I. Campese; M.P. Lynagh,
N.C. Farr-Jones (capt.); R. Lawton, T.A. Lawton,
A.J. McIntyre, S.A.G. Cutler, D. Frawley,
J.S. Miller, S.N. Tuynman, S.R. Gourley

Scorers – Tries: Campese (2), Miller, Lynagh,
Walker, Tuynman; Conversions: Lynagh (5);
Penalty goals: Lynagh (2)
Referee: G. Maurette (France)
Attendance: 40,000

MATCH 16: 25 NOVEMBER 1989 AT TWICKENHAM

Barbarians 10 New Zealand 21

Barbarians: A.G. Hastings; T. Underwood*,
S. Hastings, J.C. Guscott, R. Underwood;
A. Clement, N.C. Farr-Jones; D.M.B. Sole
(capt.), B.C. Moore, D. Young, W.A. Dooley,
P.J. Ackford, P.M. Matthews, P.T. Davies,
G.W. Rees

Scorers – Try: Matthews; Penalty goals: A.G.
Hastings (2)

New Zealand: J.A. Gallagher; C.R. Innes,
N.J. Schuster, W.K. Little, T.J. Wright; G.J. Fox,
G.T.M. Bachop; S.C. McDowell,

S.B.T. Fitzpatrick, R.W. Loe, M.J. Pierce,
G.W. Whetton, A.T. Earl, W.T. Shelford (capt.)
(Z.V. Brooke), M.R. Brewer
Scorers – Tries: Innes, Brooke, Loe; Conversions:
    Fox (3); Penalty goal: Fox
Referee: C. Norling (Wales)
Attendance: 60,000

MATCH 17: 28 NOVEMBER 1992 AT
TWICKENHAM
Barbarians 20 Australia 30
Barbarians: M.A. Rayer; I. Hunter, W.D.C. Carling
    (capt.), I.S. Gibbs, T. Underwood; S. Barnes,
    R.N. Jones; N.J. Popplewell, N.N. Meek*,
    J.A. Probyn, I.D. Jones, N. Hadley,
    M.G. Skinner, B.B. Clarke, I.R. Smith
Scorers – Tries: Hunter, I.D. Jones, Probyn;
    Conversion: Rayer; Penalty goal: Barnes
Australia: M.C. Roebuck; P.V. Carozza, J.S. Little,
    T.J. Horan, D.I. Campese; P.R. Kahl, P.J. Slattery;
    D.J. Crowley, P.N. Kearns, E.J.A. McKenzie,
    R.J. McCall, T. Coker, V. Ofahengaue, B.T. Gavin,
    S.J.N. Scott-Young
Scorers – Tries: Horan, Crowley, Kearns;
    Conversions: Roebuck (3); Penalty goals:
    Roebuck (3)
Referee: J.M. Fleming (Scotland)
Attendance: 54,000

MATCH 18: 4 DECEMBER 1993 AT NATIONAL
STADIUM, CARDIFF ARMS PARK
Barbarians 12 New Zealand 25
Barbarians: A. Clement; A.G. Stanger, S. Hastings
    (capt.), I.S. Gibbs (C.P. Scholtz*), N.K. Walker;
    E.P. Elwood, G. Armstrong (R. Howley*);
    N.J. Popplewell, T.J. Kingston, E.J.A. McKenzie,
    P.S. Johns, O. Roumat, R.I. Wainwright,
    L.S. Quinnell, N.A. Back*
Scorer – Penalty goals: Elwood (4)
New Zealand: J.K.R. Timu; J.W. Wilson, F.E. Bunce,
    L. Stensness, V.L. Tuigamala; M.C.G. Ellis,
    S.T. Forster; C.W. Dowd, S.B.T. Fitzpatrick (capt.),
    O.M. Brown, I.D. Jones, S.B. Gordon, B.P. Larsen
    (M.R. Brewer), Z.V. Brooke, A.R.B. Pene
Scorers – Tries: Dowd, Tuigamala, Jones;
    Conversions: Wilson (2); Penalty goals: Wilson (2)
Referee: P. Robin (France)
Attendance: 55,000

MATCH 19: 3 DECEMBER 1994 AT
LANSDOWNE ROAD
Barbarians 23 South Africa 15
Barbarians: J.E.B. Callard; S.P. Geoghegan,
    M.R. Hall, S. Hastings (P.W. Howard),
    P. Saint-Andre; C.M. Chalmers, R.N. Jones
    (capt.); N.J. Popplewell, K.G.M. Wood,
    P.M. Clohessy, I.D. Jones, S.D. Shaw*,
    A.J. Charron (G. Manson-Bishop*),
    R.I. Wainwright, N.A. Back
Scorers – Tries: Saint-Andre, Geoghegan;
    Conversions: Callard (2); Penalty goals: Callard (2);
    Drop goal: Chalmers
South Africa: A.J. Joubert; G.K. Johnson,
    P.G. Muller, J.C. Mulder, C.M. Williams
    (J.T. Stransky); H.P. le Roux, J.H. van der
    Westhuizen; J.P. du Randt, J. Dalton, I.S. Swart,
    J.J. Wiese, M.G. Andrews, J.F. Pienaar (capt.)
    (R.A.W. Straeuli), C.P. Strauss, R.J. Kruger
Scorers – Tries: Kruger, Muller, Johnson
Referee: W.D. Bevan (Wales)
Attendance: 49,500

MATCH 20: 7 DECEMBER 1996 AT
TWICKENHAM
Barbarians 12 Australia 39
Barbarians: T.R.G. Stimpson (J.T. Stransky);
    N.K. Walker, A.G. Bateman, G.P.J. Townsend
    (M.C. Allen*), T. Underwood; C.R. Andrew
    (capt.), R. Howley (A.P. Moore); N.J. Popplewell,
    N.J. Hewitt, D.J. Garforth*, J.C. Quinnell (G.W.
    Weir), I.D. Jones, D.L.M. McIntosh*,
    L.S. Quinnell, N.A. Back
Scorers – Tries: Bateman, L.S. Quinnell;
    Conversion: Andrew
Australia: M.P. Burke (S.J. Larkham); D.I. Campese,
    D.J. Herbert, T.J. Horan (capt.), J.W. Roff;
    P.W. Howard (R.C. Tombs), S.J. Payne;
    D.J. Crowley, M.E. Caputo (M.A. Foley), A.T.
    Blades (A. Heath), D.T. Giffin, T.B. Gavin,
    O.D.A. Finegan, M.C. Brial (B.J. Robinson),
    D.J. Wilson
Scorers – Tries: Burke (2), Roff, Campese, Horan;
    Conversions: Burke (4), Penalty goals: Burke (2)
Referee: E.F. Morrison (England)
Attendance: 60,000

THE BARBARIANS

MATCH 21: 10 DECEMBER 2000 AT
MILLENNIUM STADIUM
Barbarians 31 South Africa 41
Barbarians: C.M. Cullen; M.P. Burke,
   B.G. O'Driscoll, D.J. Herbert, C.E. Latham
   (I.R. Balshaw); C.J. Spencer (N.R. Jenkins),
   A. Pichot (B.T. Kelleher); R.L.L. Harry
   (P.M. Clohessy), A.E. Drotske (M.G. Hammett),
   M. Reggiardo, N.M.C. Maxwell (M.E. O'Kelly),
   D.T. Giffin, R.W. Williams (A.J. Ward),
   R.T. Cribb, L.B.N. Dallaglio (capt.)
Scorers – Tries: O'Driscoll, Pichot, Latham, Cullen;
   Conversions: Burke (4); Penalty goal: Burke
South Africa: G.S. du Toit; B.J. Paulse, R.F. Fleck,
   J.C. Mulder (A.J.J. van Straaten), C.M. Williams
   (C.S. Terblanche); P.C. Montgomery, J.H. van der
   Westhuizen (D.J. van Zyl); R.B. Kempson,
   J.W. Smit (C.F. Marais), W. Meyer (A-H. le
   Roux), P.A. van den Berg, M.G. Andrews,
   C.P.J. Krige (W.G. Brosnihan), A.N. Vos (capt.)
   (A.J. Venter), A.G. Venter
Scorers – Tries: Paulse (3), Williams (2), le Roux;
   Conversions: Montgomery (4); Penalty goal: van
   Straaten
Referee: R.G. Davies (Wales)
Attendance: 70,000

MATCH 22: 28 NOVEMBER 2001 AT
MILLENNIUM STADIUM
Barbarians 35 Australia 49
Barbarians: P.C. Montgomery (C.J. Spencer);
   B.J. Paulse, S. Glas (M.S. Rogers), P.W. Howard,
   C.S. Terblanche; A.J.J. van Straaten, R. Howley
   (capt.) (W. Swanepoel); D.R. Morris
   (C.W. Dowd), R. Ibanez (R. Cockerill), D. Young,
   I.D. Jones (T.S. Maling*), M.G. Andrews,
   C.P.J. Krige, P.C. Miller*, O. Magne (P. Lam)
Scorers – Tries: Paulse (3), Glas, Lam; Conversions:

van Straaten (5)
Australia: C.E. Latham; B.N. Tune, S. Kefu, R.S.T.
   Kefu, S.N.G. Staniforth (S.J. Larkham);
   E.J. Flatley (M.H.M. Edmonds), G.M. Gregan
   (C.J. Whitaker); W.K. Young, B.J. Cannon
   (M.A. Foley), R.C. Moore (B.J. Darwin),
   J.B. Harrison, T.M. Bowman (P.R. Waugh),
   M.R. Connors, D.J. Lyons (O.D.A. Finegan),
   G.B. Smith
Scorers – Tries: Staniforth (3), Latham, Flatley,
   R.S.T. Kefu, Tune; Conversions: Flatley (5),
   Edmonds (2)
Referee: C. White (England)
Attendance: 40,000

MATCH 23: 4 DECEMBER 2004 AT
TWICKENHAM
Barbarians 19 New Zealand 47
Barbarians: M.S. Rogers; C.E. Latham (A. Tuilevo),
   L. Tuqiri, M. Turinui (G. Bobo), S. Bobo;
   M.J. Giteau (W.W. Greeff), J.W. Marshall (capt.);
   W.K. Young (A. Lo Cicero), B.J. Cannon
   (G.G. Botha*), S.J. Rautenbach, D.J. Vickerman,
   P.A. van den Berg (A.J. Venter), S.W.P. Burger
   (U.R. Samo), X.J. Rush, P.R. Waugh
Scorers – Tries: Rush, Lo Cicero, van den Berg;
   Conversions: Giteau, Rogers
New Zealand: J.M. Muliaina; D.C. Howlett,
   C.D.E. Laulala, M.A. Nonu, R.L. Gear;
   A.J.D. Mauger (capt.), Q.J. Cowan
   (P.A.T. Weepu); S. Taumoepeau (C.J. Hayman),
   K.F. Mealamu (A.D. Oliver), G.M. Somerville,
   R.D. Thorne (C.R. Jack), A.J. Williams, J. Kaino,
   S.P. Bates (M. Tuiali'i), M.R. Holah
Scorers – Tries: Gear (2), Holah, Nonu, Laulala,
   Kaino, Weepu; Conversions: Mauger (5), Weepu
Referee: A.D. Turner (South Africa)
Attendance: 58,597

II

MATCHES AGAINST OTHER NATIONAL TEAMS

ARGENTINA
17 November 1990 (Cardiff) W 34–22

BRITISH ISLES
10 September 1977 (Twickenham) L 14–23

CANADA
17 November 1962 (Gosforth) D 3–3
12 June 1976 (Toronto) W 29–4

ENGLAND
29 September 1990 (Twickenham) L 16–18
27 May 2001 (Twickenham) W 43–29
26 May 2002 (Twickenham) L 29–53
25 May 2003 (Twickenham) W 49–36
30 May 2004 (Twickenham) W 32–12

FIJI
24 October 1970 (Gosforth) L 9–29

GERMANY
12 August 2000 (Hanover) W 47–19

IRELAND
18 May 1996 (Dublin) W 70–38
28 May 2000 (Dublin) W 31–30

ITALY
26 May 1985 (Rome) W 23–15

PORTUGAL
10 June 2004 (Lisbon) W 66–34

RHODESIA
26 May 1969 (Salisbury) W 24–21

SCOTLAND
9 May 1970 (Murrayfield) W 33–17
26 March 1983 (Murrayfield) W 26–13
7 September 1991 (Murrayfield) D 16–16
17 August 1996 (Murrayfield) W 48–45
31 May 2000 (Murrayfield) W 45–42
24 May 2001 (Murrayfield) W 74–31
1 June 2002 (Murrayfield) W 47–27
28 May 2003 (Murrayfield) W 24–15
22 May 2004 (Murrayfield) W 40–33

THE BARBARIANS

WALES

17 April 1915 (Cardiff) W 26–20
6 October 1990 (Cardiff) W 31–24
24 August 1996 (Cardiff) L 10–31
20 May 2001 (Cardiff) W 40–38
29 May 2002 (Cardiff) W 40–25
31 May 2003 (Cardiff) W 48–35
26 May 2004 (Bristol) L nil–42

ZIMBABWE

4 June 1994 (Harare) L 21–23

Full details of individual matches, teams and scores
can be found on www.TheBarbarians.co.uk

III

OTHER OPPONENTS (BY COUNTRY)

ARGENTINA AND URUGUAY
South American Barbarians

CANADA AND USA
Alberta, Atlantic All-Stars, Bay Area Touring Side, British Columbia, New England, Ontario, Quebec, Saskatchewan

ENGLAND
Bath, Bedford, Birkenhead Park, Blackheath, Bradford, Bradford & Bingley, Bristol, Cambridge University Past & Present, Carlisle & District, Cheltenham, Combined Services, Corinthians, Cornwall, Coventry, Devonport Albion, Devonshire, East Midlands, Exeter, Gloucester, Hampshire, Hartlepool Rovers, Huddersfield, J.E. Thorneloe's XV, Leeds, Leicester, Liverpool, London, London Irish All-Stars, London Welsh, Midlands XV, Moseley, Old Dunelmians, Oxford University Past & Present, Percy Park, Plymouth, RAMC, Rockliff, Shoreham Camp, South Shields, Swinton, Wasps, Waterloo, West Hartlepool, West of England

FRANCE
French Barbarians, Le Havre, Racing Club de France, Stade Français

IRELAND
Cork Constitution, Dublin University, Old Wesley, Ulster, Wanderers

ITALY
Lupi, Zebre

JAPAN
Kansai President's XV, Kobe Steel

NEW ZEALAND
New Zealand Barbarians (at Cardiff)

RUSSIA
Krasny Yar, CIS

SCOTLAND
Border League, Glasgow Academicals, Melrose, Stirling County

SOUTHERN AFRICA
Combined Transvaal, East Africa, Natal, Northern Transvaal, Quaggas, South African Barbarians, South African Country Districts, South African Services (at Richmond), Southern Universities, Transvaal, Western Province, Western Transvaal

WALES
Cardiff, Llanelli, Neath, Newport, Newport & District, Penarth, Swansea

SEVEN-A-SIDE
TOURNAMENTS

V

INDIVIDUAL RECORDS

MOST APPEARANCES

30 – A.J.F. O'Reilly (1955–1963)

25 – C.R. Jacobs (1953–1965)

25 – D.P. Rogers (1961–1971)

24 – M.P. Atkinson (1913–1923)

24 – P. Maud (1890–1896)

24 – A.G. Ripley (1972–1981)

24 – F.M. Stout (1897–1906)

23 – A.R. Smith (1955–1962)

23 – J.S. Spencer (1969–1977)

23 – R.M. Wilkinson (1972–1984)

22 – A.R. Dawson (1957–1964)

22 – J.A. Waters (1933–1943)

22 – R.H. Williams (1954–1959)

21 – S.F. Coopper (1901–1908)

21 – M.S. Linnett (1989–1997)

20 – P. Bennett (1970–1980)

20 – A.B. Carmichael (1966–1976)

20 – W.P. Carpmael (1890–1897)

20 – D.J. Duckham (1969–1975)

20 – G.W. Hastings (1955–1959)

20 – H.L. Glyn Hughes (1913–1926)

20 – A.A. Mulligan (1956–1962)

MOST TRIES

38 – A.J.F. O'Reilly

27 – D.J.K. McKay

22 – P.H. Thompson

19 – D.J. Duckham

17 – H.E. Rees

17 – J.J. Williams

16 – A.R. Smith

15 – D.A. Stark

13 – A.R. Irvine